Inside the Gate

Inside the Gate

SIGRID UNDSET'S LIFE
AT BJERKEBÆK

Nan Bentzen Skille

Translated by Tiina Nunnally

University of Minnesota Press
Minneapolis
London

Published in Norwegian as *Innenfor gjerdet. Hos Sigrid Undset på Bjerkebæk*; copyright 2003 by H. Aschehoug & Co. (W. Nygaard). Originally published in English by H. Aschehoug & Co. (W. Nygaard) AS; copyright 2009 by H. Aschehoug & Co.

First University of Minnesota Press edition, 2018. Published in agreement with Oslo Literary Agency.

English translation copyright 2009 Tiina Nunnally

Published by the University of Minnesota Press
111 Third Avenue South, Suite 290
Minneapolis, MN 55401-2520
http://www.upress.umn.edu

Printed in the United States of America on acid-free paper

The University of Minnesota is an equal-opportunity educator and employer.

24 23 22 21 20 19 18   10 9 8 7 6 5 4 3 2 1

Library of Congress Cataloging-in-Publication Data
Skille, Nan Bentzen, author. | Nunnally, Tiina, translator.
Inside the gate : Sigrid Undset's life at Bjerkebæk / Nan Bentzen Skille ; translated by
    Tiina Nunnally.
First University of Minnesota Press edition. | Minneapolis : University of Minnesota Press, 2018.
    | Includes bibliographical references.
Identifiers: LCCN 2017054254 | ISBN 978-1-5179-0496-8 (pb)
Subjects: LCSH: Undset, Sigrid, 1882-1949. | Authors, Norwegian–20th century–Biography. |
    Bjerkebæk (Lillehammer, Norway). | BISAC: BIOGRAPHY & AUTOBIOGRAPHY /
    Literary. | BIOGRAPHY & AUTOBIOGRAPHY / Women.
Classification: LCC PT8950.U5 S6513 2018 | DDC 839.823/72–dc23
LC record available at https://lccn.loc.gov/2017054254

Contents

Introduction

One day in 1979, when I was working at the University Library in Bergen, my colleague Maya Thee showed me something she had found in one of the old boxes stored on the fifth floor. It was a yellowed issue of *The New York Times Book Review* from 1943 which contained an article by Sigrid Undset entitled "The Books That Last Forever." She had written the essay at the Hotel Margaret in Brooklyn while her thoughts were on occupied Norway and her home Bjerkebæk, which at the time had been taken over by the Gestapo. For me, the discovery of "The Books That Last Forever" was the start of a long and passionate interest in Undset's writing, her life story, and eventually also her home. I thought it was only natural to view these three facets together – rather like a handshake, a hand, and a glove, to use one of Undset's own images.

This book has two goals. First, I want to present some of the source materials that I've gathered over the past years, both through my work with the Sigrid Undset Society, which I headed for five years after its founding in 1997, and through my work documenting the Bjerkebæk site history from 1998 until 2003. For this reason, I have largely made use of letters and photographs that have not been used in earlier Undset biographies. Second, I want to offer a portrait of Undset in stereo. My work with the physical estate and the biographical materials has been very enriching for me, as I have attempted to "read" the values and attitudes expressed in the artist's home along with the story of her life.

My thanks to Maihaugen, the Sandvig Collections, and the Friends of Maihaugen, who awarded me the Anders Sandvig Museum Stipend in 2000, and to Eckbos Legater for additional financial support. Thank you to all who have contributed to this book by providing access to Undset materials that have not been previously known. Some of the new source material came from Susanna Bøe and her sons Allan and Karsten, who have preserved the letters and photographs left by Bjerkebæk's housekeeper, Mathea Mortenstuen Bøe. They also allowed me to examine her large collection of books from Bjerkebæk. Research librarian Tone Modalsli at the Norwegian National Library has kept me informed about acquisitions to the Manuscript Collection during the past few years. Especially intriguing were the letters that Sigrid Undset wrote to Marjorie Kinnan Rawlings in the years after the war. Jarle Bragelien had the presence of mind to bring home to Norway copies of a collection of letters that Sigrid Undset wrote to Magny Landstad-Jensen in the United States. A special thank you to Harald Bentzen and Tore Skille for their patient assistance, useful comments, and steadfast support.

Nan Bentzen Skille

Lillehammer Station
– Disembark on the right

The train from Kristiania arrives daily in Lillehammer at 4:42 p.m. and 8:05 p.m.

This small announcement was regularly printed in Lillehammer's local newspaper during the summer of 1919. At the main train station in Kristiania (now Oslo), the northbound passengers prepared for departure. The locomotive spouted a few tentative clouds of white steam and slowly but surely began moving away from the platform. It chugged along, one kilometer after another, past apartment blocks and wooden houses with gingerbread trim, sawmills and iron foundries, stands of Norway pine and fields of grain, medieval churches and small farms. The train passed the paddle steamer on Lake Mjøsa, and after 180 kilometers it finally slowed and then came to rest at the small town of Lillehammer.

Each day livery drivers and local residents came to the station to pick up goods and guests, because during this particular summer the traffic to the valley town was busier than it had been in a long time. After four terrible years of war in Europe and everything the fighting had entailed – including high prices, shortages, reckless speculation in stocks, and bitter financial losses – life had finally settled into a regular routine again. But as the world war came to an end, the Spanish flu epidemic struck, and tuberculosis was still raging without mercy. It was tempting for many Norwegians to turn their backs on the capital, with

Lillehammer Station.

its cramped apartments and dust-filled streets, and reserve a seat on the train to head for healthier regions out in the country. The numerous sanatoriums and countless small, private residences offering rest and respite in eastern Norway were enjoying a lucrative period, and Lillehammer, located on the threshold of the Gudbrandsdal region, with its deep valleys and spectacular mountain ranges, was a particularly popular destination.

The local newspaper provides a lively picture of the situation for the arriving passengers and their hosts. One column after another presents news of great world events intermixed with small, local concerns. In the issue of *Gudbrandsdølen* for Thursday, May 22, 1919, the Tourist Hotel advertises for "a boy who is an experienced driver," perhaps to pick up guests at the station, while the Skogly Sanatorium seeks to hire a maid. The newspaper reports that during the peace negotiations in Versailles, the parties are quarreling worse than Cain and Abel about *who* should take responsibility for *what*. The article recounts that "Clemenceau is of the opinion that Germany has previously, though indirectly, admitted guilt; so there is no use saying anything else at this point."

On this very day, Sigrid Undset was staying with her two children at the Breiseth Hotel, only a stone's throw from Lillehammer Station. She may have taken the time to plow her way through the long article in *Gudbrandsdølen* about the "benefits of vaccination" in the fight against smallpox, a disease that according to the journalist was claiming half a million lives a year in Europe alone. On the next page she could have read that the local city council had agreed to "an increase in fees at the Lillehammer tuberculosis home from 3 Norwegian kroner per day to 4 kroner for local patients, and an increase from 4 to 5 kroner for out-of-town patients." On several occasions Undset's husband, the painter Anders Castus Svarstad, had entered a sanatorium outside Kristiania for treatment, and it could have been interesting for his wife to compare the prices in Lillehammer with those in the capital.

Yet it was unlikely that sanatorium prices were Undset's greatest concern on that day, because what she and her children needed most of all was a place to live. Her personal problems might seem trivial and petty compared with international politics and epidemics, but it was no joke for a family with five children to be evicted from their apartment in Kristiania. It was true that Svarstad had recently purchased a small house, but it wasn't yet vacant, so they had to find a temporary solution. As Undset sat over her morning coffee in the Breiseth Hotel, her thoughts drifted to her husband, who turned 50 on that very day,

Anders and Mosse 1919.

May 22, 1919. As the dutiful wife she was, she no doubt felt a pang of guilt about everything that she had fled: preparations for a celebratory birthday dinner with her stepchildren and her own offspring; visits from in-laws and friends, all filled with anticipation; congratulations offered by colleagues who secretly shook their heads at the guest of honor, whispering to each other that he was in the middle of an artistic crisis.

Undset carefully studied the classified ads in the paper, concluding that she was not alone in her search for living quarters; many others were advertising for a house. A couple of days earlier, she had found herself among the crowd of passengers disembarking at Lillehammer Station. Presumably she had a firm grip on the hand of her six-year-old son Anders, while she carried four-year-old Maren Charlotte on one arm. In the midst of the teeming vacationers, she didn't particularly stand out from the rest of the people on the platform; there must have been others with tired children and a heap of big suitcases at their feet. A discreet glance at the well-known author from Kristiania – the writer who some years earlier had caused such an uproar with *Jenny*, her "immoral" novel about a woman artist – would have revealed that she had a third child on the way.

A few passengers put their heads together, whispering. Wasn't that the woman whose first novel opened with the daring statement: "I have been unfaithful to my husband"? What was her name again? Mrs. Marta Oulie? No, that was the title of the book! The author's name was Sigrid Undset. She was the daughter of the archaeologist Ingvald Undset, a renowned scholar who had died far too young. The daughter was apparently interested in history too; at any rate she had written a story set in the Viking Age, full of blood and violence, something about a pair of unhappy lovers. Now she was married to one of those painters who preferred to depict factory smokestacks and telephone poles instead of beautiful landscapes. Wasn't his name Svarstad? A divorced man with three children from his previous marriage. Three stepchildren! And how was she supposed to be addressed? As "Mrs. Undset" or "Mrs. Svarstad" or "Mrs. Undset Svarstad"? It was probably best simply to say "Ma'am."

She was tall and straight-backed – a full head taller than the other women on the platform – and she moved with an easy grace, in spite of the bulk due to her pregnancy. She certainly didn't look like some mousy office secretary, even though it was well known that she had written a collection of stories called *Fattige skjebner* (Poor Fates) about just such women. And the book had actually received excellent reviews. But why was she here in Lillehammer? Was she visiting someone or just taking a vacation in the country? Or perhaps she was set on writing another book of an "immoral" ilk.

Sigrid Undset with Anders and Mosse.

No doubt she had friends who turned up at the train station to help her with the children and baggage, perhaps one of the town's best-known artists, the painter Alf Lundeby, who lived in a little red house with no kitchen up on Nordseterveien. Undset had met him on her first trip to Italy. She was twenty-seven back then as she left her mother and sisters and the hated office job in Kristiania to set out into the world, all on her own, determined to create a career for herself as a writer. In Rome she was immediately welcomed into the colony of Norwegian artists, and for the first time in her life she experienced what it meant to be young and free and much in demand. Then, on Christmas Day in 1909, she met Svarstad. "I think I need to lie down and kiss the ground in all humility – I think I need to serve every living thing – because I am happier than I ever knew a person could be." That was what she wrote to a good friend when she was struck by the great love, the kind that recognizes no rules, but breaks them all.

While abroad, Undset had become friends with Lars Jorde, another painter belonging to the artist colony in Lillehammer. She was introduced to him in

Paris, where she had agreed to meet Svarstad in secret, on her way back to Norway from Rome. In rue St. Honoré she had bought a bonnet which she wore when she posed for her lover. Svarstad kept that portrait as he struggled to obtain a divorce from his first wife and arranged to have his children placed in an orphanage. Two years later, when all the arrangements were made, the painting was sold for 2,000 Norwegian kroner, and the money was put to good use on the couple's honeymoon.

Sigrid Undset and Anders Castus Svarstad were married at the Norwegian consulate in Antwerp on June 30, 1912. From there they went to London, where they spent several carefree months. He painted and she wrote, they went to galleries and museums and enjoyed watching people on the streets. With the approach of winter they went back to Italy, to their "old" apartment on Via Frattina in Rome, where they had met for the first time. It was there that Anders junior was born, barely seven months after their wedding. He was a delicate little creature who almost didn't survive his first few months of life.

Back in Norway and a couple of years later, Maren Charlotte was born, and now Undset was expecting her third child. In Lillehammer, nine years after meeting Svarstad, the memory of their first ecstatic time together was still vivid, but daily life with all its demands had caught up with Sigrid Undset. Now she knew, just as Jenny did, that "no love turns out as they had dreamed of it when they kissed for the first time."

On that day in May 1919 it was most likely Helene, one of Undset's women friends, who welcomed the little group of travelers from the capital as they arrived in the town on Lake Mjøsa. Helene was a pianist and the daughter of Oluf Fagstad, a Lillehammer merchant who took a great interest in art. She was now the newly married Mrs. Frøisland. Helene, too, belonged to the circle of friends Undset had met in Rome; she had provided numerous character traits for the beautiful and impulsive Francesca in Undset's novel *Jenny*.

Helene and Sigrid had spent many a late night sharing both worries and sweet secrets over a bottle or two of Chianti, but now Helene had settled down after marrying Frøis Frøisland, another native of Lillehammer who had returned home from the big world. Frøisland had spent five exciting years in Paris as the war correspondent for *Aftenposten*. He was then promoted to editor at the newspaper's head office in Kristiania – and now, at the age of 36, he was a new husband. The marriage had taken place on May 16 in Kristiania, and the following day all of Norway had celebrated Independence Day with flags and banners and rousing music. The private celebrations for the newlyweds no doubt continued in Lillehammer, where the families of both the bride and

Sigrid Undset in Rome, 1909–10.

Anders Castus Svarstad, self-portrait.

groom were prominent citizens, and Sigrid Undset took advantage of the occasion to visit with her old friends.

Helene, 34 years old and newly married, probably had just as much to recount now as when she and Sigrid were impressionable young ladies in the Eternal City. Their bonds of friendship had withstood both great differences in temperament and the natural wear and tear of time. Back in Kristiania they had continued to be good friends, and now, here in Lillehammer, they had an excellent opportunity to renew contact since Helene's days as a single woman were over.

The end of the war, the marriage, Independence Day, and summertime were all good reasons for cracking open the champagne and drinking toasts to brighter times. But for Undset it couldn't have been as easy as it was in the "old days" to listen to everyone else's plans and hopes for the future. Now she was the one who was in need of a confidante. What with illness, the loss of her home, and marital conflicts, she had plenty of problems to contend with. Worst of all was her concern for her daughter, four-year-old Maren Charlotte, or Mosse, as she was called. The child suffered from epileptic fits, which had started when she was only two. She didn't talk, and she was still in diapers. Mosse had undergone extensive tests at the National Hospital in Kristiania, but the doctors were unable to say anything specific about what illness might have hindered her development.

Undset couldn't bear to see the slight body of her daughter ravaged by vio-

Hanna and Oluf Fagstad with their children; Einar on the far left and Helene on the far right.

lent convulsions and worried so much that she made herself sick. In the fall of 1918 she had spent several weeks at a fashionable health spa in the hills above Kristiania. Her well-to-do friend Nini Roll Anker was the one who had urged her to go there, and of course it did help – for a while. But back home in their apartment in the Sinsen district, Undset's husband, their two children, and her three stepchildren were waiting. Then came the eviction notice, and they had to pack up all their furniture and belongings and prepare to move. By then Undset was just as worn out as before, and pregnant again as well.

The children's father, Anders Castus Svarstad, focused most of his attention on his own work, just as "all" fathers usually did, while Sigrid took care of the family. If the children had all been healthy and the family's finances had been more or less stable, this type of division of labor would have been acceptable. But for this particular family, with five children from two different marriages and with one child from each group developmentally handicapped, plus finances based on the highly unreliable income of two artists, it was too much of a strain.

Undset had begun to enjoy the company of Ebba and Gunhild, the teenage girls from Svarstad's first marriage, but of course they required a good deal of daily attention, as well as food, clothing, and guidance. The youngest stepchild, Trond, was eleven but showed clear signs of being disabled – though not in the same way as Mosse. Trond had trouble learning even the simplest things, and he had serious behavioral problems. In addition, a shadow had been cast over his birth, since Svarstad wasn't certain that he was actually the boy's father. The three children couldn't expect much help from their own mother, because as a divorced woman Ragna Moe Svarstad was having trouble even providing for herself. It was Svarstad's mother, who lived on a small farm in Røyse near Tyrifjorden, who took care of the three young children during vacations and at times when they became too much for their parents to handle.

By nature Svarstad was a taciturn and reserved man, and lately he had begun closing himself off more and more from his spouse. He was thirteen years older than Sigrid and had always done a good deal of traveling – to the United States, Denmark, Germany, Belgium, and France, as well as to England and Italy. He was accustomed to spending long periods abroad, but the war and his new family had curtailed his freedom, and after staying home for several years he was now feeling restless. As an artist he had reached an impasse, but even so he fought fiercely against the prevailing modernists and staked

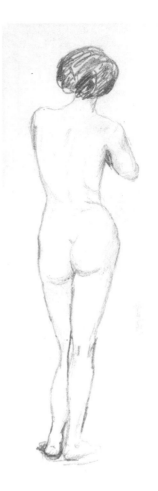

Nude by Anders Castus Svarstad.

everything on becoming Christian Krohg's successor as the head of the Art Academy in Kristiania. Svarstad was deeply frustrated over what he perceived as the misguided direction the world was taking and expressed his opinion through attacks in the press against Bolsheviks and Prussians and Jews. In 1918 he published an article with the title "The Revenge of the Jews" in the journal *Samtiden*, in which he spouted the most rabid descriptions of the "anatomical defects of this race" and leveled crude accusations against them for conspiring and destroying European culture.

Sigrid Undset was headed in quite a different direction. She had always had sympathy for those who were outsiders and helpless – life's "flotsam," as she

Svarstad with his son Anders on the roof of Via Frattina 138 in Rome.

called them. And because of Mosse's fate, her feeling of personal responsibility had increased toward those who were less fortunate. In her daily life she found herself left on her own to handle her worries and care for the children, both the three from her husband's first marriage and the two that they had together. During the first few years of their marriage she and Svarstad lived in a small house in Ski, about twenty kilometers south of Kristiania, where Ebba, Gunhild, and Trond only occasionally came to visit. But when they moved to Sinsen, closer to the center of town, they took in the three children, and this was an enormous burden, even with the help of a very capable maid. Asta was a real treasure, available round the clock, but Undset also had her share of the work to do. "Every once in a while when she would come to visit us for the day, she would be streaked with fatigue, but her will was as indomitable as ever," said Nini Roll Anker about her friend during those years.

It was difficult for Undset to find time for her own work, yet she had to write in order to secure the family's finances. By sitting up late at night, she had somehow managed it, and almost every year – even after she had children – a new book by Sigrid Undset would be published. In 1914 *Våren* (Springtime) appeared, followed by *Fortellinger om kong Artur og ridderne av det runde bord* (Tales of King Arthur and the Knights of the Round Table) in 1915, *Splinten av trollspeilet* (The Splinter from the Troll Mirror) in 1917, and *De kloke jomfruer* (*The Wise Virgins*) in 1918. In the long run, such a ruthless exploitation of her own energies naturally took its toll on both her health and her marriage, and she couldn't afford to go to expensive health spas every time she felt run down. It was the last straw for Undset when their landlord in Sinsen decided to evict them. Svarstad had bought a small property on the east side of town, in Kampen, but there was still the matter of where they could live until this house became vacant. Something had to be arranged, and quickly, since the new baby was due in August.

In this difficult situation Sigrid Undset packed her suitcases and boxes of books and filled the baby carriage with diapers and toys. It finally dawned on her that if she was going to provide for herself and her children, she would have to give up her attempt to keep the whole family together. Her husband was selling his paintings at good prices, but there were long gaps between each sale. The family needed a stable income, and from personal experience Undset was acutely aware of what it meant to be without money. In her own childhood home, where early on her mother became a widow with three daughters, the constant refrain was always: "We can't afford it." The Undset family had possessed a wealth of education and culture, but in terms of everything else they had been forced to scrimp and save. For ten years, after finishing secondary school and business school, Sigrid Undset had worked as an office secretary in

Prof. LEOPOLD MEYER

DEN FØRSTE BARNEPLEJE

POPULÆRT FREMSTILLET

MED 15 AFBILDNINGER

FJERDE OPLAG

KØBENHAVN
DET NORDISKE FORLAG
BOGFORLAGET: ERNST BOJESEN
1902

Sigrid Undset was well prepared to be a mother – in theory.

Kristiania in order to supplement her mother's scanty income. Now, after seven years of marriage with much strife and struggle, she simply couldn't go on.

Filled with bitterness toward Svarstad, she left Kristiania. In a great fury – at her husband, his children, his first wife, and her own inadequacies – Undset wrote to Nini Roll Anker: "There he is in Kampen, with that woman's frightful boy; he doesn't even know whether it's his – and all *my* efforts to help him with the burden have merely destroyed us both and torn me apart – more than anyone could know."

In spite of this bitter defeat, Undset had not given up on her marriage, but she alternated between hope and despair. In 1918 she had written the short story "Gunvald and Emma," in which she depicts the struggle to rebuild a new Garden of Eden after a terrible marital disappointment. Emma is Gunvald's second wife and cannot possibly measure up to his first when it comes to eroticism. She realizes that for her husband she is no seductive Eve but rather a nurturing Mary, and eventually she accepts this. In the last section of the story, we see Emma as a Madonna figure with her son in her arms. Wearing a blue dress she stands in the garden bathed in sunlight, and "the sun brought forth a faint reddish sheen" in her hair, gleaming like a halo. In a very telling detail in this scene, the stepdaughters are pictured outside the fence that protects the little patch of garden belonging to Emma and Gunvald. There they are playing with some of the children who live on the street, having been sternly warned not to get dirty.

Like her husband, Undset also had her birthday in May, a day that was usually celebrated with the first caraway-sprout soup of the spring as appetizer to the meal, and with exciting packages of books as dessert. On May 20, 1919, Sigrid Undset turned 37. This time it was no occasion for celebration, since the entire household had been packed up for an indeterminate length of time. But "from the thickets lining the road the jubilant birds sang, gentle and springlike, all day long until dusk," and the child she was carrying was earnestly giving signs of life.

In this situation Lillehammer must have seemed like a place where Undset and her family could make a new start, on a smaller scale and with less toil than in the capital. No doubt she listed all the advantages for Svarstad. The town could offer benefits for all of them: a healthy climate, a liberal artist milieu, good schools, and a tranquil working environment. Anders and Mosse had delicate health, and Svarstad himself had suffered from lung problems for years. This was the sanatorium town where both he and the children could grow strong and healthy. Lillehammer was also the town of painters; they had artist friends there who could help them get settled and perhaps provide Svarstad with new inspiration. In Kristiania the class divisions were strictly maintained, with invisible barriers between civil servants and academics, merchants and artists, the nouveau riche and old money, workers and poor people. In Lillehammer social relationships were less strictly regulated and more liberal; there artists could consort with civil servants as well as farmers, with craftsmen and merchants.

And last but not least: in Lillehammer Undset would have the peace to write, and she would be closer to the material that she now intended to use in a new book. She was planning a lengthy project, a historical novel, in which Gudbrandsdalen would play an important role. This was something that she'd been thinking about for several years, but in order to get started, she first had to find a place to live. In *Gudbrandsdølen* for Thursday, May 22, 1919, a little ad caught her attention:

Nice house.

Unfurnished timbered house
on the northern outskirts
of town, one-year lease.
Contact **Hjorth**, Victoria Hotel.

Sigrid Undset
makes herself a home

On Nordseterveien, just outside the town of Lillehammer itself, the business-man Ola Aasen had placed a timbered house moved from Gudbrandsdalen in 1918. It was a building that had originally been part of a farm further north, in Kvam, but now it stood on the outskirts of the town on property that had once belonged to the old estate of Lysgaard. After being moved here, the building had been meticulously adapted to its new life as a family home. On the inside, the walls had been given wood paneling, and a veranda facing south was added to the ground floor. A combined woodshed and outdoor privy had been erected close to the road, but the site itself, which had been an outlying field at Lysgaard, had remained untouched as a rocky scree covering 1.25 acres, with old birch trees towering high above nettles and thickets. A little stream trickled down toward town, providing refreshment for the horses and cattle that still used the area as a pasture. Less than a kilometer to the south, the rapids of the Mesna River rushed toward Lake Mjøsa, and when the river was running high, its roar could be heard all the way to Nordseterveien.

Ola Aasen sold the property to a young painter by the name of Hjorth, but before the artist even had a chance to move in, he was awarded a grant that made him change his plans. Instead of furnishing the house and clearing the land around it, he decided to go to Paris and lease the house for a year. When Sigrid Undset saw Hjorth's ad in *Gudbrandsdølen* on May 22, 1919, she contacted

Sigrid Undset bought a new hat for her meeting with Peter Nansen in Copenhagen.

him at the Victoria Hotel. They soon came to an agreement on the rent and signed a contract that would be valid until the autumn of the following year. The relief that Undset felt at finding a place to live, a place where she could make herself a home even though it was intended to be temporary, was evident in the letter she sent to her friend Nini:

> Now everything looks brighter – everyone in Lillehammer says that I've been unbelievably lucky. Normally there aren't any houses for rent here, or any domestic help either. I had almost decided to buy a small house, for more than it was worth, of course – and then a young painter, Sverre Hjorth, put in an ad offering to lease his 5-room timbered house for a year. We called on him at once, and now we've settled on the lease, will pay 2,500 kroner for 15 months; that's not expensive for here. It's an old farm from up the valley that was moved here and refurbished with a kitchen, a small dining room, and a big, lovely living room on the first floor, with 2 small bedrooms and one large one upstairs. The whole place looks comfortable, and the location is delightful, right across from the Jorde and Lundeby homes – unfortunately on the wrong side of the town boundary, which passes right through the property. One other snag is that no one has lived in the house yet, and it's not quite finished – but at least I'll have the summer months to figure out all the flaws. A further snag is that the site hasn't been fenced or cleared; the house stands at the edge of a big horse pasture with huge old birches and a dense alder thicket...

"We" called on the young painter, Sigrid Undset writes in this letter dated June 10, 1919. Who does she mean by "we"? Did Helene Frøisland drive around with her to look at houses? Or had her husband come to Lillehammer? Undset was then seven months pregnant, and Svarstad must have been worried about her. And perhaps he didn't care for the idea that she was thinking about buying her own house, and for a price that was too high, at that. She does, though, say that "I" have been unbelievably lucky, and "I" am going to use the summer months to transform the house into a home. It's clear that this was Sigrid Undset's own project from the very beginning.

Her choice of where to live was not as coincidental as it might seem, nor was the sole motivation friendship or practical considerations. This landscape where she now sought to establish herself possessed a culture and a history to which she felt strongly tied through personal memories and familial bonds. There were natural reasons why she might choose to make herself a home here with her children. Many years later she published a collection of essays called *Selvportretter og landskapsbilder* (Self-Portraits and Landscape Pictures). As is evident from the title, she was aware of a connection between an individual's identity and her surroundings, between a person's self-perception and the environment in which she chooses to settle. This connection is also apparent in her relationship to Gudbrandsdalen and Lillehammer.

In its former life, the house into which she now moved had actually stood only thirty kilometers or so from the birthplace of her paternal grandfather. Halvor Undseth was born in Sollia, a little mountain village at the base of the Rondane Mountains, halfway between the two long valleys of Gudbrandsdalen and Østerdalen. Sigrid had been named after one of Halvor's ancestors, Siri Pedersdatter, and was proud of this kinship. Half-jokingly she said that she was probably related to every single person in Sollia, and she took great pleasure in the stories about the "hard-toiling" settlers who lived there. She bragged that they were a spirited bunch who caught bears with their bare hands, fought with gypsies, spat snuff, and drank their liquor straight from the bottle.

From her childhood and youth she had many fond memories of traveling through the region on the way to visit her grandparents. As an adult, Halvor Undseth had settled in Trondhjem (now Trondheim), and his son Ingvald came north from Kristiania to visit his parents on several occasions, bringing along his Danish-born wife Charlotte and their three young daughters: Sigrid, Ragnhild, and Signe. The easiest route was to take the train up through Østerdalen, but as an archaeologist, Ingvald Undset (who dropped the "h" from the family name) was particularly fond of Gudbrandsdalen. This region encompassed many ancient sites and traces left behind by Olav Haraldsson, the Viking king who had introduced Christian law to Norway and survived in the national consciousness as Saint Olav. Even as a boy, Ingvald Undset was fascinated by the king who became a saint, and it was only natural for him to share his knowledge and interest with the whole family. Especially with his daughter Sigrid, who early on showed signs of possessing an extraordinary sensitivity and imagination. The girl also had an astounding memory and loved to show off the expertise that her father had taught her – just as long as no one laughed.

In 1889, when Sigrid was seven, the family traveled by train from Kristiania to Eidsvoll, and then to Lillehammer on board the paddle-wheeler *Skibladner*. From there they continued northward by horse and wagon. During their stay in Sel, at the north end of Gudbrandsdalen, they heard the locals recounting stories about "Stor-Ofsen," the terrible flood that a century earlier had carried off a large number of the valley's farms and cost 70 people their lives. One of

the farms that had disappeared in the foaming torrents of water was Jørundstad, which stood on the bank of the Låg river in Gudbrandsdalen.

Much later, after becoming an author, Sigrid Undset resurrected the farm as the estate of "Jørundgaard." It was here that Kristin Lavransdatter had her childhood home, but Undset placed the narrative of the trilogy farther back in time, at the beginning of the fourteenth century, that period of the Middle Ages when life in Norway was at its peak.

In the novel Undset describes how on a May night Kristin and her father are awakened by the rain and the rushing of the river:

> The sky was a heap of tangled, surging rain clouds; there was a seething from the woods, a whistling between the buildings. And up on the mountains they heard the hollow rumbling of snow sliding down.

Sigrid Undset and her sisters Signe and Ragnhild.

Lavrans lies awake, thinking uneasily about a prophecy he has heard that someday in the distant future the farm will be swept away by a huge flood – something that actually happened in 1789. Here the author allows her imagination free rein, and with great elegance she plays with various time periods. The seed for this scene had lain dormant in her mind for years and came to fruition long after she had heard about Stor-Ofsen as a child.

Yet the most exciting part of the family's visit in 1889 was being allowed to go riding with her father, to see him pointing toward Sollia many kilometers to the east, and to hear him talking about his own father, who had been born there in the mountains. Halvor had lost his father when he was very young, so he and his mother went back to live with her family on the Undseth farm in Østerdalen. Some years later they moved to Trondhjem, where Halvor began his training in the military. He attained the rank of sergeant major, married Kristine Øllegaard Dahl, and settled with his wife and three children on the Vollan estate, where he was employed as the superintendent. This estate was a

Halvor and Kristine Undseth with their three children: Kirsa, Halma, and Ingvald.

Sigrid Undset as a young secretary.

reformatory for fallen women, i.e., prostitutes and young girls who had ended up "in trouble." Undset provided a glimpse of her memories from Vollan in an article published in the Danish newspaper *Politiken*:

> Sigrid Undset herself recounts how, during visits to the home of her paternal grandfather, she could never understand what exactly was going on with these elegant young "ladies," who would arrive one evening in a carriage, wearing bustles and tight-fitting jersey bodices in keeping with the highest fashion. But the next day they were put to work in the laundry, wearing the institute's gray garb and under the stern command of the deaconess!

Ingvald Undset grew up on the Vollan estate, but if we're to believe his own account, it was not ladies wearing jersey bodices who filled most of his boyhood dreams, but rather the Norwegian national saint, Olav the Holy. Along with his best friend Henrik Mathiesen, he explored the ruins of Nidaros Cathedral in Trondhjem. The two boys clambered and climbed all around the church, "until they knew every nook and cranny... much better than the sexton himself." The boys pretended to be archaeologists, pounding the ground in search of secret chambers, measuring the remains of columns, and making copies of all sorts of ornamentation. With great enthusiasm they wrote down nearly illegible inscriptions, and went searching for the grave of St. Olav. Some years later it was decided that the church, in spite of vehement protests from anti-Catholic factions, should be restored, and Ingvald Undset was among those who rejoiced the most. Young Sigrid found much food for her imagination in all of these stories from the lives of her father and grandfather, and she never forgot them.

During the ten years that Sigrid Undset worked as a secretary in Kristiania, she made several stops in Lillehammer on her way to her much-coveted vacations in Gudbrandsdalen. With her sisters or her Swedish friend Gösta af Geijerstam, she would roam around in the mountains for days, taking along

Gösta af Geijerstam and Sigrid Undset sitting by the hearth at Laurgardseter.

only a change of clothes, a book, and a pack of cigarettes in her pocket. At least that was how she remembered these vacations. During one of the excursions her sister Ragnhild became engaged to Einar Wiberg, another charming Swede.

When evening fell, the young people would join the local inhabitants around a fire and listen to ghost stories. They heard about the *utburd*, the child who screamed and wailed at night after being left to die in the woods and denied burial in consecrated ground. Sigrid once boldly bet that she would dare go alone to a mountain pasture that was said to be haunted, but this was a bet that she ended up losing. Halfway there, she felt "something" grab her, something ice-cold and menacing. Terrified, she turned on her heel and ran back to the others, her face white as chalk and glistening with a cold sweat. "As if smeared with melted lard," remarked Gösta with a grin.

After her years as a secretary, Undset entered a period when she had money in her pocket, at first from a writer's grant and later from the royalties she received for her books. She traveled south through Denmark to Germany, Italy, and France, to Belgium and England. The world opened up for her, and she made steady progress in her development as a writer. But she always carried the landscape of her homeland with her – it had become part of her identity.

Sigrid Undset in the mountains.

When she wrote letters home from her travels in the big world, the Norwegian mountains were the yardstick by which she measured everything she saw. Such was the case, at any rate, in 1910 when Sigrid Undset and Anders Svarstad, in all secrecy, met as lovers in Paris. There he took her up in the tower of Notre Dame to show her the view of the city. One by one he pointed out the landmarks to her, but what Undset depicts in her letter home, published in the newspaper *Morgenbladet*, is not Montmartre or the Seine or the famous rooftops of Paris. Instead she writes:

> The little people who clamber up a slope and look out over the endless mountain plateau try to make themselves at home – to get their bearings. There is Vestronden, and beyond it lies Rondeslottet... And we quarrel with each other over Jotunheimen and the names of the peaks that we can see.
> There to the north are the Romsdal Mountains. But right in front of us Jetta greets those of us who are familiar with the area, and those three little knobs there, they are Heimehaugen and Anaripig and Karihaugen, and down in that direction is where we live.

The last time that Sigrid Undset visited Lillehammer before she actually moved to the town was in 1917. She brought her children Anders and Mosse with her, taking lodgings in the mail-coach inn at Sel so she could write. Her work progressed badly, because the summer heat was nearly tropical, but she did see Gösta af Geijerstam again. He was now living at Romundgard, where he had set up house with his lovely wife Astri. The old friends took an excursion to Sandbu in Vågå, and there Undset wrote numerous notes about the old farm and the magnificent landscape – information and observations that she would later put to good use. These preliminary investigations were important, because she had now started work on what would be her great historical novel, set in the first half of the fourteenth century.

The material was not new to her; it was something that she'd had in her desk drawer for years. In a letter to her Swedish penpal Dea Hedberg, she mentions that she sometimes finds fragments of this story in old books and on scraps of paper from her childhood. But as a very young girl, when she was struggling with "the big, lengthy monster," the main characters were Danish and named Maiden Agnete and Svend Trøst. Back then she had never really managed to breathe life into the figures or to make the details seem real, even though she had envisioned how everything ought to be:

> The whole time, you see, the reader should know where he is, how the land looked, as well as the houses and the people and the animals and the clothing and the weapons and saddlery, and you should quite naturally and easily enter into the life, see and understand why these people are this way, how they feel and why they behave as they do; and all of this without pedantic lectures about the era and the spirit of the times and all that muck that can make a story so inartistic because it's historical.

She had set so high a standard that it became too difficult for her, and so she put the material away in a drawer.

Next Sigrid Undset attempted another huge project, the precursor to the four-part novel *Olav Audunssøn* (titled in English *The Master of Hestviken*, and published in four separate volumes: *The Axe, The Snake Pit, In the Wilderness, and The Son Avenger*). This "big brute" was also based on material from the Danish Middle Ages, but Aage Nielssøn of Ulvholm, which was the name of the main character in the earliest version, never saw the light of day. In 1904 the manuscript was rejected by the Gyldendal Publishing Company in Copenhagen, which was the largest publisher at the time, also for Norwegian authors. Editor-in-chief Peter Nansen offered Sigrid Undset several comments, which she later in her life portrayed in a manner that he would never have recognized. According to Undset, Nansen supposedly told her with a shrug that she ought to stay away from historical novels, but she might try her hand at "something modern" – you never could tell. She took his advice, which in actual fact had been phrased with far greater delicacy.

From her debut novel *Fru Marta Oulie* (Mrs. Marta Oulie) in 1907 and up until 1919, when she left the capital and headed for Lillehammer, Undset published ten books, most of them based on contemporary material. But all were published by Aschehoug in Kristiania, which promoted itself as a publisher of Norwegian authors, and in particular of young women authors. Undset always had a hard time forgiving anyone who failed to show her proper respect.

After finalizing the house lease with Hjorth the painter, Sigrid Undset was ready to make a new attempt with the historical material about Agnete and Svend, but this time with Norwegian characters named Kristin and Erlend. Here, on the threshold of Gudbrandsdalen, she could breathe in the smells and hear the sounds along the path taken by her fictional characters, and it was in this landscape that they gradually emerged from the shadows to acquire color and life.

One of the advantages with setting the historical novel in Norway was that Undset could then make use of what she had learned, not only from her father but also from her father's younger cousin, Ove Dahl. Uncle Ove, as he was called in the family, had studied the Norwegian language as it was spoken in the Middle Ages, and in 1888 his dissertation about *Homilieboken* (The Homily Book) was accepted by the university in Kristiania. *The Homily Book* is a collection of sermons and freely revised stories in Old Norwegian; it's a text that truly provides a vivid insight into the minds of people during the Middle Ages – "how they feel and how they behave," as Undset put it. From Ove Dahl she learned how Norwegians had expressed themselves six hundred years earlier, the types of words and sentence constructions they used, the rhythm and tone of their speech. In the story about Kristin and Erlend, the language was terribly important for establishing a sense of verisimilitude, and even though Undset was not able to write the novel in the way that Norwegians actually spoke during the fourteenth century, the text had to contain authentic traces of the old speech patterns.

By 1893, when the Undset sisters lost their father, Ove Dahl had given up his philological studies for the sake of another passion of his: botany. In that year he was hired as an assistant at the university's Botanical Museum in Kristiania. When he had some free time he would occasionally take Sigrid along and set out on botanizing expeditions in the nearby fields and woods. The combination of Norwegian botany and Old Norwegian philology became Dahl's specialty, and Undset put both these fields of knowledge to good use in her work about Kristin Lavransdatter. By making Gudbrandsdalen the focal setting of the novel, she was able to draw on all the knowledge she had acquired; now she could finally put the thousands of details together.

Although the landscape in which Undset had now established herself was closely tied to memories of the past and plans for the future, both personal and professional, the physical reality was "here and now." When she arrived in May 1919, the town of Lillehammer had grown, and not just in size; it had also changed character since she had last traveled through with her mother and

father. The center of town still consisted mostly of blocks of two-story buildings with shops on the first floor and residences on the second, as had been
decided when the town was founded in 1827. But in 1912 new regulations
regarding the outlying areas of town were adopted, and they followed completely different principles. The plan now was to focus on single-family dwell-
ings, and the houses were to be positioned along streets and roads that followed
the terrain. The new catchwords of the day were: "diverse," "natural," and
"picturesque." Inspiration came from the English garden cities, where the intent
was to build healthier and lusher residential areas than what had developed as
a result of the explosive industrial growth of the nineteenth century. In Scandinavia the English ideas had their counterparts in the "Movement for Home
Ownership," of which Undset was an ardent supporter. In her treatise entitled
Et Kvinnesynspunkt (A Woman's Point of View), which was the first thing she
wrote after moving to Lillehammer, she says:

> The Movement for Home Ownership is one of the pet ideas of the day; and
> by the way, it's also one of my own cherished ideas. For most ordinary citi-
> zens, one of their deepest wishes is without a doubt to have their own home
> with a little garden. Owning a home is an extremely desirable thing – for
> many reasons. One is that when the house is your own, you can more easily
> accept its flaws and with staunch cheerfulness go about fixing everything
> that can be fixed. Another is that in terms of experiences, a child thrives
> better when allowed to grow up in one place, without changing environments.
> A child's ability to take an interest in everything around him is wrapped up
> in the objects of daily life, like roots around a rock. Any sort of uprooting
> or transplanting will always be followed by a period of stunted growth.

As a child, Sigrid Undset had been constantly on the move with her parents,
and she wanted to spare her own children the same sort of upheaval. She had
a desire to settle down for her own sake too; she was 37 years old and "could
no longer deal with having everything be so uncertain," as she wrote to Nini
Roll Anker.

In Lillehammer the building sites that had been set aside for residential areas
in accordance with the new regulations were very spacious, with plenty of room
for fruit trees, berry shrubs, flower beds, chicken coops, and woodsheds with
outdoor privies. Many of the houses were designed by skillful young architects,
but just as often it was the contractor himself who was in charge of the planning
and design. Ola Aasen, who had erected Hjorth's house, was one such contrac-

tor. As was the custom in Gudbrandsdalen, he often re-used old buildings. He would travel north in the valley and buy up reasonably priced timbered structures that he would then dismantle, log by log, and transport to town, where he re-constructed the building in a suitable design. The quality varied, and the house from Kvam was definitely not one of the best, but with the new paneling most of its flaws were well concealed.

You might think that these types of houses, which had been moved from other sites and were then rebuilt, would be considered second-class structures, but that was not the case. On the contrary, they were highly regarded, especially by well-to-do citizens and self-assured artists, who preferred to have a home marked by "genuine" Norwegian peasant culture. They rejected the idea of a "foreign-looking" house with gingerbread trim or a house decorated in *dragestil*, an Old Norse style inspired by the stave churches, often with dragon heads on the roof. What Undset wanted was a home characterized by excellent workmanship and old tradition, but it had to be authentic. In this she shared the views of Natalie, in the novel *Den trofaste hustru* (The Faithful Wife), who frowned upon anything that was plucked out of context and pretended to be Norwegian even though it wasn't. In Natalie's opinion, her parents' dining room is, at worst, the most horrible room in the world, and at best, merely amusing in its ugliness:

> The boards of the walls had been painted a glistening blue-green and the wainscoting the reddish color of whey cheese. The furniture was machine-made in a type of dragestil, and the sideboard was simply a miracle of oddness – the lower cabinet looked like a little sports hut, and the upper cabinet like a miniature storehouse with balconies on the sides where all of Mamma's electric coffee pots and egg cookers and other items she had won at the bazaar stood, turning yellow... It had never occurred to Pappa that there should be a coherence between objects... that made everything beautiful, or that the style was based on a craftsmanship that couldn't be replicated in a factory.

There were many painters, authors, and composers, both in Norway and in the neighboring countries, who thought as Natalie did. The weekly press presented as contemporary models the homes of such artists as Karin and Carl Larsson, who lived at Sundborn in Sweden, and Sigrun and Gerhard Munthe, whose house was just west of Kristiania in Lysaker. Larsson and Munthe were visual artists who, along with their wives, had created original and highly personal homes, with special emphasis on the excellent quality of craftsmanship in all the details. Svarstad had also made an attempt in the same direction; he had designed a canopy bed for the first home that he and Sigrid Undset furnished together, hiring a carpenter to do the work. But Svarstad never made a name for himself as a designer, perhaps because he himself paid such little interest to his environment. It was the high-profile and leading painters of the day who had an influence on the trends in taste, both in terms of exterior and interior design, and the furniture that they created was displayed and sold through the Artist Association in Kristiania. This combination of good design and fine craftsmanship won broad appeal during the big exhibition at Frogner Park in 1914, when the centennial of Norway's constitution was celebrated.

Through this exposure "Lunde Furniture" became a well-known concept, for in Einar Lunde's workshop in Lillehammer furniture was produced in accordance with the ideals of the Arts and Crafts movement. William Morris was the Englishman who first formulated the desire to combine the best of design and craftsmanship in quality products for "everything" that was needed in a home, from chairs and tables to cushions and curtains. The idea was to create an alternative to all the poor-quality factory-made goods that were flooding the European market. The Arts and Crafts Movement had developed quickly ever since the 1860s and had broken new ground for British decorative arts. It had also spread to other countries, finding its way to Scandinavia – and even to Lillehammer.

In the fall of 1902, the Norwegian painter Fredrik Collett invited to his home in Lillehammer some of his friends who were interested in art. In front of the fireplace he read aloud from his own translation of the work of the movement's foremost theoretician, John Ruskin. Collett's friends thought it was all well and good to translate the writings of the Arts and Crafts Movement, but the style itself had to be "translated" too – from English design to patterns and colors that would appeal to Norwegians, and that was of course much more difficult. It was true that excellent models could be found in the heritage of Norwegian national romanticism, but there was no point in holding on to the past, even in a town like Lillehammer where Anders Sandvig had won great praise for his collection of old applied art. His museum at Maihaugen was filled with fine wood-carvings and cabinets painted in the traditional floral rosemaling patterns. Einar Lunde wrote in a catalogue that his goal was not to copy the furniture that was produced in Norway "in the old days," but to satisfy the demand for Norwegian goods of a more personal character than was typical of factory-made pieces. "People do not have to kneel in obeisance before the machine, which is what is now happening everywhere. Consequently, what we surround ourselves with and fill our homes with are nothing more than corpses."

Undset was keenly interested in the conflicts taking place at the turn of the century, when "old and new attitudes and emotions vied for prominence in people's minds; a new economic order stretched out its tentacles to win control over a wild and powerful nature; a less pleasing building style and cheap industrial products tried to force out the magnificent old wooden architecture and the most precious products of Norwegian folk art." Undset's interest in the Arts and Crafts Movement had taken root long before she arrived in Lillehammer. As a newly married couple, she and Svarstad had lived in William Morris' old neighborhood in London, where the Hammersmith Socialist Society, which he had founded, was still very much alive and active. In the evening there were frequent meetings in the area with "salvationists and anarchists, socialists and anti-socialists, the Catholic mission and one thing and another." In the daytime the newlyweds took the opportunity to visit galleries where they could study the paintings of Morris and his friends. These Pre-Raphaelites, as they were called, specialized in an exquisitely detailed realism which they combined with atmospheric and symbolic motifs from the Middle Ages, not unlike the approach that Undset used in a literary sense in her medieval novels.

She was also familiar with the literary works of William Morris. One of the books he had published was a poetry collection called *The Defence of Guenevere and Other Poems*, which was based on the legends of King Arthur and the knights of the Round Table. Undset published her own version of the same material in 1915 because she was just as fascinated as Morris was with the tales about King Arthur, who was betrayed by his best friend, Sir Lancelot, and about Guenevere, who loved two men. "For customs and traditions may change greatly, in accordance with the tastes of the time; and the beliefs of people also change, and they may think differently about many things. But the human heart never changes as times go by." This is how Undset ends her book about the brotherhood of knights, and these lines remained her creed ever afterwards. It is her most famous quotation.

When Sigrid Undset moved to Lillehammer, it was through Einar Lunde and his friends that she once again encountered the influence of the English circle around William Morris. This was a cultural climate that she knew well and was inspired by as she set about furnishing her own home.

Others who had shaped contemporary styles were the feminists, those strong-willed women with whom Undset had such a strained relationship, because, as she said, they were using childbirth and motherhood for political purposes. It was no coincidence that the housing ideals in the new century took shape at the same time as the women's movement took off, both in England and in Scandinavia. Women in the new century wanted to focus on functionality, health, and well-being rather than placing emphasis on the home as an arena for entertaining on the husband's terms. For a long time the so-called "gentlemen's rooms" had existed, filled with heavy, upholstered furniture, dark wallpaper, and voluminous drapes, while the ladies' "salons" were meant to have light furniture and bright colors. Gradually the big, luxurious, work-intensive houses, with their differentiated rooms – the so-called boom-period mansions – went out of fashion. For most people, in any case, they had represented an unattainable dream, with their elaborate floor plans encompassing everything from a dining room, parlor, conservatory, and library, to a kitchen, pantry, maid's room, nursery, bedrooms, and dressing rooms. The new female ideals and regard for the demands of daily life gradually won out. A home should be designed with a view to economic concerns, labor-saving features, health, and hygiene. For most women the home was also their workplace, while for men it was still primarily a place for rest and social life. But in the case of artist couples, both spouses might have their workplace in the home, and perhaps this was a contributing factor behind the focus on their residences as contemporary models.

In the work of Sigrid Undset, the difference between male and female ideals regarding living quarters is clearly presented in the autobiographical story *Tolv år* (Twelve Years), an unfinished manuscript found at Bjerkebæk in 1998. Undset's alter ego, Ingvild, is the main character of this story. As long as Ingvild's father is alive, their home is crammed with furniture and filled with books; it is dark and confining, with a good parlor that marks their social status but is only seldom used. When Ingvild's mother is widowed, she and her three daughters move to a smaller apartment, and there the style is completely different. Light and air and plants are allowed into the rooms, and the demand for function takes precedence over entertaining and prestige. The mother has to sell most of the family's belongings after her husband's death, but she keeps the most beautiful of their possessions, "and it was much easier to see them, because here the sun shone into the rooms all day long," says the daughter, almost with a guilty conscience.

So it was not only the architects and building contractors but equally the artists, craftsmen, and feminists who demonstrated how people should live in the new century. In Lillehammer it was the painters, in particular, who designed unique homes that also functioned as their workplaces. The thought must have occurred to Sigrid Undset that if Svarstad had his own studio, he too might consider living in Lillehammer and thus share in creating an artist home. But Svarstad's place in the new household was unclear. The matter remained unresolved, and Undset concentrated on setting the house in order before the new baby arrived. All the same, she furnished the new house on Nordseterveien with great care. She had always loved beautiful things, and many times she allowed her emotions to take precedence over her good sense when it came to surrounding herself with beauty. Even as a young, impoverished secretary, she had begun to collect antiques. And even in those places where she was going to live for only a short time, such as in London or Rome or Paris, she always had to have something beautiful to look at. Here in Lillehammer she was going to stay for all of fifteen months. Or so she thought.

Svarstad arrived from Kristiania with a load of furniture and household items and stayed for a week to help out his wife. The blue canopy bed was set up in the big bedroom on the second floor with a view to the west. He had also brought along the birch chest of drawers, which had been Undset's bridal chest during the years that she was secretly engaged. In these drawers she had put everything that had been embroidered and marked with her initials during the engagement period – pillows, sheets, tablecloths, and napkins. Afterwards, when they were newly married, Svarstad had decorated the front with two spirited Pegasus figures, one male and one female. Now the chest of drawers was placed in the living room. The mirror above it was flanked by pictures of Undset's two grandmothers in oval frames: Clara Petrea Severine Gyth of Kalundborg in Denmark, and Kristine Øllegaard Undseth of Trondheim in Norway. This room would have to serve as Undset's workroom, because she was determined to do as Jane Austen had done: to sit in the middle of the living room and write as her family and the household help swarmed about her. The alternative was to write at night.

Her desk, work chair, and bookcase, all of which she had inherited from her father, were brought into the house. Undset placed the green-painted desk in front of the living-room window so that she could look down toward the town and across the valley and the river, to the blue mountains on the other side. To the left of her desk, on her father's bookcase, which had sides made from woven willow branches, she had room for her reference books and her treasures, such as the lovely photograph album that was a gift from her maternal grandfather Gyth in Kalundborg. On top of the bookcase stood a photo of her mother, Charlotte Gyth Undset, taken in 1882, the year of Sigrid's birth.

As always, Undset gave a great deal of care to her potted plants. In front of

Sigrid Undset with her sister Ragnhild and their mother in 1907.

the triple-pane windows in the living room, white-painted bookshelves were installed below the windowsills so there was room for two rows of pots. To ensure that the plants received the most possible light, the curtains were made of the lightest type of material. In this Undset was following the recommendations of the magazine *Urd*, which advised its readers: "See to it that you have the walls painted in light colors as much as you can, and put up thin, lightweight curtains; don't let heavy draperies cover the windows. Remember that here in Norway we have so much fog and darkness that we need every meager ray of sunshine that we can get."

Svarstad needed some of the furniture from their former apartment in Sinsen for his new household in Kristiania, and so Undset had to make some purchases. At Lunde's shop in Lillehammer she found both furniture and textiles after her own heart – items that had been designed by Norwegian artists and produced by skilled craftsmen. The small dining room between the living room and kitchen was furnished with a bench, six plain chairs, and a solid chair with arms for the head of the family. That was where Undset herself sat. Svarstad largely stayed in Kristiania.

The relationship between the spouses had now turned extremely cold. Undset recounts in a letter to Nini, who had gone through a divorce herself and was now married for the second time, that when she had taken off her wedding ring to have it repaired, little Anders had gone quite pale and solemn-eyed. He asked, "Mother, why aren't you wearing your wedding ring? You're not going to divorce Father, are you?" Undset didn't answer him, because she was uncertain about any future that she might share with Svarstad. It was becoming more and more clear that they were moving in separate directions, both politically and personally. Both of them were at odds with the fashionable trends of the day – for her part, it had to do with the women's movement; for his part, it was his view of modern art. Svarstad had long been hoping that the position of director of the Art Academy in Kristiania would become his, and so he refused to move out to the provinces. Undset, on the other hand, was delighted with her own work situation, because she now saw an opportunity for acquiring some help, both with the housework and childcare. Filled with optimism, she wrote to Nini:

> But stroke of luck no. 2 – as of July 1, I'll have a Swedish white-cross sister, meaning she's trained in the care of infants and children. She happens to be free at that time, so I've hired her for at least half a year... I can hardly believe that things are going to work out so well for me! Now if only I could find a maid, everything would be arranged so that I could enjoy some good days for a while.

In the midst of all the work involved with moving into Hjorth's house, something was worrying Undset. She wondered how she was going to finish a collection of essays in which she clarified her views regarding the women's movement. She had long been at odds with the feminists, whom she found both elitist and naive, and now she wanted to put five of her earlier published articles in a book, adding a longer, newly written "Afterword." This work was close to her heart, and she also needed the money. "If I get some help, I think I'll manage to have it published, even if I have to write *lying down*," she confided to Nini.

Things didn't go completely according to plan. The Swedish "Sister Sia" couldn't come at the agreed-upon date, and when she did arrive, she turned out to be a disappointment. There was soon a long list of housekeeping problems, because the residence on Nordseterveien was certainly no palace. The water pump in the cellar was constantly failing, and the children couldn't be allowed outside on their own because the property lacked fencing, which meant that cattle and horses often plodded all the way up to the buildings.

It was Charlotte Undset, Sigrid's Danish-born mother, who had to step in and offer assistance, "That meticulous little woman, the Archduchess," as Christian Elling calls her in his memoirs. She looked like a lady-in-waiting from olden times, he thought, "erect as a candle, her head held high, with a towering coiffure, as artificial as a wig from Versailles. She had a proud profile, she had more of a nose than most Danes, and more backbone too." Yet the "Archduchess" was not afraid of hard work, and she valiantly assisted her daughter with the housework for a full six weeks during that first summer at Bjerkebæk.

Even so, Sigrid Undset had little patience for her mother and her countless strong opinions, so the time they spent together was not easy. Charlotte Undset, for her part, was worried about her daughter's health, and she complained that Sigrid had worn herself out trying to create a home for both her own children and her stepchildren back in Sinsen. Loudly she voiced her annoyance with her sons-in-law, who she thought gave greater priority to their work than to their families. Svarstad was now planning new travels, financed by a grant, while Sigge Pantzerhielm Thomas, who was married to her youngest daughter Signe, was busy working on his doctoral dissertation and had buried himself in his studies of the Roman Gracchus lineage. Undset laughed at her mother's tirades, writing to Nini:

> And yet she's incomparable; she manages the most amazing things and wants to do it all – and rages about my stepchildren and about Sigge Thomas who has taken Signe and the children out to the country without any maid so that he can putter about in peace with his Gracchi – "those foolish beasts." She speaks of Sigge and the Svarstads in exactly the same tone of voice she uses for the black bull that wanders about outside the house – and occasionally she stands at the window and talks to the bull and the cows as if she had Sigge and the Gracchi mothers before her. And the cows stop grazing and stand there gaping up at her with immeasurable astonishment. The whole thing is enough to make a person both laugh and cry, you know – but I suppose it's a good sign that I find four-leaf clovers every time I go into town.

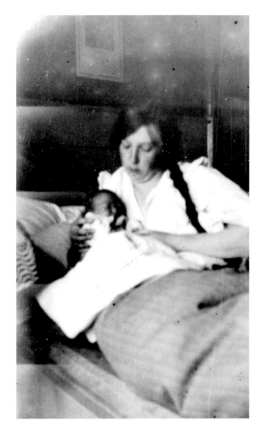 

Sigrid Undset shortly after giving birth to her third child in August 1919.

The Swedish nursemaid with Hans.

And luck was with her during the birth of her third child. On the morning of August 27, 1919, Sigrid Undset gave birth to a big, healthy boy, who from the very first moment knew how to make the most of life's blessings. A couple of months later he was christened Hans Benedikt Hugh Svarstad – "Hans" after Johannes [John] the Baptist, "Benedikt" after the founder of the Benedictine order, and "Hugh" after the English Catholic writer Hugh Benson. It was Helene Frøisland who held the child with the propitious names at his christening. Sigrid Undset rejoiced at the fact that she had finally fulfilled her dream of being able to say "my sons."

With an office in "Norway's most beautiful home"

"My sons," says Sigrid Undset so proudly, immediately awakening associations with women in the sagas and Norway as the birthplace of giants. There was nothing wrong with her sense of the dramatic, nor with her eye for set design. As a young woman she had put these talents to good use when she finally had her own room and made her first attempts at interior decorating. She was then nineteen years old and working as a secretary in Kristiania. She'd already had a good deal of theater experience in the nursery – as an actress, director, script-writer, and set designer for the plays she produced for her sisters and girlfriends. She loved the National Theater and loved hearing about the stars of the day; she may even have dreamed of becoming an actress herself.

Undset sent a sketch of her room to her penpal Dea, and in the same letter she reports with enthusiasm about an "enthralling" actress that she has recently seen. Her room she describes as if it were a tableau from the stage, and she places Dea and herself in appropriate roles and positions:

> I had it painted the exact blood-red color that I wanted, and since the walls are wood-paneled and the furniture of the simplest kind – which I painted a brilliant green color that suits the walls so well – it has all turned out so charming. A "corner sofa" draped with an old Italian rug, one of Father's old wicker bookcases, and over by the stove a lovely "peasant bench" where

Sigrid Undset at her desk in the living room, 1922.

I wish you were sitting right now with a cigarette so we could have a good chat, instead of me having to write down every word that I would have said to you. And I have my books and flowers and shelves with ceramics and pots and lots of pictures – all of them pictures that I've either bought myself or taken from Mama's huge collection of photographs of Renaissance paintings – so you see, everything has a personal meaning for me and suits my own taste.

The letter is interesting for many reasons, and not just because it shows Undset's sense for dramatizing her own life. We can see how the interior of her room reflects a personality and taste that are generally the same in Kristiania in 1901 as in Lillehammer twenty years later. The details and style of her room as a young woman correspond to an astonishing degree to the home that she created as an adult. Even though she quickly abandoned the strong color scheme, the overall style and even a few of the objects, such as her father's bookcase and her mother's pictures, reappear at Bjerkebæk.

It's clear that Sigrid Undset, both early in her life and later as an adult, placed great emphasis on an interior that was personal. As if she were a child of Romanticism but born too late, she wished to be unique and original, surrounding herself with objects such as the Italian rug and the bench harking back to a Romantic view of the peasantry. Her ideals pertaining to education and her social class can also be read in the interior. The travel traditions of the upper class are evident in her remark regarding Renaissance art from "Mama's huge collection," while the culture of the academic class is represented by the books that she has placed on "one of Father's old wicker bookcases." The fact that Undset smoked cigarettes and collected ceramics demonstrates that she nevertheless was a modern woman.

We find another glimpse of Undset's thoughts regarding furnishings in an article that she wrote in 1922 when she was in the process of shaping her home in Lillehammer. One day she paid a visit to Ingeborg Janson, a talented woman who had started an evening school for young girls, to teach them something about the decorative arts and interior design. In her article, Undset recalls her own youth and how she and her girlfriends would get together to do needlework after their workday at the office, and how they strove to make their meager lodgings comfortable. She admits that the result usually failed:

It was often so difficult to make things look the way we had so clearly imagined they ought to be. It was easy to see that our rooms, which we wanted to seem "personal" and "artistic," as we expressed it back then, were merely clumsy and untidy... The sofa covering and cushions were not the sort that greeted us pleasantly every time we entered the room, nor could we arrange our belongings in such a way that we could avoid thinking every second about how cramped the room was.

In the article Sigrid Undset praises the efforts of Janson's evening school, because to be successful as an interior designer, an individual has to have both technical knowledge and an awareness of "the legitimate harmony of lines, of mass and weight, of space and how to fill it in a pleasing way." Ten years of marriage to a painter had clearly left their mark.

The home that Undset created in Lillehammer reflects not only her own taste and personality; it also says something about the relationship between private and public space that was typical for the time. Previously, a home had primarily been a place of refuge that provided shelter and security, but gradually it came to be regarded as an extension of the owner's identity – and even part of the public stage. For many cultural figures, their home was an important part of marketing themselves as artists, and Bjerkebæk came to function in the same way for Sigrid Undset. After the dissolution of the union between Norway and Sweden in 1905, and against a backdrop of growing industrialism and the First World War, Undset donned her "bunad," the Norwegian national costume, and had herself photographed in front of the old timbered buildings, often with her children. Specially chosen journalists published lengthy articles about her, with photos of some of the rooms and the garden at Bjerkebæk. In this way the author, whose fame was steadily growing, was able to convey the values that she esteemed most highly. By shielding certain parts of her home from public view while emphasizing other features, she allowed Bjerkebæk to function as a stage set that made it possible for her to live up to her own myth. And why not? "I thought life was so much, so grand and so beautiful, that we ought to make ourselves into works of art," she had written to Dea at the age of nineteen. In Lillehammer it was not herself but her *home* that she set out to transform into a work of art. The buildings surrounded a courtyard on three sides, as if it were a stage. The fence functioned as an essential controlling element, because it was of course only on specific occasions and under special circumstances that Undset would open the gate and allow the public inside. On a daily basis, she wanted the least possible attention to be directed toward herself and her family.

Before Undset could go about shaping the stage set of her home as a mature artist, she needed a substantial income, and that was something she had to accomplish by using her pen. It's not known whether she actually had to lie in bed while finishing *A Woman's Point of View*, but the essay collection was published in the fall of 1919, thereby ensuring her finances – at least for a while. The lease on Bjerkebæk was extended for another year, and Sigrid wrote to Nini: "I have filled all the windows with roses and pelargonias and oleanders and English geraniums and abutilons and stars of Bethlehem and fuchsias – my potted plants have never thrived the way they do here. If only I could stay in Lillehammer!"

Over the next five or six years Sigrid Undset pushed herself to the limit, impelled by thousands of personal demons, driven by creative joy and ambition, as well as the need to pay the bills and provide for her family. The result was a creative rapture without parallel, in which great art and a unique home took shape under her strong-willed hands. The pace she set for herself was formidable.

The publication of *Kransen* (*The Wreath*), which was the first volume of what would become the trilogy entitled *Kristin Lavransdatter*, caused a sensation in the autumn of 1920, and it was both a literary and commercial success. Through her contemporary stories, Undset was already known as a talented interpreter of the psyche of her time. Now she surprised her readers with this portrait of a medieval universe and with her impressive ability to create an epic narrative. The depiction of a relatively stable life and the fully formed characters in *The Wreath* appealed to readers who were living in a world marked by ever-growing secularism, brutality, and rootlessness. Some did question the novel's historical authenticity, while others claimed that the underlying eroticism of *The Wreath* was both immoral and pernicious reading material for young people. But most realized at once that the book presented a rare literary quality, and that it clearly had to be deemed a masterpiece.

The novel went through many printings, and sales were brisk – not just in Norway but all over Scandinavia. Praise came streaming in, and it meant a great deal to Undset that she was now recognized as a prominent artist. As if to emphasize that Kristin's creator was no light-weight, she wrote a solid scholarly article about Nordic folk ballads, which won her academic respect as well.

Because of the numerous printings of *The Wreath* and the professional security she now had gained, Undset experienced a new freedom, also financially. This was something that was much needed, since all indications were that her marriage to Svarstad was coming to an end. He stayed in Kristiania or spent time abroad and refused to hear any talk of living together in Lillehammer. In general, he didn't want to discuss any marital problems at all. For her part, Undset wanted to clarify the situation, and in December 1920 things came to

The living room, as it looked until 1924.

a head, resulting in a complete break between the two. Undset took this as a bitter defeat, but she still had both the self-discipline and the strength of will to go on alone. It was her future as an artist that was at stake, after all.

Hjorth, the painter who owned the house on Nordseterveien, decided to sell it, and in July 1921 Sigrid Undset signed the purchase agreement. The property measuring 5,113 m² was hers for 27,000 Norwegian kroner. For the first time in her life she was now living in a place where she could move walls and doors, install stoves and baths without asking anyone for permission.

What gave her the courage to take on this financial risk was that her work on *Kristin Lavransdatter* was going better than she had ever expected. The second volume was received with marvelous reviews, though it did nothing to soften Svarstad's frame of mind to see that the book about Kristin's unreliable husband Erlend and his opposite, her honorable father Lavrans, was dedicated to Ingvald Undset.

The income from the second volume, *Husfrue* (*The Wife*), also streamed into Undset's bank account, making it possible for her to ensure Mosse's future by taking out a life insurance policy. Finally she felt that she had the wherewithal to begin a new chapter in her own life, a chapter as the proprietor and mistress of her own property. It was now that she gave her home the name of "Bjerke-bæk." Since there was both a small "bæk," or creek, on the site and many old "bjerke," or birch trees, it may seem a natural choice for a name, but subsequently a different explanation has been handed down. It was said that Undset actually had in mind a well-known Danish vaudeville figure, a certain Herr Bjerkebæk, who appeared in a musical as a caricature of a "Nordic Norwegian from Nor-way." If the choice of names proved annoying to her Danish-born mother, Sigrid Undset seemed not to mind.

The same autumn that she purchased the property, Undset began planning improvements at Bjerkebæk, and a contractor named Grønvold supplied the blueprints. But before the carpenters could get started, Christmas had to be celebrated, with the seven traditional types of cookies and visitors from Kristiania. It was a wearisome holiday season, with Undset's mother as a "rather nerve-wracking companion," as she wrote to Nini. In addition, the well had run dry again, and they had to carry water in buckets from Postmaster Lieungh's house down below. The children were put to bed, one after the other, with bad colds. Even so, Undset had time to read a big stack of new books from the fall season, and whatever books she didn't care to keep, she packed up and sent off to hospitals, schools, and nursing homes. It was probably good to have her own work as a means of escape.

During the winter and spring of 1922 she continued to work on the third volume, *Korset* (*The Cross*). Undset must have felt an enormous sense of satisfaction that the trilogy about Kristin Lavransdatter, the first great literary ambition of her youth, was now approaching completion. "I wrote eight different versions of those books, and by hand – not on a typewriter. Now and then, when I was struggling most with the work, I would think back almost with longing to my days at the office." Undset made this remark many years later in an interview with a German student who had turned up at Bjerkebæk. It was probably not meant in all seriousness!

For someone who had a great need of quiet in order to concentrate, the living room at Bjerkebæk was, of course, a poor workplace. And the problems of daily life were not always as charming as the impression she gave to Dea in the following letter:

Hans is starting to rebel against garden fences and nursemaids – his little friends Arne and Magne, 4 and 5 years old, show up all on their own in my workroom while I'm sitting there writing, or they come in while we're having dinner, bringing along a chair and asking for food as if they were in their own home – once in a while a curtseying sister who's a few years older turns up to ask if we know where Magne is. Or has Arne been here today? You can see that I truly live out in the country.

By the time her work on *Kristin Lavransdatter* was nearing an end, Undset had figured out how Bjerkebæk should be changed to suit the family's needs. Contractor Grønvold was asked to expand the small outlying building, while at the same time work proceeded on the main house. A new, two-story veranda was erected, with an enclosed garden room on the first floor and an open veranda on the second. That was where Undset sat for the Danish painter Harald Slott-Møller when he and his wife Agnes came to visit during the summer of 1923. The portrait had been started while Undset was in Copenhagen earlier in the spring, but the landscape that was meant to form the background had to be painted on-site, and the veranda offered a relatively peaceful place to work.

It must have been a strange experience for Undset to pose for a painting again, as she had done so many times for Svarstad. It probably annoyed her that the work took so much time, but William Nygaard, the head of Aschehoug Publishing Company, insisted on acquiring a portrait of his best-selling author. Undset's books now completely dominated the Norwegian book market, and she had secured Aschehoug's position as the country's leading publisher. "The Nobel Prize? She'll certainly get it," said Nygaard – and he ordered two railroad cars of paper for the reprinting of her books. Slott-Møller's portrait was given a place of honor in the publisher's vestibule, where it still hangs today.

If she had wished to do so, Undset could certainly have afforded to pay for the portrait herself, because her tax returns show a staggering increase in her income during those first years at Bjerkebæk. In a very short period of time she exchanged a financially strapped existence for the life of a prosperous woman. The documents from the county tax offices in Fåberg show both the beginnings of a personal fortune and a solid annual income even in 1921. It was from this time that Bjerkebæk started to take on the character of an "enterprise," with significant income and significant expenses, and with many people and countless projects to manage. One of them was Undset's subscription to a news clipping service. From this point on, all articles and mentions in the press that had anything to do with her work were glued into big, black binders, and over the years the collection grew to 22 volumes. The contents include newspaper clippings from both Norway and abroad, with everything from book reviews

DEN NYE SVALGANG

Lillehammer 4-10 1921 L. Grønvold

Contractor Grønvold's drawing for the new veranda, dated October 4, 1921.

and news of the Nobel Prize to letters from readers and trivial observations in the best tabloid style.

Another activity that became systematized at this point had to do with the household finances. All bills were put in ring binders and roughly sorted according to topic: groceries, bakery goods, beverages, electrical bills and insurance premiums, furniture and handicrafts, books, paintings, sporting goods, dental treatments, photography, work in the garden, indoor renovations, cab expenses (often for several trips each week), dresses and undergarments, doghouses, plumbing work, electrical items, advertisements, and flowers.

This detailed material offers insight into the most personal of matters. For instance, an ad was placed about a "lost cat" – Mosse's pet – in January 1924, and 40 bottles of red and white soda were purchased on January 23, 1926, which was the day before Anders' thirteenth birthday. He must have had an extra number of guests that year when he became a teenager. We can see that Mosse's sealskin coat cost 247 kroner, which was a large sum for a child's garment, and that it was bought in Kristiania, or Oslo, as the capital was renamed in 1925. We can draw so many conclusions from the bills. For instance, January 1929 must have been an extremely cold month, since there were constant calls to the plumber – with subsequent bills for "thawing water pipes and the rent of thawing transformers." We can wonder what film it was on December 12, 1931, that made Undset pay 3 kroner to be driven by taxi round-trip to the movie theater. These are the sorts of odd questions that keep popping up when you sit with the household binders in front of you. A few of the receipts are so revealing of intimate matters that you hurry to page past them, murmuring a quiet apology to Sigrid Undset.

Other receipts that are much easier to peruse cast a light on Undset's professional life. She must have devoured large quantities of newspapers and journals, both local and national, of all genres, ranging from cultural publications and parish newsletters to women's magazines. There are incredibly long lists of purchases of books from both Norway and abroad, fiction and nonfiction, theological publications and art books. A bill that she received dated December 31, 1924, for a year's worth of purchases from a bookstore in Kristiania shows no less than 101 entries. It includes the letters of the historian P.A. Munch, a Latin

grammar, pocket calendars, dictionaries, books by Fridtjof
Nansen and Hans Christian Andersen, *Shakespeare's Works*,
and books by Norwegian poets. In addition to what she
bought personally, Undset constantly received packages of books from Aschehoug Publishing Company
and from the Authors' Union, and she was a regular
customer at the bookstore in Lillehammer. So it's
easy to understand why bills keep appearing for new
bookcases for the house too.

The ring binders bear witness to another matter:
Sigrid Undset's strong belief in doing good deeds. It's
impressive how many receipts there are from those
she helped by giving them money – people who were
ill or unemployed, poor families with talented children in
need of aid in order to go to school or take music lessons,
and needy colleagues who were given a helping hand through the
relief fund of the Authors' Union. She made large contributions to her own
family members and to close friends, and her stepchildren and sisters enjoyed
the full measure of her generosity. "Send me the bill," was her customary refrain.
Once a large sum was "given by Mrs. Sigrid Undset to Mrs. Charlotte Undset
and delivered to St. Ringgate 16, Sogn Haveby," where her mother was living
with Undset's sister Signe and her family. And to distribute her favors equally
between her two sisters, Undset made sure that Ragnhild and her Swedish
husband received a comparable sum.

Gösta af Geijerstam was one of her old friends who benefited greatly from
Undset's generosity. He was constantly short of cash and received help in the
form of commissions for paintings, presents, and loans. And then there were
all the others. Receipts show that over just four weeks in 1926 Undset paid the
grocery bills for nine families in the Hamar region, families who were most
likely members of the Catholic congregation there. The more she earned, the
more individuals she had on her "payment list." Eventually there was so much
to keep track of that she allied herself with a cleric named M. Lüdemann, who
took over some of the distribution and ensured that the money went to those
who needed it most. The total of all the gifts that she made over the course of
many years must have added up to a huge sum, but Undset insisted on discre-
tion, so not many knew of these activities. The recipients often didn't know

Sigrid Undset in the late 1920s.

where the help came from, but a few thank-you letters did find their way to Sigrid Undset all the same and were archived in the Bjerkebæk binders.

Large sums were gradually allocated for the household's own use too, and from the receipts it's evident that 1922 was in many ways a year marked by significant home improvements. In addition to Grønvold's work on the outbuilding and veranda, we see that Undset received a bill for the construction of a rustic fence, which meant that she didn't have to worry any longer about allowing the children out to play in the yard at Bjerkebæk. Plumber Ramsøi sent a bill for a new pump and for cleaning out the sewer line. A big new "bear stove" was purchased, a cast-iron stove the size of a bear standing on its hind legs that could cope with even the most bitterly cold temperatures. And in the living room the walls and ceilings were covered with sacking and then painted.

Sigrid Undset was now a frequent customer at Einar Lunde's store, and while the bill in 1921 was 529 kroner, it was almost double that amount in 1922, with a total of 985.20 kroner. She also shopped in Kristiania. At Christmastime in 1922 she purchased from Groseth the antique dealer a furniture set consisting of six chairs and a couch. Old Groseth was very fond of his customer, and many years later he recounted: "She'd been coming here ever since she was a little girl with a braid down her back. I always noticed her. She would stop outside and pick out a specific item. Then she would come in and ask how much that item cost. As a girl she bought only small things. The first larger item she purchased was an English cabinet, an unusually fine cabinet. After that she bought more and more large items."

Undset's new wealth was welcomed by her closest family members, and the number of visitors increased. In the summer of 1923 she writes to Gösta af Geijerstam that her house is full of children, her own three and two belonging to her sister, Ragnhild Wiberg. In the spring of that year Ragnhild had fallen seriously ill, and "Aunt Sigrid" immediately brought to Lillehammer four-year-old Ulla and her little brother Ingvald from Stockholm. They stayed at Bjerkebæk for six months, "so there's not much peace to work here – and my work this year is translation, which is harder than I had envisioned," she wrote with a heavy sigh.

Peace and quiet were what Undset sorely needed, and for several reasons. While working on *Kristin Lavransdatter*, she had done a great deal of research about the customs and teachings of the Catholic church as it was in Norway before the Reformation in 1536, and gradually she developed a desire to become a member herself. After writing the monumental story about Kristin, that reluctant servant who in spite of all guilt and shame clings to her pact with God, Undset began receiving instruction from parish priest Kjelstrup at the Catholic church in Hamar. She must have had a great need for a place of retreat where she could gather her thoughts, and in July 1923 she put the following ad in the local paper:

Wish to purchase,

for removal and rebuilding, a house made of solid timbers, preferably 2 stories, with space for the furnishing of one large and two or three smaller rooms on each floor. Offers including information regarding price, the age of the house and its dimensions, distance from a railroad station, etc. to be sent to this newspaper, marked "House for removal."

There was a building for sale on the Nordre Dalseg estate in Gudbrandsdalen, a magnificent old timbered building that had not been occupied for many years. The first floor consisted of a large open space of 50 m² and a narrow room, an alcove, running the full width of the house. A fireplace was situated in one corner of the big room, in accordance with the traditional layout of an Akershus type of cabin. New studies have shown that the timber used for the building was felled sometime between 1702 and 1704, and most likely the house was constructed shortly afterwards.

Undset bought the Dalseg house for 7,000 kroner – which was far too much, according to her friends, but her curt response was: "I can afford it." As soon as the deal had been made, contractor Grønvold prepared the blueprints for the new project, with corridors and stairs that would connect the two main buildings. The house was disassembled, log by log, and transported to Lillehammer by rail. Then Bjerkebæk was invaded by a whole army of workers. The first thing to be built was a dry, frost-free cellar for the storage of fruit and vegetables. Next, terraces made of flagstones were created in the courtyard in front of the buildings. Parts of the creek were lined with stone, and that job alone required almost 700 man-hours. The heavy flat stone that had lain in front of the entrance at Dalseg was also brought to Lillehammer, and the old soapstone fireplace had to be reconstructed, so there was a great need for workers. Little Hans claimed that the fireplace was as huge as a "a horrid pig," while his mother went even farther and said it was as enormous as "a medium-sized room."

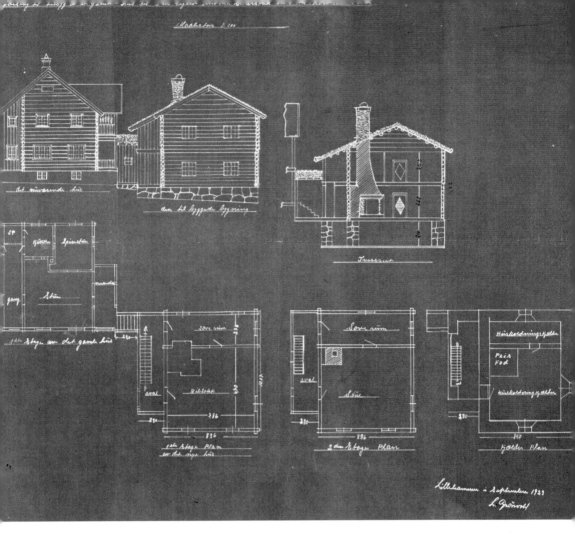

Grønvold's blueprint of Bjerkebæk with the Dalseg house.

Undset was looking forward to having the peace to work, because she was now dreaming of completing the other big project from her youth. She wanted to take up again the manuscript that the Gyldendal Publishing Company in Copenhagen had once rejected. Now this material would also be "translated" to a Norwegian setting, just as she had done with the trilogy about Kristin Lavransdatter. The author had decided to turn the Danish knight Aage Nielssøn into the Norwegian Olav Audunssøn. But the work conditions at Bjerkebæk got much worse before they would get better. Undset complained vehemently to her friend Gösta that there was such a commotion all around her now that she honestly wished herself far away:

For one thing, all summer long people have been treating my house like a train station, and I've gone about like some sort of hostess, serving coffee, tea, and dinner with and without wine, etc. – and haven't been able to work at all except at night. In addition, I've had a garden put in. Now it's true that I've had a man to look after the garden. But somebody has to look after the man. Third, they're working and building full steam ahead on my new house, which is a whole story unto itself, but I hope you'll all have a chance to come and see it for yourselves sometime. It's a Gudbrandsdal building of high quality – and farmers from the valley keep coming up to have a look at it, sighing over their own stupidity – over what they've once had themselves and ruined, and they talk about when an auction was held after their grand-mother died, and about when they renovated their own house – and now it's done and what was ruined is ruined.

The positioning of the fireplace in the big timbered building soon presented a problem, but they found a solution by reversing the blueprint from the original plan. Otherwise the goal was to change as little as possible. The lovely paneling with the wide trim was put up again, following the traditional method of alter-nating the planks so that the wide end of one abutted the narrow end of another. In this way the difference in width was evened out. The bench was affixed to the wall as before, and the low, wide entrance doors were re-installed. In the alcove, next to the hearth room, the walls were covered with sacking and then painted. Witty gossips claimed that this was because of vulgar words and draw-ings that had been scratched into the walls. Another modification that can be explained with greater accuracy was that the ceiling of the alcove was lowered so as to create an insulated space of 80 centimeters between what was to be Undset's study and the boys' bedroom above. Like most brothers, the boys bickered and fought, so their mother had to take these necessary measures if she was going to be able to work in peace, as she so longed to do.

As the icing on the cake, Undset had a brazier make door handles in the shape of animals for the new doors in the house – fledgling birds and baby seals that fit the hand perfectly. Nini Roll Anker was so enthused by these brass door handles that Undset had to order the same kind for her friend's house in Asker.

Work on the Dalseg house continued all winter and spring, and even on into the summer. Everything looked wonderfully promising, and the museum founder Anders Sandvig came to visit and heaped warm praise on the project. By August 1924 the restoration had progressed so far that Undset allowed herself to be photographed on the slope in front of the buildings. In the picture she is standing hand in hand with her household help, and all of them are wearing "bunads," the Norwegian national costume. Their attire had to suit the stage-set, of course.

The last phase of the project, when the rooms were to be furnished, must have been a true shopping spree, because Undset's financial state now allowed her to pick and choose from the very best that the galleries and antique shops had to offer. Without blinking an eye she paid 4,500 kroner for a single painting, a landscape by I.C. Dahl. Then it occurred to her that this might be a good investment for her two sons, so she bought another. Three antique chests were brought home, one for each child. Little by little the house was decorated with beautiful paintings by Kristen Holbø, Nikolai Astrup, and Gerhard Munthe, while drawings by Gösta af Geijerstam filled one entire wall of the alcove. Sigrid Undset purchased tapestries and chests, brass lamps and silver candlesticks, and on the top shelf in the hearth room she put her collection of old glasses, which she set side by side with the newest examples of ceramics.

She had a sense for the practical too. The electrical wiring was concealed inside pipes in the walls so that modern lamps could supplement the antique chandeliers and candelabra. She bought several small electric heaters with sheets of soapstone that held the heat for a very long time, and this was a great advantage when the power went out, which happened quite often. The windows were given light and airy valances instead of side curtains, and the windowsills were filled with lush potted plants and a big collection of cacti. "The new house has turned out so beautifully that you'd have to see it to believe it. The living room and alcove on the first floor are so perfectly in accordance with my own taste that it couldn't be any better," the happy proprietor wrote to Nini. Yet she was proudest of her book collection, which had now been put in place on the specially designed shelves.

> My library turned out to include more than 1,000 volumes in addition to the works of fiction. Head Librarian Kjær, who was up here to help me do the cataloging, was so delighted by it that I was just about to burst with pride. So there, in any case, is a small fortune for the children. I'm so looking forward to sitting by the fireplace and reading; but most of all to having a peaceful study.

The house that Undset had leased in 1919 had primarily offered her and her children a roof over their heads and a corner where she could put her desk.

The Dalseg house during construction in the summer of 1924.

The "new" house, on the other hand, was a project that gave her the chance to create an environment that reflected her own personality and taste. Here she could present herself to the outside world as "the artist in her home," because now she was the mistress of her own property. In the rooms that were intended for socializing, Undset seized the opportunity to give her stage-setting talent free rein. Here she put on display her preferences, status, religious affiliation, and class position as if the house were a theater set.

Perhaps it was especially important for Sigrid Undset to create an impression of solidity and dignity now that her marriage to Svarstad was formally heading for dissolution. The immediate reason for the divorce was that in the fall of

The hearth room.

1924 Undset had been accepted as a member of the Catholic Church, and she had immersed herself in this new role with the greatest solemnity and fervor. The neighbors watched with surprise as Bjerkebæk began receiving visits from priests and nuns from Hamar, and the rumor spread like wildfire that mass was even held in the new hearth room.

More important than the exquisite furnishings in the Dalseg house was the fact that Undset was now able to organize her daily life so that it was easier to combine her roles as artist and mother. In many of her works she presents the conflict between the female artist's need for creative development and her family's need for a responsible and attentive mother. This dilemma is handled most clearly in *Splinter from the Troll's Mirror*, which contains two novellas from 1917. Uni, who is the main character of the first novella, entitled "Mrs. Hjelde," toys with the idea of leaving her husband to return to her career as an actress. Even though she loves her children, she admits to herself: "They just aren't *enough* for me!" All the same, in the end Uni decides not to shirk her obligations to the children, though she would have preferred another option, because "didn't we long for both? If we had been given the choice: either the pain of arrogant pride or the humbly bowed head of happiness – God knows which we would have chosen."

In her private life, Sigrid Undset was aiming for her own solution after the break with Svarstad. He was now "outside the gate." but she was intending to take care of her home and her children at the same time as she wanted to be an artist – a great artist and not merely a "pen-wielding lady," as she wrote in a letter to Dea in 1902. As a single mother with particularly demanding children, she took on a hazardous task that no outsider can properly judge. As an artist she was heralded as "the reigning queen of literature."

When the house from Dalseg was finished, Sigrid Undset had for the first time a "home office," and her tasks as both mother and artist could be literally integrated under the same roof. She even gained the opportunity to work undisturbed during the daytime – although of course it wasn't easy to change old habits. "I had a guest arriving by the night train, and for that reason I couldn't work late but had to go to bed early – before 1 a.m.," she writes in a letter. So she clearly continued to work far into the night. But now the household tasks could at least be relegated to specific areas in the home, and so there was more peace for working, as well as more distance between the mistress of the house and the domestic help. An impatient Sigrid Undset writes to her friend Nini:

This week I move in... And then – I'll have peace, with only my boys close by – and I won't have to hear and see and smell strangers close by around the clock. It's no doubt because my hour of liberation is so near that I suddenly don't think I can stand it another day. Just imagine being able to sit in the alcove and work in the evenings, hearing and knowing that my boys are upstairs – no one else!

Olav Audunssøn (the four-part novel entitled *The Master of Hestviken* in English) was the first work that she wrote largely in the peace and quiet of her new workroom, far away from the noise and commotion of the household help and her children. Here Undset could shift her gaze from the woods and birds and mountain slope outside and look inward, into the human heart, which "no matter what the era... never changes." All of a sudden the distance to Oslo seemed to have increased. Now she was far away from "all that pseudo-artistic hogwash" in the capital, with its tumult and carousing, a milieu that in her opinion was "the most wearisome company one has to protect oneself from being ensnared by."

The hearth room.

Yet she wasn't able to completely isolate herself from people in the years to come. In the Dalseg house Undset received author colleagues, fellow Catholic believers, and journalists. Here the priests from Hamar celebrated mass, here she invited her artist friends to a party once every Christmas and once every summer, and here the family would show up, dressed in their finest, for holidays and special occasions. But no children dared run into Undset's rooms uninvited if they had scraped their knees, and the adults wisely kept their distance from the hearth room and the alcove during "work hours." Even the publisher's representative felt a bit uneasy when he turned up with the proofs for *The Master of Hestviken* at a time that didn't suit the "reigning queen" of Norwegian literature. Bjerkebæk was now organized into two parts, one private and one public, with specific hours that were protected and others that were open. There were certain codes of conduct, and it was important to heed both the correct time and place.

In order to complete the work on the Dalseg house, Sigrid Undset wrote to

Aschehoug and kindly asked the publisher to send her a grand piano. She herself didn't play, but a piano was part of any well-to-do home. The purchase of a Steinway was immediately arranged and it was then sent to Lillehammer. When the family arrived at Bjerkebæk, full of anticipation to celebrate the first Christmas in the new house, it was hard to say who was more excited: the guests or the hostess. When the children ran toward the wide door of the hearth room, Undset stopped them and said: "Mama will go in first. I think this is the most beautiful home in Norway."

Sigrid Undset and her fellow Catholics gathered for mass at Bjerkebæk.

The "guesthouse" that became the "priest's house"

As long as there was only one house at Bjerkebæk, there was barely enough room on a daily basis for three children, two household helpers, and an author and mother who worked at home. When guests arrived, it was simply too crowded. In particular there was a lack of space for guests to stay overnight, and when Svarstad, Undset's mother, stepchildren, or her sisters and their families came to visit, the three bedrooms on the second floor were packed to the brim.

In March 1922 Undset took the first steps to solving the problem of lack of space when contractor Grønvold was asked to remodel and expand the small outbuilding. The blueprints might be read as one last attempt to save her failing marriage, since they show a large room with a great deal of light coming through windows facing south and west, a room that would be ideally suited as a studio for a painter. But Svarstad was not the sort to take orders from anyone, and the room was never used for anything but guest quarters. In an ironic twist of fate, the family's finances were secured that very spring when the Norwegian parliament granted Sigrid Undset a lifetime author's stipend. From that moment on, Svarstad's role as breadwinner was for all intents and purposes over. Undset celebrated the stipend by purchasing twelve loads of topsoil; now she could create her own paradise without any help from her spouse.

A couple of years after the expansion, the guesthouse acquired a new function, which prompted the household help to change the name of the small

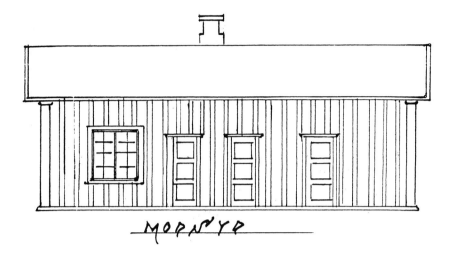

In March 1922, contractor Grønvold presented this suggestion for the renovation of the outbuilding.

building from "gjestehuset" (the guest house) to "prestehuset" (the priest's house). This was because it was used as lodgings for clerics with odd and foreign names such as Bechaux, Lutz, and Vanneufville. They were all Catholic priests, a breed that had hardly ever been seen before in the streets of Lillehammer. But interest in Catholicism was growing all over Norway, and one of the most vital areas of activity was in Hamar, 60 kilometers south of Lillehammer. The curiosity of the local citizens was so great that when Bishop Smit was to celebrate mass during Easter in 1923, he had to lease Hamar's largest meeting hall to make room for the 900 people who showed up.

Later that summer the visit of Cardinal van Rossum from the Netherlands attracted much attention, because this was in fact the first official visit of a Catholic cleric to Norway since the Reformation, over 400 years earlier. Cardinal van Rossum was greeted with friendly curiosity everywhere he went, and there was extensive coverage in the press. He was even granted an audience with King Haakon. But it was only as a tourist he visited Nidaros Cathedral, the old church that had been the destination of so many pilgrims in the past. The good Lutherans of the Norwegian state-supported church would not condone any sort of worshipping of saints, not even Olav the Holy. One had to draw the line somewhere, after all!

The St. Torfinn congregation was established in Hamar, and Undset became one of the most active members of the church. She had long been interested in Catholicism and had personally witnessed the daily customs of the church among the faithful that she had encountered on her travels. This had undoubtedly made an impression on her, but her fascination with the Catholic religion can be traced even farther back, all the way to her childhood. At the age of fourteen she wrote a melodramatic story with the title: "*Ora pro nobis! Virgo Maria!*" for a school newspaper. It was about a fervent and beautiful nun who, after many years of solitude and unselfish acts, dies in the arms of the love of her youth, Father Pietro. As a schoolgirl, Sigrid must have been curious about the exotic creatures wearing monk's garb and nun's habits who were part of the urban scene in Kristiania. They belonged to Vor Frue Hospital and St. Olav's Church on Akersgaten, located not far from the neighborhood where her family lived. One woman who frequently went in and out of the hospital gates was someone that Undset would meet several decades later at St. Torfinn's Church in Hamar.

Mathea Bådstø (1868–1959) was a photographer, artist, nurse, masseuse, and Catholic who had even been to America. She was an unusually resourceful woman and a bit of an adventurer. At the age of twenty she left her home on the Bådstø farm, which also functioned as a coach stop and inn near Tretten just north of Lillehammer. Her excuse for leaving was the very proper intention of taking a housekeeping course, one of the few opportunities available to young women at that time. The next step for Mathea was a position in Lillehammer as photography apprentice with the Barth sisters, who belonged to a group of particularly talented female photographers. Mathea Bådstø worked both behind and in front of the camera, and the pictures that have been preserved show a beautiful, stately woman, at times coquettishly costumed and with a mischievous glint in her eye, at other times with her face displaying an open and frank expression to the camera. There is an air of fortitude and steadfast character about her.

After several years with the Barth sisters, Mathea Bådstø went to Kristiania, to Vor Frue Hospital in Akersgaten, where she trained to be a nurse and masseuse. Here she encountered Catholicism first-hand, and after receiving instruction, she converted. But she continued to use the camera, now as assistant to Andersen, the royal photographer. He counted many famous actors among his steady clients, and through them she often obtained free tickets to the theaters. America proved even more enticing, and in 1905, Mathea traveled to New York. There she stayed for three years, until she had to make a hasty return home to Tretten to take care of her dying father and to help her mother and siblings on the farm. After that she settled at Bådstø and took an active part in local concerns. She helped to establish a school for adult education and a local women's

Sanitary Society. She also acted as librarian for the local lending library, and she was often called upon to take photographs at weddings and funerals. With her camera and flash in her bag, Miss Bådstø traveled around from one village to another, taking pictures. One of her specialties was making portraits of the deceased in their coffins. She never married.

Mother Fulgentia.

Mathea Bådstø and Sigrid Undset got to know each other through their work with the Catholic congregation in Hamar, where a small clinic and maternity home had been opened, run by the nuns of the Dutch Order of St. Charles Borromeo. In charge was Mother Fulgentia, who was not only a skilled and energetic administrator but also a wise and wonderful person beloved by all. The large membership enjoyed by the congregation in Hamar, especially after Cardinal van Rossum's visit to Norway, enabled the Catholics to consecrate their own house of worship on May 29, 1924. One of the guests present at St. Torfinn's Chapel for the dedication ceremony was Sigrid Undset, who had brought along her older son Anders, then eleven years old, for the solemn event. Undset herself was studying with the newly installed parish priest Karl Kjelstrup, but Mother Fulgentia also acted as an important conversant for her.

Before Sigrid could be received into the church, there was a certain problem that had to be solved. She was married to a divorced man, and in the view of the Catholic Church, he was forever bound in his marriage to his first wife, Ragna Moe. She and Anders Castus Svarstad had taken vows to remain together until death, after all, and both were still very much alive. For that reason, the Church regarded Svarstad's second marriage as invalid, even going so far as to state that it had never taken place. Svarstad reacted sharply to this point of view, but in order to be accepted as a Catholic, Undset had to obey the Church. She petitioned the civil authorities for a divorce from Svarstad, but the formalities took a long time, and the marriage was still not legally dissolved by the time

Mathea Bådstø (1868–1959).

she had completed her course of instruction with the parish priest. In late October 1924, word came from the central office of the Catholic Church that dispensation had been granted and that everything was in order so that Undset could convert.

This meant that she had only a couple of days to make the last-minute preparations, because Father Kjelstrup was about to travel south for the winter. The last, decisive step over the threshold was a difficult one, and Undset hesitated, turning to Mother Fulgentia to confide her doubts. In all haste, Father Kjelstrup sent a telegram to summon Mathea Bådstø, who was willing to assume the role of godmother for the convert. On Saturday, November 1, All Saints' Eve, Sigrid Undset delivered her confession of faith and her declaration of loyalty to the Catholic Church. The ceremony was a highly emotional experience, for behind her reserved facade, Undset harbored feelings that could be quite intense and reach great heights. Her conversion to Catholicism marked a true revolution in her life.

The next day, when Undset as a new Catholic was to receive communion for the first time, two others knelt beside her at the altar in St. Torfinn's Chapel. She knew both of them, they were the children of a Catholic friend in Lillehammer and schoolmates of her own son Anders. One was eleven-year-old Hetty Henrichsen, and the other was Hetty's nine-year-old brother Christian. It was a solemn moment for the three who received the sacrament on that day, because among Catholics, the first communion is as important an occasion as confirmation is for Lutherans.

Hetty and Christian's French-born mother was deeply moved for several reasons. When Edith de Castro became engaged to Sigurd Henrichsen, a dentist from the barbaric land of Norway, she had promised her parents that if her marriage was blessed with children, all of them would be accepted into the true faith. On this day she made good on her promise.

After mass, an emotional Sigrid Undset went over to Mrs. Henrichsen and embraced her so warmly and for such a long time that Hetty thought it looked as if her petite mother was about to drown in Undset's capacious arms.

Then they all had breakfast and celebrated with gifts. For the occasion Hetty was photographed in her new white dress with white stockings and shoes, and wearing a white veil over her hair. Sigrid gave her a picture of the Virgin Mary as a remembrance of the event, and from Mother Fulgentia the children each received a rosary and a little prayer card with a French text. Sigrid Undset asked for a photograph of Mother Fulgentia herself – and this request was granted.

In the years following her conversion, Undset and her godmother Mathea

Bådstø met often, since both were important figures in the Catholic network in Norway. Undset presented generous gifts to the congregation in Hamar; first she paid for a bell tower for the chapel so that the exterior of the building would look more like a proper church. To adorn the interior, she had a Danish artist make a copy of the famous St. Olav altarpiece in Copenhagen, and she ordered a silk banner embroidered by the nuns of St. Birgitta in Rome. She even purchased a house to serve as the rectory for the church, with an office and living quarters for the parish priest. In this way she saw to it that the sisters who ran the maternity home and clinic were able to use more of the rooms in the original building for their own activities.

In Gudbrandsdalen no permanent Catholic congregation had yet been established, but several times a year one of the priests from Hamar would come to Bjerkebæk or to Bådstø to instruct confirmands and celebrate mass. On these occasions Sigrid Undset and Mathea Bådstø were regular guests in each other's homes, as they also were at other times. When the priests came to Bjerkebæk, they stayed in the guesthouse in the garden, and for many years it was customary for a couple of the sisters from the clinic to spend their vacations there in the summer.

Hetty Henrichsen dressed for her first communion.

Undset didn't have time to entertain these summer guests herself, but the household help was told to take good care of them, and at mealtimes the mistress of the house would sit down with her guests at the table.

The reactions to her conversion must have come as a surprise to Sigrid Undset; in any case, she couldn't have foreseen that the response would be so strong. The fact that she had returned to Norwegian history and its medieval setting in her fiction, was perceived by many as a revitalizing of old values that had long been ignored but not forgotten. In addition, belief in progress and the blessings of industrialism had suffered a serious setback during the First World War, and many people thought, as did Undset, that it was essential to revert to the old cardinal virtues: Truth, Peace, Justice and Mercy, Faith, Hope, and Charity – God's beautiful daughters. Yet it was regarded as near treason

In her novel *Gymnadenia*, Sigrid Undset describes in detail this rosary, which belonged to Edit de Castro Henrichsen.

that in her personal life Undset would turn toward "the dark Middle Ages" and join the Catholic Church.

One person who changed his mind about her writings after it became known that she had converted was Professor Edvard Bull. Originally he had displayed an unqualified enthusiasm for her novels. Right after *The Wreath* was published, criticism was leveled at purported historical errors in the text, and the book was also labeled immoral. Professor Bull immediately came to the author's defense. In the newspaper *Social-Demokraten*, a certain Mr. Stilloff had written an unfavorable review of the novel. But the professor, who was a historian specializing in the Middle Ages, defended the book's authenticity as well as its artistic merits. He maintained that *The Wreath* offered a love story filled with a healthy and refreshing sensuality, and he snorted at Stilloff's bourgeois prudishness:

> Is there anyone outside the circles of morality societies, so removed from real life, who still holds the view that we must make young people believe that human beings propagate through the help of storks or by germination? Mrs. Undset's book is entirely free of all sultriness or lewdness, and the task of a literary critic is not to act as nursemaid for six-year-olds... My second objection is to Mr. Stilloff's assessment of the book's historical content, and in this area I dare claim, in all modesty, to possess greater expertise than Mr. Stilloff. I venture to say that I have never read a historical novel that has greater authenticity than this one. Both in terms of tone and pure facts, Mrs. Undset has, in my opinion, portrayed the character of the time most admirably; and I have not found... a single real historical error. It is clear that Mrs. Undset has not only read modern historical accounts; she has also worked with the actual sources, and in such an insightful way that she has truly mastered the material; she knows the time period and is able to make it come alive for us.

A few years later, Edvard Bull became the fore-most critic of Undset's medieval characters: "even the temperaments of the people are not medieval but modern," the professor then claimed. He had decided that Kristin resembled a progressive woman who had grown up in the capital, someone who "had spent her youth in an office and whose knowledge of nature is from Sunday excursions to Nordmarka. She has the typical disposition of so many women from the big city: she is 'peevish.' And her morals and conscience are infinitely far removed from both heathendom and from the Catholicism of the Middle Ages." Bull issued these objections in 1927, which prompts specula-tion as to whether Undset's conversion in 1924 and the subsequent anti-Catholic campaigns of the day may have influenced his change of opin-ion. Or perhaps he had heard rumors that the Swedish Academy was not unanimously enthused by Undset's "intimate" novels? A few members of the Nobel Prize jury felt that she'd had prob-lems with the psychology of the historical novel and that her characters were too "modern." In addition, they felt that she had allowed religion

The card that Christian Henrichsen received from Mother Fulgentia at his first communion.

to play much too dominant a role – the same arguments that Edvard Bull now espoused. No doubt it was difficult for many, both in Norway and in Sweden, to accept that a Catholic might be a candidate for the Nobel Prize in Litera-ture.

After Undset's conversion, mass was celebrated in the new hearth room at Bjerkebæk whenever an opportunity presented itself. She had contractor Grøn-vold build an altar that could be set up in the room and then removed as needed. Sculptures of John the Baptist and the Virgin Mary were placed in the alcove on either side of an Italian Renaissance chest, and inside the chest were stored censers, basins for holy water, and other objects to be used during mass. From Paris she ordered twelve prie-dieux, or kneeling chairs, which she paid for herself.

Not many Catholics lived in Lillehammer, but one person who was always informed any time mass was to be celebrated was Edith de Castro Henrichsen.

The hearth room as chapel.

She usually came to Bjerkebæk with her two eldest children, and her daughter Hetty has described what went on:

We always arrived early in the morning, having fasted, and one by one we entered the alcove, closing the door behind us so that we could make our confession. The priest usually sat in Sigrid Undset's chair at the desk, and then we would kneel down in front of him to confess our sins. Only after everyone had been in to see the priest and everything was ready would Sigrid Undset come downstairs from her bedroom. She had undoubtedly made her confession the evening before, because for these early morning masses the priests always used to spend the previous night in the 'priest's house." Sigrid Undset had covered her head with a piece of black lace, and she looked neither to the right nor the left but knelt down on a prie-dieu and clasped her hands. Only after the mass was over and we had received the sacrament did we greet her. Then we all went to the dining room, where a lovely breakfast was served.

Sigrid Undset often went to mass; she prayed the rosary every day, and eventually also the canonical offices. She usually stayed in her room until late in the morning, and when she finally came downstairs to eat, the household help would go up to straighten her room. The maid noticed that the red velvet cushion on the prie-dieu was always well flattened from the morning prayers.

In March 1928 Undset was accepted as a lay sister in the third order of St. Dominic, and she chose *Olave*, after her old hero, St. Olav, as her new name. The Dominican sisters lived a semi-cloistered life, which meant that they remained in their own homes and did not have to take oaths of celibacy or total obedience, or relinquish all personal possessions. Their daily task was to pray the canonical offices at specified hours of the day and, in accordance with a long-honored tradition, it was their special obligation to protect the properties of the Church. This suited Sigrid Undset well, because she felt that prayers were not enough to make someone a true Christian – deeds were required for that. "Where are the deeds that should bear witness for you on the last day, showing that you were a link in God's church? The good deeds which will bear witness that you belong to God?" These are the questions that Kristin Lavransdatter envisions in St. Olav's eyes as she lies prostrate, dissolved in tears, in front of the altar in his church. Guilt and atonement are two themes that wind like a red thread through all of Undset's work, and the Fall is something that marks all her major characters, from Marta Oulie, Kristin Lavransdatter, and Olav Audunssøn to Catherine of Siena, who was the last figure about whom she wrote a major work. In her own life, Undset went about doing good deeds at a level that would make the average person blanch with admiration and perhaps also horror. It's impossible not to speculate what the reason might be behind her lifelong display of penitence. What wrong could she have done that would require such acts of atonement? Many people have searched for hidden sins in Undset's life without finding anything dramatic. Could it be that she was attempting to pay the debts of others?

Father Bechaux, August 15, 1925.

In *Den brennende busk* (*The Burning Bush*), her novel of conversion, Undset discusses several times the idea that sacrifice by proxy is possible. When little Erik dies, she writes that the boy's father accepts, though not without a struggle, the explanation of the church, which is based on the notion that an innocent child is chosen to pay the debts of the entire lineage. Erik is atoning for the sins of others and passes away "in order to receive his reward from Christ." If Sigrid Undset thought that she could make partial payments for the sins of the world through her good deeds, she certainly had a Sisyphean task before her. It's impossible to know whether she had more specific concerns in mind.

The garden – "the third loveliest thing" in the world

No matter where in the world Sigrid Undset lived, or for how brief a time, she always made an effort to surround herself with plants, even if it was only a few pots on the windowsill or on the terrace. Her literary works are filled with garden motifs: people who stray from a garden, people who strive to grow a new garden or who are locked behind a garden gate against their will, or who experience an almost ecstatic joy just at being a living organism among other life forms. In Undset's very first book, the main character Mrs. Marta Oulie says with a sigh: "How lovely it is to have a garden. I will appreciate it if we ever have one again." Another character, Uni Hjelde, in the novella "Mrs. Hjelde," thinks that her children shouldn't grow up on a busy city street, because she wants them to have "memories of fields where they played ball, of enclosed gardens brimming with fruit that they dreamed about and desired, and stole on dark autumn nights...." There seems to be very little distance between the voice of the author and that of her characters when gardens are the theme. Associations with the Garden of Eden are easily made, resonating like a distant chord in the consciousness of the reader.

After her first year as Hjorth's tenant in the house on Nordseterveien, Undset's windowsills were overflowing with blooming plants, and she was itching to realize her dream of having her own, proper garden. To her friend Nini, who had cultivated a large, lush property just outside of Kristiania, she writes:

> I think you are so fortunate to have a house and a husband whose whereabouts you know, and in general anchoring points in the world. I read with the

Thekla Resvoll (1871–1948).

greatest envy your chronicles of your garden. I think it must be the loveliest – the second-loveliest thing in the world, no, the third-loveliest, to be able to plant a little tree in the ground somewhere, and then have good reason to assume that you'll be able to watch it grow.

Undset's interest in plants was something she'd had even as a very young child. Sigrid had trotted along beside her old Aunt Signe when she tended her two gardens in Kalundborg – one for edible plants, the other merely for pleasure. With a little help from her mother, eleven-year-old Sigrid had planted her first flower bed outside their apartment building on Observatoriegaten; and she frequently went off on lengthy botanizing expeditions in Nordmarka. At the Ragna Nielsen School, Sigrid was often bored, but she paid close attention whenever the lessons were devoted to the natural sciences. The teacher Thekla Resvoll, who was an excellent young botanist, made a strong impression on the pupils. Her lessons were completely free of any pedagogical dryness, and with great skill she introduced her students to the wondrous world of plants. In 1899 Resvoll took a university degree, and over the years she wrote several textbooks as well as a doctoral dissertation entitled "Om planter som passer til kold og kort sommer" ("On Plants Suited to a Cool and Brief Summer"), (1917). Perhaps it was this pioneering woman who inspired Undset's youthful dream of becoming a gardener, "a proper gardener – the kind with soiled hands and ragged clothes," as she expresses it in her novel *Springtime*. But her mother vetoed the idea. Sigrid had to find a profession that would ensure a more stable income, and so she spent a year in business school instead.

Among her own family members Undset found someone with botanical expertise: her father's cousin Ove Dahl. When Ingvald Undset died, "Uncle Ove" tried to give the three fatherless girls a little extra attention. Sigrid was allowed to go along on field expeditions to look for wild plants, and she learned to identify the species they found. Dahl was in his element whenever he was able to expound on the Swedish botanist Linnaeus, or Carl von Linné, the scientist who had created a way of systematizing plant life. Later, when the two hundredth anniversary of Linné's birth was celebrated, Dahl published a book titled *Carl von Linnés forbindelse med Norge* (Carl von Linné's Ties with Norway), (1907).

Ove Dahl and Thekla Resvoll were both important mentors for Sigrid Undset, but it was Linné himself who had the greatest influence on her as a teacher. She was delighted to discover that he'd taken the same intense and sensual joy in nature that she herself felt. It was said in jest about the professor in Uppsala that he could describe the sex and propagation of plants with such fervor and sensuality that it approached "botanical pornography."

Ove Dahl (1862–1940).

Linné's classification of all plants in a taxonomic system gave an order and regimen to nature, and Undset took to heart his idea that each plant has a pattern inherent in its cells. This gives even the smallest creation a purpose: to realize its *telos*, its innermost norm. If you read Undset's novels with this idea in mind, you will understand that she used Linné's teachings not only as she tended to her garden and her potted plants but also in her writing and in the methods she used to raise her children.

For Undset, the biological nature of human beings is always an essential factor. One individual might be like a lily while another is like a dandelion, but what is most important for all of them is to develop into a vigorous and handsome example of their species, and then propagate so that their species will endure. This way of thinking makes it especially important for parents to understand their child's *telos*. Professor Liv Bliksrud expresses it this way: "This formative principle also entails the idea that a norm or a pattern exists for every individual, and it is imperative, first for the parents and then for the person herself, to find out what that may be and respect it. A pedagogical consequence is that children require different types of upbringing, and some must be raised with greater discipline than others."

Something else that Sigrid Undset learned was that all the beauty of nature must be conquered by the senses before reason can have a chance. This is the mechanism that Torkild in the novel *Springtime* understands. He flings himself down on a carpet of white anemones and feels the power of the earth seep into his body through his clothes, thinking: "No heavenly dreams could the soul create unless the body, the senses, had gathered the material." Deductive realism is both the young man's and the author's way of acquiring knowledge; they draw conclusions from their perceived experiences. But it's not just the wondrous impressions that come to us via our sensory apparatuses; Undset acknowledged that everything ugly is perceived in the same way, and that could be genuinely troublesome. As a child she was often scolded by her mother because she complained that things "smelled." When the family had to move from Lyder Sagens Gate to Keysers Gate because of her father's illness, it was the disgusting stink of the privy in the stairwell and the smells from the kitchen facing the back courtyard that Sigrid hated most. She retained her acute sense of smell all her life, even though she smoked like a chimney, and as an old woman she would often rub the leaf from a plant between her fingers, hold it up to her nose, and take a good sniff.

If her sense of smell was particularly acute, there was certainly nothing wrong with her eyesight either. When Sigrid was young, her girlfriends probably thought she was bluffing when she claimed to be able to tell the difference between an elm and an ash, a linden and a beech, even in the winter when the trees had no leaves. The truth was that she had both exceptionally sensitive sensory perceptions and a keen intellect. Like Linné, she could take in impressions as both ecstatic experiences and as rational facts, a combination of passion and science. Both of these ways of regarding nature show up in countless situations in her writings, sometimes even in the same sentence. In the novella "Fru Waage" ("Mrs. Waage") in *Splinter from the Troll's Mirror*, Undset has Harriet describe her illicit, adulterous love affair, using the image of a carmine-red rose with velvety petals: "I think my heart is like the Richmond roses I didn't dare buy and fasten to my clothes," thinks Harriet. "But I wear them inside my breast – concealed from everyone except the one who has seen my heart. It's like a rose now – with red petals stretched open, and a little golden sun in the middle. That is happiness, that quiet little golden point sitting deep inside my blooming heart, just as the organs of life sit deep inside, in the center of the flower."

Having botanical knowledge and experiencing an ecstatic perception of nature is one thing; designing a garden on 1.25 acres is something else entirely. Where was Sigrid Undset to find both the models and the labor force for such a project? To obtain help with the planning stage she allied herself with a professional gardener, Lorentz August Sveberg. He was a skilled and expertly trained landscape gardener with many irons in the fire; he planned school gardens, tended the summertime plants in Lillehammer's parks, and designed many of the town's residential gardens. In his old age Sveberg often talked about the work he did for Sigrid Undset, explaining that she took a special interest in the planning and that she always watched with interest as the work progressed.

At first it was mostly a matter of heavy manual labor carried out by hired help. After she purchased Bjerkebæk, Undset immediately went about having the property cleared and a fence put up. Load after load of rocks had to be carted away – almost 2,000, it was said. Some of the rocks were used to construct the terrace closest to the house and to form a wall along the creek, but countless cartloads still had to be removed. Topsoil was transported in the opposite direction, because a great deal of site work had to be done before it would be possible to plant a single shrub, never mind the much-longed-for "third loveliest" trees. According to the Bjerkebæk archives, from November 1922 until November 1923 invoices were sent from Thorvald Stuve's transport company for 45 loads of topsoil, 77 loads of manure, 16 loads of gravel,

Lillehammer's city gardener, Lorentz August Sveberg.

and 17 loads of clay. In addition, Undset purchased 12 loads of topsoil to celebrate her author stipend – a total of 167 loads of material for creating her garden.

Undset was so eager to get started on the planting work that she couldn't wait for all the landscaping to be finished. In the fall of 1922 she spent 400 kroner on perennial shrubs, and from Nini Roll Anker she received a sackful of cuttings, including several hundred blue-and-white forget-me-nots, or "loving memories" as she called them. She planted more than 200 violets and 20 peonies – creamy white, pink, violet, and red. The following spring, as she waited for the snow to melt and reveal what had survived the winter, she tended her potted plants with extra care. To her sister Ragnhild in Stockholm she wrote about all her preparations for the transplanting: "Last week I had a great deal to do – all of my flowers had to be repotted, cut back, and I really have no idea how many pots I have, but there must be far more than 50 – there are 12 with roses alone. Right now they're practically piled on top of each other, but when spring comes I'll put many of them out in the garden."

Because of the shortages during the war and with her own financially uncertain past still fresh in her memory, it was no wonder that Undset would place an emphasis on including edible plants in the landscaping work. The usual method was to grow potatoes where a future flower garden was planned so as to prepare the soil, and by 1922 the rough work had progressed far enough to make this possible, at least in a small section of the property. To Gösta af Geijerstam Undset writes with obvious satisfaction:

This summer I had the ground tilled, and I planted potatoes in the small section that was cleared in time. My first attempts at cultivation brought blessed results – and since my family in the city claimed that it wasn't worthwhile to send them potatoes, because they're so inexpensive this fall and since no one wanted a gift of potatoes from me and no one is buying any, my entire household cellar is still full of potatoes in barrels and crates, even though we eat all that we can manage – because I don't want a single one of my home-grown potatoes to go to waste. In the spring I'm going to plant fruit trees and bushes – and then I hope that I'll have enough self-awareness to realize on my own when I can no longer write well; by then the trees will have grown big enough so that I can sit at the marketplace in Lillehammer on Wednesdays and Saturdays, selling fruit and vegetables in the summer. I am so looking forward to that!

The busiest work years were 1923 and 1924, because it was then that the timbered house from Dalseg was also moved to its new foundation. The planting of fruit trees and berry bushes was given high priority, and in the vegetable garden below the outbuilding both yellow and white currants were planted, along with raspberries, black currants, and rhubarb, and all sorts of vegetables and herbs.

After the Dalseg building was put in place, it was finally time for the perennials and roses. Gardener Sveberg's designs for other Lillehammer gardens testify to his preference for strict lines and formal discipline, but then he was a stern man himself, who demanded respect, especially from the pupils in the town's school gardens. But at Bjerkebæk he had to concede to his employer's wishes for less symmetry, greater lushness, and softer lines, because Sigrid Undset knew what she wanted, especially with regard to the flower garden. Like Mrs. Marta Oulie, she disliked "desolate gardens with a gazebo in one corner, where it was clear that no one would ever sit." Undset couldn't abide geometrically designed gardens of the sort that "everyone" used to have when she was a child. At Lyder Sagens Gate 10 in Kristiania, where the Undset family lived for several years, there was this type of standard garden in front of the house. It was a large rectangular plot with a flowerbed in each corner as well as one in the middle. Not only were the flowerbeds the same in every garden, they were also planted in the same way from one year to the next. As Undset describes it in *Elleve år* (translated into English as *The Longest Years*), there were

Sigrid Undset inside the gate.

Iris sketched by Sigrid Undset
in her youth.

"stock in one, asters and carnations and verbena in the others, and a gardener came to plant the center bed: hemp and corn and tobacco plants with a surrounding border of yellow-leaved pyrethrum and blue lobelia."

In the same book, which is an autobiographical story about "Ingvild" and her childhood, the author writes with great warmth about "Mr. Wilster," who lived on the ground floor of Lyder Sagen Gate. Otto Winter-Hjelm, which was his real name, often came home with big bunches of roses that he had bought at an auction – roses with foreign names such as Ulrich Brunner, Captain Christy, Souvenir de Malmaison, and Louise Oudier. "But most fun of all was the flower bed that he dug up each year and planted with mixed seeds that had cost 10 øre. White forget-me-nots sprouted up along with morning glories, cornflowers, and poppies, and flowers that even Mr. Wilster couldn't name for Ingvild."

With her enthusiasm for "natural" elements in her garden, Undset was right in step with the ideals that had become fashionable at the beginning of the new century. Once again the influence was from England, where the "Cottage Garden" was the new creation of the day. It had started with the Irishman William Robinson, who in 1870 aroused attention with his book *The Wild Garden*, in which he rejected carpets of flowers laid out in neat geometric patterns and the use of delicate and exotic hothouse plants. Robinson thought that outdoors the emphasis should be placed on plants that could survive on their own, without having to spend the winter in hothouses or cellars. He recommended hardy perennials in colorful borders where the plants could grow in groups and intermingle with each other so that it looked as if Nature herself had been the gardener. Instead of defined lawns that demanded a great deal of work, he suggested meadows where spring-blooming bulbs could spread freely, and where swaying grasses and summer flowers would take over later in the season. According to Robinson, wild plants could be used advantageously in the garden to create a soft transition between cultivated and natural zones.

While William Robinson's garden revolt was a truly radical break with everything that smacked of artificiality and pretense, landscape architects and horticulturists gradually found their way to a style that combined formal elements, such as terraces and stairs and long beds of perennials placed close to the house, with informal plantings and the use of wild plants, especially in the outer sections of the garden. Sigrid Undset's property is an example of this style, which is known as "New Formalism."

The person who first popularized these ideas from England in Norway was the English-born Queen Maud. In the royal gardens at Bygdøy, with assistance from Charles Hubbard, a gardener from her native country, she designed a garden that became a clear forerunner. "People around here are imitating us, Hubbard!" Queen Maud supposedly said. Upon hearing this remark, the gardener wrote to his family in England that he had begun to look around "and sure enough, gardens have been popping up like mushrooms. The garden at Bygdøy and the plants we used there have made a big impression." Her neighbors were not the only ones who admired the queen's garden; it was also photographed and described in the journal of the Norwegian Gardening Association. Eventually many people were inspired to follow the queen's example, including Sigrid Undset.

One important element in the new garden style was the extensive use of roses – as hedges or in wide borders, which was the case at Bjerkebæk, or in a separate rose garden, as in the queen's garden. Another new creation was the mountain garden, in which plants that grew naturally on the Norwegian slopes were planted among stones that were spread over a flat area of the site. Undset placed this type of garden on the eastern side of Bjerkebæk, just outside the veranda room. Here she even outdid the queen by using plants like white dryas, saxifrage, lady's slippers, pasque flowers, and a few orchids. The neighbor's boy Ole Henrik Moe, who shared Undset's interest in botany, says that she once phoned him to say that he had to hurry and come over because one of the beauties in her garden had just bloomed: her Adonis vernalis, or yellow pheasant's eye. It was a plant that she had personally smuggled into Norway after a visit to the island of Gotland. Her hatbox had proved useful in more ways than one.

Of course Sigrid Undset didn't have a royal gardener to assist her in planning the garden at Bjerkebæk, but during the busiest times she did have four or five men working for her, as well as carts that delivered goods and materials. From the gate at the bottom of the garden she had a gravel path put in, and on one side of it she planted old-fashioned perennials such as larkspur, poppies, peonies, and globe-flowers, martagon lilies, daylilies, and columbine. On the other side she put in white narcissus and squill along the outer edges, with more roses inside. A large number of plants were required to fill the long, wide beds, and it took a great deal of work to make sure that they thrived. The garden work was eventually relegated to Oscar Mikkelsen, a neighbor whose job it was to plant and sow, water and weed, cut the grass, and move shrubs according to instructions from the mistress of the house. Mikkelsen was also responsible for

Sigrid Undset received a good deal of "help" from the children in creating a mountain garden behind the house.

providing firewood for the winter. Normally his wages were 90 øre an hour, but for heavier work, such as putting up fences and the gate facing Nordseter-veien, he received 1 krone and 20 øre per hour.

At times there were as many as 400 potted plants at Bjerkebæk, and the garden was unusually beautiful and well-tended, so the household help and Mikkelsen certainly had their hands full, both indoors and out. Undset took as active a part in the work as her schedule permitted, and even when she left most of the tasks to others, she still took a great interest in what went on. The maids noted with amazement that the mistress would get up in the middle of the night to see whether one of the cacti in her collection, a plant that rarely flowered, had bloomed. She showed such a keen interest that sometimes it could take a toll on both her hands and her health, as she explains in a letter to her sister in Sweden:

> Without a doubt, I've caught another cold, I've been running up and down the cellar steps, seeing to the transplanting. The repotting itself I did in the kitchen, but I have all sorts of pots and various kinds of soil and sand stored in the cellar, and I was down there mixing for the various types of plants. In

any case I must have gotten rid of that awful rash that I had on my hands because I didn't have any outbreaks after I got a thousand cactus spines in all my fingers and actually everywhere else too – but now I'm really hoping for great results. By the way, it's unbelievable how much time flowers take – I've replanted in three different stages, and still have a lot left to do; for instance my camellia, which hasn't quite finished blooming, but when the last rose falls off, I will get to it.

Much of what Undset needed for her garden could be obtained from local gardeners, even though interest in gardening was a relatively new phenomenon in Gudbrandsdalen. The Fåberg and Lillehammer Gardening Club was founded in 1895, and during the war years, from 1914 to 1918, the group had attracted a large membership of amateur gardeners. Everyone was concerned about increasing their food supplies, and they tried to meet household needs as much as possible from what they could grow on their own property. In Lillehammer lectures were held and courses given; there were exhibits and contests with certificates and prizes. All homeowners were warmly encouraged to keep chickens, and Undset, who was a member of the Gardening Club for many years, thought this was a good idea. To Mathea Mortenstuen, who would eventually become Bjerkebæk's legendary housekeeper, she writes in January 1928: "Well, we certainly have chickens now, let me tell you! Over the winter they're living in the old cellar room where we used to store coal, and they're already laying eggs, so we're keeping ourselves supplied. It's funny to hear them from up in the dining room cackling all day long!"

Gunhild's daughter, Brit, among the lilies in the garden.

Like most garden-lovers, Sigrid Undset was always planning new projects. The chickens were moved over to a chicken coop that was put up at the edge of the woods right across from the creek, and a dog run was built behind the house. A long stone wall was placed parallel to the garden path and covered with plants such as stonecrop and saxifrage, pinks and houseleeks. The vegetable garden, which was at first placed below the outbuilding and close to Nordseterveien, was later moved closer to the creek, and a strawberry patch was planted – a luxury that was meticulously cared for and tended. Even so, it wasn't to protect the garden from youths intent on stealing berries or fruit that a new fence was put up facing the road. The rustic fence across from the guesthouse was replaced with a high wall of planks placed close together, because after Undset won the Nobel Prize in Literature in the fall of 1928, the gawkers started to become annoying. They would come wandering along Nordseterveien individually or in groups, and the boldest of them would stop and take out their Kodak cameras. The new fence created an enclosed courtyard, where the maids could sit outdoors with their work and remain undisturbed when the weather was good. Undset's handicapped daughter could also be outside in the fresh air. As Mosse began having more trouble getting around, one of her favorite pastimes was to sit in a deck chair up near the house and toss a ball down the garden slope. Then whoever was taking care of her would have to run after the ball and bring it back to her – over and over and over again.

Watering the large garden was of course an important and time-consuming job. The maids had to carry buckets of water every evening, and in dry periods Sigrid Undset herself would take a turn at night. To her sister Signe she writes in June 1932:

> My garden is looking lovely this year. Of course a lot of branches have dried up on the bushes, etc., but everything that has been in the ground is coming up much more lush than ever before; my lilies look like they're going to be magnificent, and the row of phlox has been planted and is looking good – we move the water sprinkler around from the moment the sun sets and until I go to bed in the early morning hours.

To make the work easier Undset had many meters of water pipes buried in the ground, with a couple of taps attached at strategic places, and that must have made the job more manageable.

Sometimes Undset was so busy that she didn't have time to be outside very much. But particularly in the evening, when the air was mild and sated with the scent of flowers, she liked to stroll in the garden with the family dogs at her heels. From what she wrote in letters and in her novels, it appears that she had a special fondness for fragrant trees and perennials, such as violets and lilies of the valley, lilies and phlox, lilacs, bird cherries, roses, and mignonette,

The stone wall in full bloom.

as well as aromatic herbs such as sage, hyssop, and thyme. In any case, she displays an extraordinary degree of observation when it comes to various smells, and a unique talent for describing them. The same talent was shared by Erik Axel Karlfeldt, the Swedish poet who wrote a "summer sermon" titled "Smells and Scents," in which he extols the nose and feels sorry for anyone who can't tolerate the scent of flowers. "Those who have a weak sense of smell or none at all seem to me impoverished," he writes. In his summer sermon, written in July 1930, Karlfeldt mentions that "the odor from the burning bush (Dictamnus) can be ignited like a gas." Perhaps this was where Undset found the idea for the title of her novel, *The Burning Bush*, which was published in the autumn of the same year.

There is no question that Karlfeldt, who was not only a poet but a botanist and head of the Swedish Academy, held a special place in Undset's heart. He was the one who sent her the telegram on November 13, 1928, to tell her that "the eighteen" of the Academy had decided to award her the Nobel Prize in Literature. Only a few hours after the announcement, Bjerkebæk reeked like an overfilled chapel, and for once there were actually too many flowers, even for Sigrid Undset! Perhaps she told Karlfeldt about her flower garden when they met in Stockholm for the award ceremony. They may have even had a chance to chat about gardening during the banquet, for Karlfeldt had established a garden on his own property, called "Sångs i Sjugare," at about the same time that Undset was creating hers at Bjerkebæk. "The garden is my summertime joy and my wintertime worry," lamented Karlfeldt, and with that the Nobel Prize winner undoubtedly concurred.

One person with whom Undset shared many of her joys and concerns regarding her plants was Astri af Geijerstam, who had a large garden to care for at her home near a fjord in western Norway:

> We've had sunshine now for almost three weeks, but it freezes at night, so the snow is only slowly receding. It will probably be quite a while before I can start to look for snowdrops or think about the garden. It's always so exciting here in the middle of the Oppland district when spring arrives – to see what has survived and what has not. Hans waits just as eagerly as I do – he knows just about every plant in the garden. And so it's exciting to see when we'll be able to get to work in the vegetable garden – of flowers I have only perennials.

It wasn't so strange that the long, cold winters in Lillehammer caused Sigrid Undset concern, but even in the summertime the weather could be bad: "We've had terrible weather here this summer," she writes to Gösta af Geijerstam in September 1928, and goes on:

> I've always thought that Holy Bishop Thorlak was one of the most admirable of all saints – according to the legend about him, he never complained about the weather... Give my greetings to Astri – I wish she could have seen my garden in August. Strangely enough, in spite of the cold, my flowers have never been so splendid – the delphiniums are twice my height and it's that way everywhere, the rue anemones that I got from her have grown into a whole thicket. But nothing has come of my vegetables, the beans and others are just blossoming now.

A year later Sigrid Undset presents a delightful view of the weather, which for once has been perfect:

> We have summer here. Signe said last year that she hoped God had put away in the bank for us all the sunshine and warmth that He has so stubbornly denied us for several years. It's really as if an angel were standing up there in heaven every morning, from the time the sun comes up until it goes down, doling out the golden hours with a generous hand – here you are, the balance owing with plentiful heavenly interest, and interest on the interest. We've had a couple of rain showers every time it looked like things were getting too dry (yesterday it poured down from midnight to midday). Today the sun is shining again, and everything looks freshly washed. The roses had begun to bloom, even before Midsummer – I can't remember that ever happening before; your blue irises are almost finished, and now the red lilies are coming out.

Undset was also interested in what was growing outside her own garden fence. She loved to go for drives, using a taxi several times a week, and she often went on trips to neighboring villages. After a summer excursion in the region, she would always come home with big bouquets of wildflowers – lush, hastily gathered bouquets. And she frequently took cuttings from a roadside ditch or a meadow. From one of these excursions it was a rare bellflower from Brøttum that she brought home – and it can still be found at Bjerkebæk today. Another time it was a cutting from an unusual plant from Tretten, an Agragene sibirica. From her trips abroad she brought back botanical souvenirs, even though it was actually illegal to do so, such as the Adonis vernalis from Gotland, which

Linné had described. And from Stockholm she once sent enough asparagus seeds to supply the entire neighborhood. In April 1928 she traveled to England, and there she witnessed the amazing springtime flowering in the parks and gardens. Undset tells her friend Astri that she took the opportunity to order 2,000 bulbs "of a type of squill that grows wild in the woods over there; it's their spring flower instead of the blue anemone. I've never seen them in gardens here in Norway, although they may be known in the western regions." Now the squill bloom by the thousands all over the slopes of Bjerkebæk every spring.

Her trips abroad gave Undset the opportunity to compare the growing conditions away from home with what she knew, and this could be a frustrating experience for a garden-lover. To Mathea Mortenstuen, who shared her employer's interest in plants, she wrote from the health spa at Montebello in Jutland, Denmark, about the residential gardens that were "filled with hyacinths and daffodils and primroses, and a plethora of lovely blossoming bushes – Alpine currant and forsythia. It makes a person quite envious, to see what abundance they have here, the likes of which are not to be found in Norway – not in Oslo, and I won't even mention Lillehammer." When she was feeling particularly gloomy she would dream of moving to warmer climes, and in January 1929 she confided to Astri that she was thinking of leaving Gudbrandsdalen. "Here the winter is so unbelievably long, and winter isn't much fun when a person starts getting older... But of course I'll never really do it, the house here is *too* nice, as is the garden that I've had cleared myself..." When the garden came to life in the spring, Undset forgot all about such thoughts. She had planted a hardy bird cherry as the courtyard tree, and she rejoiced every time it blossomed like "one huge bouquet." And it still does today.

In the fall of 1935, however, she began to think seriously about moving south. Anders had gone to Birmingham to train as an engineer, and Undset herself had much more to do in Oslo after being elected chair of the Norwegian Authors' Union. Yet the growing political unrest was one of the reasons that she still chose to remain at Bjerkebæk, because the home had become a haven for her entire family. In addition, Undset was dependent on circumstances that would allow Mosse to get the care she needed, and this she primarily received from their housekeeper, Mathea Mortenstuen.

In spite of all its drawbacks, Undset always yearned home to her own garden whenever she was traveling. In April 1937, she sent the following missive to her housekeeper from England:

Sigrid Undset inspects her vegetable garden.

I'm going to send home some flower seeds to try out – although I have no idea where we'll find room for them! The flat seeds in the little translucent bag without a label are something that I got recently at Kenilworth, so I truly hope that they'll sprout. Mikkelsen will have to sow some of them here and there, not too deep I think, since the seeds are so light – a few in the border near Anders' bush, some in the new bed near the south wall, some in the bed in front of the kitchen door and main entrance, perhaps a few in the rock garden. It's a flower that the English call Honesty, and it's very beautiful and pleasant and old-fashioned, and in the fall it has seedpods that look like tiny mirrors.

It was hard to find more room for flower beds, and it didn't help matters that Undset, in 1936, had the opportunity to lease an adjoining property consisting of one acre above the buildings at Bjerkebæk. On the other hand, she now had the joy of taking walks in her own woods. Thickets and trees were allowed to grow freely over by the creek, and anything that rotted provided fertile soil for the abundant and bird-friendly insect life. Sigrid Undset liked to putter about on the small paths with her binoculars hanging around her neck, observing the birds that had settled in as tenants. She made careful note of which bushes provided seeds for the various birds, she set up several feeding trays, and at Christmastime eight to ten sheaves of grain were hung at the windows. From her desk in the alcove she had an excellent view for making ornithological observations. "A strange thing – I've seen almost no birds all Christmas," she writes to her sister Signe one January day in the late 1920s. "Now today they've arrived in huge flocks. There are yellow buntings and chickadees – the sheaf at the edge of the well is one big whir of wings and bobbing tails as they jostle each other aside. The whole lot of them has probably made the rounds of the district, going from one farm to the next."

In spite of botanical disappointments and meteorological travails, Sigrid Undset enjoyed many moments of pure, intense joy inside the gate of her garden. Signe Thomas Ollendorff tells a story about one time when she was visiting Bjerkebæk as a child. She and her aunt were sitting alone at the table one morning, eating breakfast and chatting as they glanced out the window. The air was cold and damp, and the garden and woods were glittering white with frost. Suddenly they saw an entire flock of waxwings swoop in over the treetops. The birds circled several times, flying in elegant formation, before they landed in the crown of a tree. Hand in hand, Sigrid Undset and Signe crept out onto the steps, where they stood for a long time, staring with enchantment at the birds rocking back and forth as they perched on the branches, making the ice crystals sparkle in the sharp spring sunlight. After a while aunt and niece went back inside, and Signe was sent to the kitchen to get bread for the birds. When she returned with a bowl full of bread crumbs, she stopped short in the living room. There sat her Aunt Sigrid, shivering and with her eyes open wide. Signe asked if she should bring her aunt a shawl. "No, no, my child," replied Undset. "I'm not cold. I'm just shaking with happiness, you see, because I've always wished to see the waxwings when they're migrating." Signe Ollendorff says that she remembers feeling suddenly so impoverished. "We had seen exactly the same thing, the two of us. And I thought it was a beautiful sight too. But *I* wasn't *shaking with happiness*!"

She was intense in so many ways. "Sigrid Undset communed with plants. She communicated with them," writes Ole Henrik Moe. And it might be added that she sometimes even introduced them to her friends. When the American author Willa Cather became acquainted with Sigrid Undset in the United States during World War II, she noticed that her Norwegian friend sometimes had a personal relationship to individual plants:

> I am sure that in the years to come, at home, she will often remember certain trees and flowers as one remembers people one has met – people who have stimulated or charmed one.... It was pleasant to talk about trees and flowers to Undset because she had personal relations with them, but she was by no means the sentimental "lady botanist." She took a keen pleasure in learning all there was to know about these new forms which interested her so much.

When Undset was in the United States, she often thought about everything she would do when the war was over and she could return to Bjerkebæk. Along with Willa Cather and Hope Emily Allen, she planned "An American Garden," and when she finally returned home after five long years abroad, she tried to realize this dream of hers. She asked her friends to send her seeds and cuttings, but the experiment was not particularly successful. Some of the plants did flourish, of course, but some, like the dogwood tree, which had overwhelmed her with its marvelous blossoms, did not. She soon realized it would be useless to try replanting it. No doubt the most important aspect about her dream of an American garden was that it helped her endure those long years of exile.

The children at Bjerkebæk

"We don't like this Lillehammered place!" Peevish and sniffling, the twins trudged up toward the house, making their way through the raspberry bushes and the nettles, scrambling over big boulders, and scraping their knees. The closer that Lotte and Sigrid came to being rescued, the louder they howled. In the baby buggy outside the living room window, the twins' little sister lay sleeping, while cousin Hans stomped around behind the house with a walking stick turned upside down. Dashing around the legs of the two-year-old boy was a little kitten that kept batting at his legs with its paws. When little Hans heard his cousins wailing, he dropped the stick and peered cautiously around the corner to see what was going on – and then quickly retreated.

Lotte was the first to reach the stairs where Sigge and Signe Thomas came into view. "Waaa!!" the child bellowed with renewed vigor when she caught sight of her parents. Her father immediately lifted her up in his strong arms. Signe ran past the buggy and down the path toward little Sigrid, who had sat down and was screaming with rage and pain. She had been bitten by mosquitoes and her arms and legs were swollen and red.

On the stairs stood Aunt Sigrid, hastily taking in the whole scene.

"That doesn't look good! I think I'd better call the doctor at once."

They all went inside. Except for Hans. Reluctantly he toddled toward the stairs, then stood for a moment at the open door, listening to the twins crying

Hans in 1920 or 1921.

Signe and Sigge Thomas with little Signe and the twins, Charlotte and Sigrid. The year is 1921.

and the adults speaking in soothing tones. Then something began rustling inside the buggy! The little boy quickly went over and reached for the handle, just managing to grab it with his fingertips. The cries of the infant got louder, but now Hans managed to make the buggy move just a bit. All of a sudden it flew out of his hands and raced down the slope. It gave a leap and jolted a little farther along before it toppled onto its side and lay there, with two wheels whirring in the air. The boy covered his ears, because screams were now coming from the bundle inside the flannel blanket, and there came the grown-ups rushing out again!

It's not certain that this was exactly what happened that summer when Sigrid Undset bought Bjerkebæk and had a visit from her sister and brother-in-law and their three daughters from Kristiania. But it *is* true that the twins Charlotte and Sigrid didn't like "this Lillehammer place," and that little Sigrid had to go to the hospital because of mosquito bites. And Hans did send the baby buggy racing down the slope in front of the house; these stories are part of family lore from those first summers at Bjerkebæk.

At times there were too many children in the house. In addition to Undset's own three, her stepchildren were regular visitors, and the offspring of both of her sisters came for vacations and holidays, or if a family member was ill. For many years the children of the Catholic families in the district received their confirmation instruction in the hearth room, and during the Winter War of 1939–40 in Finland, three young siblings from Koivola were taken in at Bjerkebæk. Undset was also asked to be godmother for the children of many of her friends, including the Frøislands' daughter Anne-Marie, and the Geijerstam's daughter Sunniva, and she took these responsibilities very seriously. She wrote letters to her godchildren, sent them books, and gave them presents. Judging by the receipts in the Bjerkebæk household archives, she made regular purchases of traditional silver brooches at the handicrafts shop in Lillehammer for many years.

Concern for her own children was one of the most important reasons behind Sigrid Undset's decision to continue living in Lillehammer. Soon after moving there in 1919, when she published the essay collection *A Woman's Point of View*, she chose an epigram for the book that signaled the role she was now about to accept – as a single mother with the primary responsibility for the welfare of her children, their material needs as well as their social and spiritual upbringing. The quote, from an old ballad, is as follows:

> *Hossi kan grase paa jori gro,*
> *naar sonen maa inkji mori tru?*
> (How can the grass grow on earth,
> When the son cannot trust his mother?)

Even the Virgin Mary, she who shows mercy to all the miserable sinners of the earth, closes the heavenly door "to this one, the mother who has betrayed her son's trust," says Undset in her essay. She had chosen a very high standard by which to measure her actions.

Child-rearing was something that had interested Sigrid Undset long before she had children of her own. In 1910 she wrote a travel account from Rome about "The Children in Aracoeli," those free-spirited children who every Christmas presented their poems in honor of the infant Jesus at the church of Santa Maria in Aracoeli. When Undset saw how freely and naturally the Italian children were allowed to develop, and without interference from the adults, it made her think about "the poor Norwegian children whose mothers go to meetings to find out how they can win their children's confidence." Undset thought that adults needed to win their children's trust, not their confidence. Children should be allowed to live their own lives without having their parents nosing around and digging into everything they did. But then it's tempting to ask: "How long should they be allowed to develop freely?" Four years and one child after her experience at Aracoeli, Sigrid Undset writes: "The cultural work has to be started while the mind is young and tender." Her own sons realized at an early age that she expected a lot of them, both in terms of behavior and achievements; on the other hand, they received very few displays of physical affection. Kisses and caresses were not part of her repertoire, and she never engaged in baby-talk.

In terms of the father's role, Undset had to moderate her views over the years. In 1916 Katti Anker Møller, an activist in the Norwegian women's movement, asked Undset if she would consider contributing to an exhibition on the modern domestic setting. Undset was not at all inclined to do so. The reason for this was that she thought the feminists wanted to politicize something that she regarded as deeply private – motherhood itself. The exhibition was going to show the latest developments within obstetrics and infant care, and it was intended to contribute to improving public health care for mothers and children. Sigrid Undset was asked to equip an ideal children's room with everything that was pedagogically and hygienically correct. She refused. She maintained that children should not be subjected to the preferences of grown-ups; they should be allowed to collect "knick-knacks and flotsam, twine, rags, and colored leaves, all of which they love and we find hideous."

The opening of the maternity home exhibition was honored by a visit from King Haakon himself. According to Sigrid Undset, he was first shown a "misery room," the cramped lodgings of an impoverished family with many children, in which the father's presence was represented by a hat and where the mother was once again going to give birth "in the midst of all the family's sleeping and eating accoutrements":

> But worse than the misery room was the room that the women of the exhibition were displaying as the opposite – the "ideal children's room," in which two small beds and an infant's crib stood isolated and alone in an "artistic setting." It's said that the king asked where the thermometer for the bath was; it seems that nobody asked: Where is the mother's bed? And the father was not represented at all – only his ability to provide finances.

Sigrid Undset provoked many people, both with her opinions and the manner in which she delivered them, but she continued indefatigably to rail against the politics of childbirth and the fight for women's liberation. She insisted on seeing women's lives in light of their biological function as mothers. "This physical fact means so much in human society that there's nothing better a woman can be than a good mother, and nothing worse than a bad one," she claimed. The foremost role for women, whether they had their own children or not, was to be the culture-bearers and child-rearers of the family and society, and to live in such a way that they would deserve the respect of the young. "The higher a person's culture, the more that person will accept responsibilities beyond her own sphere," according to Undset. In her opinion, the women's movement had taken a wrong turn and become elitist. Originally it had focused on the issue of unmarried women, i.e., what remedy could be found for "the desperate plight of those women who, with the development of society in a capitalist direction, were driven out of their homes." Gradually the movement became focused on the situation of women in general and of middle-class women in particular. Undset dryly concluded that "the weakness of the movement was that from the very beginning it had a tendency to keep an account only of its gains and not of its losses."

On the debit side in her own life, Undset soon had to include the father of her children, because at Bjerkebæk the man was represented neither by a hat nor by his ability to provide financial support. After Hans was born, the house on Nordseterveien was filled to the eaves with women and children. Little Anders assumed the role of man of the house and did his best to live up to everyone's expectations. In a letter his mother reports that he "gets plenty of exercise because he flies around doing all the errands in town for me, polishes my shoes and carries water up and down to the bedrooms. He's awfully clever and sweet, but when he's not doing useful things, he gets into mischief, of course." Mosse, or Tulla as they also called her, required extra care, almost as much as an infant, even though at the age of four or five she was in relatively good health and could get around much like other children her age. But her speech was poor, she was not toilet-trained, and the fear that she would have another epileptic fit hovered like a constant shadow over the house.

The family's material security was very tenuous during the first year in their new home, and the need to improve their finances was a top priority. In order to have peace to work, Undset needed expert help in the house, and in order to afford such help, she had to write – and to write well. Only in that way could she support herself and her children. The nursemaid who came from Sweden that first summer didn't like her job much, and after only a few months she packed her bags and went home. Fortunately, Undset was able to find two excellent replacements. The first was Asta Solheim: She was nineteen, a gentle

and clever girl who had been thoroughly trained by her mother. "Extremely charming – mahogany through and through," Sigrid Undset wrote with satisfaction to Nini.

The other addition to the household was a young girl named Mary Andersen, who arrived in early October. She was from the Danish town of Randers, in Jutland, and Undset was pleased: "it's no exaggeration to say that she is truly a gem – pleasant and cheerful and as diligent as – well, not Norwegians, with the exception of Asta!" Over the next few years Undset hired other girls to work in her home for short or long periods of time, and it was always nerve-wracking to see whether the new employee would be able to handle the special challenges required of her. Right after Mary had been installed in the maid's room, Mosse had a severe epileptic attack; she screamed horribly and shook with convulsions, foaming at the mouth. And as usual during such episodes, she suffered an involuntary release of her bowels and bladder. Mary clapped her hands to her face and backed away in fright, but her employer told her firmly, "That's not why I brought you up here!" With a supreme effort Mary pulled herself together and soon became Mosse's most devoted nursemaid.

Asta and Mary brought laughter and good humor to the house, and they shared their mistress's interest in needlework and books. Mary knitted and sewed clothing for herself and the children, while Asta was especially good at embroidery. Other girls came and went, and the following ad appeared repeatedly in the newspaper *Gudbrandsdølen*:

Opening available
at the home of Sigrid Undset, Bjerkebæk, Lillehammer,
for a clever and industrious girl over twenty,
preferably a country girl, good at housekeeping and skilled in sewing.
To begin immediately.

It was important to Sigrid Undset that her household help showed some understanding for the demands of her profession, and that they protected her from disturbances as much as possible. It was hardly a coincidence that those who thrived best and stayed the longest at Bjerkebæk were the ones who took pleasure in reading. A special friendship developed between the mistress of the house and Mary Andersen, or Abba as they called her. Danish was actually Undset's first language, after all, and Abba made no apologies for the unrefined

Ulla and Ingvald Wiberg between Hans and Mosse.

sound of her Jutland dialect. Miss Rasmussen, on the other hand, was one of the many employees who lasted only a few months at Bjerkebæk. She was both snobbish and vain, but not particularly discreet. According to her employer, she had six party dresses in her closet, and she possessed a detailed knowledge of whom every bank director and company manager in the country had married or divorced. Undset reported that when Miss Rasmussen was away from the house, the mood always lifted:

> She has tomorrow afternoon off, so I'm going to take a break from my novel and Mary Andersen and I will drink tons of coffee and knit while Mary reads aloud from Ewald Fay Kristensen, who is from her home district, and it's a real joy for her to read in the Jutland dialect. We don't dare do this when the new girl is home, and I have a feeling that she regards my library as a horrifying and bewildering mixture of pedantry and grossly immoral vulgarity.

Sigrid Undset worked hard and took pleasure in whatever joys daily life might bring, but she invariably suffered from pangs of guilt regarding her stepchildren, who complained that they missed her. Svarstad had made arrangements for a housekeeper to look after them whenever he was traveling, but in no way could the woman measure up to "Mother." Undset had to steel herself, taking solace in the fact that Mosse was doing much better in the rural environs of Lillehammer than in the city. Mosse's condition was a constant source of worry, but for the longest time Undset hoped that she would continue to develop. To Nini she wrote:

> She will never be like other children, I have no illusions about that, but if only she were able to talk to us a little, to grow a little closer to us. Now I'm beginning to think that through my work I may be able to ensure her future... As for herself, she's happy to live as she does. She sings and dances and laughs practically all day long; she's talking a bit more, and she's starting to show pleasure in pretty clothes in strong colors. On Christmas Eve she was so lively and merry, and I was quite touched that both Miss Solheim and Miss Sørensen were so happy about that – after the children had been put to bed, and we were downstairs having tea, Miss Solheim said in her rather naive manner, "You know, the whole Christmas seems to be more festive because little Mosse was so happy tonight."

Sigrid Undset and her sister, Ragnhild Wiberg, with their children Hans and Ulla.

They did have some good times amidst all the work and worries. One January night after the Christmas visitors had all departed, as Undset sat down and prepared to start on her work, she reports: "I can hear the maids giggling as they wash in their rooms, and up above me the children occasionally tumble about in their beds, making a thump that reverberates down the wall." At such moments Undset seems like a mother hen who has gathered all her chicks under her wing as she vigilantly keeps an eye out for any dangers.

For a single mother with great financial responsibilities, everyday life could often be stressful and far from idyllic, and not everything could be left to the household help, especially the discipline of her children. Once again it was good to confide in Nini:

I'm so tired... God knows whether I can even write legibly – I worked until 3 a.m., and when I came upstairs little Hans woke up and made a fuss for the rest of the night... and every day I work well into the wee hours and stay in bed until noon, reading religious texts and legal code in Old Norse. I'm in quite a desperate mood, actually... Anders is getting out of hand – Anders junior, I mean. The other morning I gave him a sound spanking on his bare bottom; a lot of good that did. First he threw everything he could grab at the ceiling and walls, then I gave him another spanking – but an hour later

It wasn't easy to get Mosse to sit still when the camera was taken out.

he says with solemn affection: "Yes, Mother, you're not having an easy time with me, I can see that myself." But he's so big that it's not easy to give him a thrashing – from a purely physical standpoint, I can't handle it.

Sigrid Undset didn't use corporal punishment more than was deemed reasonable among most parents at the time, but she did discipline her children when she thought they deserved it. And she had a temper herself, so they might well receive a slap when she lost patience with them. How tough it was for her to have sole responsibility for her three children is clearly expressed in a letter she wrote to Gösta af Geijerstam in 1931:

When I came to Lillehammer twelve years ago, a couple of months before Hans was born, it was a matter of saving my life; I knew that if I died, Tulla would end up in that inhuman trash bin that is Tokerud Home for the Retarded, and Anders would land in an orphanage, or with Signe and Thomas. So there was no question of pampering my children. I had to punish Tulla with slaps, as difficult as it was for me to do that, to get her to stay clean and do everything that would keep her from sinking into an animal state. I had to punish Anders to put some mettle into the boy, in case he should lose me and end up among strangers. Only the Lord knows how hard this was for me.

The pupils at Gudrun Ørn's school in 1919 were from left: Bibbi Bruel, Hetty Henrichsen, Randi Helleberg, Anders Svarstad, and Fredrik Getz.

When Undset wrote this letter, she had just had the Geijerstams' son staying at her house for six months, and she was both frustrated and resigned about the boy's lack of discipline. She felt a strong need to call the father to task in his role as child-rearer, so we probably need to read the words with a grain of salt if we're to understand the author of this letter correctly.

It was a struggle to be both provider and mother, and it was with a certain wistfulness that Undset realized she was no longer either young or free. Even when spring arrived, she had to experience the new season from her windows, because the children and her work demanded her attention around the clock. Only in stolen moments could she slip outside and breathe in the fresh air, just as the mother does in "Vårskyer" ("Spring Clouds"), a short story that Undset wrote in May 1920. In the story she lets the narrative unfold in a stream-of-consciousness style. At the outer level, we follow an exhausted mother who takes a walk in the woods and goes up to a waterfall during the spring thaw, as she listens with half an ear to her son's ceaseless prattle. At the inner level, she is carrying on a conversation with herself, recalling in rapid succession glimpses of other springs when she was as young and unfettered as the family's nursemaid, eager to set out and test her strength in life. Now, as she finds herself ceaselessly immersed in the creative process, handling demands from all directions, she yearns for her own sense of longing and thinks somewhat hesitantly: "But I wanted nothing else."

Undset's role as mother was not made any easier by the fact that the three

Bjerkebæk children were so different. Anders, who had been quite sickly as an infant, had developed into a genuinely athletic and independent boy. He started at Gudrun Ørn's private school at Kirkegatan 8 in the autumn soon after they arrived in Lillehammer. At first he had only two fellow classmates, the girls Hetty Henrichsen and Randi Helleberg, who were both his age, but eventually the school had over 20 pupils of various ages. "Most of them came from well-to-do families who could afford to pay 40 kroner a month in tuition," explains Hetty, who more than 80 years later remembered her days at Gudrun Ørn's school in great detail and with considerable pleasure. Some of the students were sent to Lillehammer because of poor health, usually respiratory ailments. Most took lodgings with other Lillehammer families and studied with Miss Ørn for only a short time. Anders, Randi, and Hetty, on the other hand, stayed together as private students until they graduated in 1926.

Classes were held in a white-painted patrician villa just south of Søndre Park, where Miss Ørn lived with her widowed mother. The children were given instruction in Norwegian and math, as well as history and geography, in accordance with a plan specifically designed for each child. Hetty, for example, was exempt from religious instruction since her French-born mother was Catholic, while Anders and the others received the prescribed dose of Lutheran commandments and articles of faith, parables and hymns. The music lessons were conducted with everyone standing around the piano in the living room, or the "conservatory," as the room was called, while the needlework lessons for the girls took place in the bedroom shared by Miss Ørn and her mother. The girls would sit with their sewing and knitting at a big table at the foot of the beds, where thick quilts lay hidden under white crocheted coverlets. During the long lunch break the children would eat the food they had brought with them as they sat on the staircase that elegantly wound its way from one floor of the house to the next.

Miss Ørn and her assistant Signe Dahl were skilled pedagogues who made sure that the children learned what was required of them by the public school curriculum, and then a little more. They focused on the well-being of the children and on their diversity, often taking their pupils on excursions – on foot, on skis, or by sled. Occasionally they borrowed a car and drove everybody to one of the neighboring districts where they played games and botanized, ate the food they had brought with them, and sang songs. Anders showed no sign of having any particular artistic talents, but he was smart and diligent and had a fondness for math. At home he'd been given a head start in Norwegian and history, and he knew more about the Norwegian writer Henrik Wergeland than anyone else in class. Hetty Henrichsen remembers that Anders was somewhat awkward and not particularly social, and that sometimes he'd get into fights with the other boys and take a beating, but he never complained. He was by no means considered the class star, either socially or professionally, since he didn't have much to brag about, with a father who was a painter and rarely on the scene, and a hard-working mother who was a writer. The other pupils could all boast of equally lofty status symbols, whether it was a French-born mother in the case of the Henrichsen children, or a wealthy father, in Randi's case.

For Sigrid Undset it was extremely important that Gudrun Ørn tailored the lessons to the abilities of each student. Her own first teacher had been her mother, who had devised an untraditional curriculum based on the standard Norwegian history book, the comedies of Ludvig Holberg, and the stories of Hans Christian Andersen. Gudrun Ørn's lesson plan was far more systematic and goal-oriented, but Undset felt that Anders needed more contact with male teachers, and she was very critical of what she called "old-lady pedagogy." Over the years, the boy did receive instruction in woodworking and physical education along with the students in the public school, but it wasn't until he entered secondary school and later the Gymnasium that he had male teachers in other subjects.

Of Undset's three children, Anders must have been the one who was most aware of his parents' estrangement, and he probably missed his father. All the same, he undoubtedly enjoyed a pleasant childhood in Lillehammer. Daily life was marked by financial security, a sense of order, and a wealth of opportunities to experience cultural events. He had a reasonable degree of personal freedom, which he knew how to use, to his mother's relief – and consternation:

In some sense children stay children for a long time out here in the country. Anders often seems unbelievably naive and provincial compared with city children, yet in many ways they grow up quickly – looking out for themselves and making their own decisions. I know very little about where he goes or what he does when he's not home, and if I ask him how he got so wet or how he managed to get so scraped up or how he'd cut his face so badly that he was bloody from his forehead all the way down to his socks: "I fell in a pond – I climbed over a fence – I fell off the roof of the cowshed at Ersgård" – he explains in a voice cool with astonishment, as if he can't comprehend why it might interest *me* that my nine-year-old son is falling into ponds or off cowshed roofs. "Well, what were you *doing* up on that cowshed roof?" I asked him as I washed and bandaged him. "*Doing?*" his tone even more astonished. "There's nothing to *do* up on a roof!"

For the most part Anders escaped any real harm from all his exploits, because he was a down-to-earth boy with a healthy amount of good sense. He had inherited a stubborn streak from his father and showed no lack of tenacity when he set his mind to something. At home he tried out his talents as boss, a role that he evidently thought it was his duty to assume, as the eldest male. His mother allowed him to test his wings at it, but occasionally she had to intervene if he went too far. For instance, he once promised 10 øre to little Brit, the daughter of his half-sister Gunhild, if she would lick the soles of his shoes clean, even though there was horse manure on them. That was stretching the limit!

Undset liked the fact that her elder son enjoyed sports and athletics and was interested in engines and machinery – in short, that he generally showed signs of becoming a "proper man." She was easily impressed when it came to such subjects, since she herself had little skill in those areas. Judging by the receipts at Bjerkebæk, we can see that a good deal of money was spent on bicycles and skis, racing skates and soccer balls at the Helleberg Sporting Goods Store, and many of the receipts state that Anders was the purchaser. There are also receipts for the repair of sports equipment, so it was presumably put to frequent use. In the winter Anders went off skiing with his friends as soon as there was snow on the ground, and Sigge Thomas, the boy's godfather, took him along on some lengthy hiking expeditions in the mountains. Undset was most enthusiastic about her son's performances as a ski jumper, and she would watch with excitement whenever there was a competition on the slopes of Lysgårdsbakken. She saved newspaper clippings and all reports of sporting events that included his name, and it was obvious to everyone that she was proud of his courage and perseverance. When her son suffered defeats – as inevitably happened –- she suffered along with him.

Hans Benedikt was nothing like his big brother. When he was two years old, his mother said of him: "Hans is terribly sweet now, radiantly handsome, but he's sluggish and slow to catch on and awfully spoiled." In 1923 she reported to her sister Ragnhild:

> Believe me, Hans is lively and sweet, but a dreadfully fussy and pampered creature, and more mischievous all on his own than Anders and poor little Mosse put together. He always has to fidget and fumble with everything – the other day he calmly and quietly plucked off the leather from the covers of a number of my old editions of the sagas, books that are starting to peel along the spine. He received a good slap for that. And he begs for chocolate and "noranges" and cookies and sugar cubes all day long and gets very upset if

he doesn't have his way – but he really is nice and sweet… I'm doubly glad to have a garden this year since I'll probably have to give up the idea of traveling to Iceland; I don't dare go so far away from Mosse and Hans. But it was actually so pleasant last summer when Hans would sit on the steps each morning, waiting for me to come down – and then we took a long walk in the garden and woods – he remembers everything so clearly and is always asking if we can go out and eat berries "tomorrow" – his concept of time is still quite nebulous.

Hans was a beautiful child, and his mother waited a long time before cutting off his blonde locks, which formed such a soft frame around his face – and sometimes caused him to be mistaken for a girl. As it soon became apparent, he had a number of talents, including an unusually good memory. He possessed an extraordinary retentive ability that could match that of his mother and was blessed with a good imagination and sense of humor and could tell the most fantastical stories. The boy was in general quite different from most children his age, and perhaps that was the reason why he had an insatiable need for his mother's attention and company. "Hans is pestering me by following at my heels everywhere I go," Undset complained to a woman friend when Hans was six. "He has begged permission to sit here with a picture book, claiming he won't 'bother me.' So I don't have much peace or quiet for anything." On another occasion he kept jumping up and down in front of his mother's work-room window until she went out to play with him. Undset claimed that it took several days to get back into the material after that interruption.

Undset couldn't manage to give Hans all the time and care that he demanded; for his part, the boy felt rejected and began to speak of his mother with bitter-ness. Over the years it was Svarstad who became his youngest child's greatest hero. The story goes that one time when his father had come to Lillehammer for a visit, Hans strutted in front of him along Storgaten, loudly proclaiming: "Here I come with my father, the painter Anders Castus Svarstad from Kristi-ania!" The fact that the boy had a sense of self-importance that far exceeded his age and skills made him a comic figure in the eyes of many. For others, like his aunt Signe and half-sisters Ebba and Gunhild, it aroused both tenderness and concern. What would become of this gifted, sensitive, and peculiar boy?

There was another side to Hans' personality that could make people smile: he was clumsy and long-winded and terribly impractical. As a boy he had trouble with everything from tying his shoelaces to learning to ski properly, which both annoyed and worried his mother. When Sigrid Undset and six-year-old Hans were vacationing with the Geijerstam family in western Norway, she reported that Hans was truly thriving, "but he spends most of his time with Brit, who is closest to him in age, and she waits on him hand and foot. The boys are so quick-witted that he hardly can get a word in edgewise with them; before he even utters his first remarks, they've already moved on to something else." When he got older, Hans often used his helplessness as a form of coquetry. He showed up at the school skiing competition at Lysgårdsbakken dressed in a hat and overcoat, to the great amusement of his classmates. And he would moan and groan so much while pulling off his ski boots that the housekeeper, Mathea Mortenstuen, said it sounded like he was giving birth!

Something else that worried those closest to the boy was that he paid no attention to rules or admonitions. To his mother's despair, Hans shrugged off any obligations that he found tedious, and he showed no respect for any figures of authority who tried to force him to toe the line, especially teachers. On the other hand, he had a vivid imagination and a unique ability to create drama and commotion. One time when Undset was away, Hans and the neighbor's boy Ole Henrik Moe went on an expedition into the woods and found some poisonous baneberries. Hans thought they should use them to make a devil's potion, so the two little boys chopped and mashed and mixed and stirred until they'd created a type of brew. Then they each took a swallow and lay down on their stomachs in the dim alcove with Bishop Bang's book *Norwegian Witches' Incantations and Magical Recipes* in front of them on the floor. Hans knew that this work was on the Catholic Church's index of banned books and that his mother had been granted special permission to have a copy in her library. Now he proceeded to chant from the witches' incantations; he said he was going to conjure up the Devil himself. The boys thought the whole thing was terribly eerie, and they held their breath in terror when they heard heavy footsteps approaching. As Ole Henrik Moe tells it, the footsteps came closer and closer, and his heart was pounding hard when the door was brusquely thrown open. There stood Mathea Mortenstuen in all her majesty, wanting to know what those two rascals were doing in Undset's workroom! Ole Henrik thought that having Thea after them was worse than if the Devil himself had shown up, but Hans just laughed and slipped past her.

Hans grew no less conceited over the years, even though many tried to bring him down a peg. He found it only natural that others waited on him, and he enjoyed lecturing his audience about everything from religion and politics to literature and history. But these were Sigrid Undset's special areas of interest, after all, so Hans was constantly being put in his place by his mother, who was far more knowledgeable. That was not always something he accepted with equanimity, for Hans had a fierce temper that could flare up into the most intense fits of rage. He might lash out at just about anyone and would throw whatever was at hand against the wall. In fights with his brother, Hans always lost, at least when they were young, and their mother complained that they raised a ruckus "worse than the destruction of Jerusalem."

At times the brothers could be the best of friends, such as on days when the spring sun had dried the garden path in front of the guesthouse and conditions were perfect for "throwing coins." They could carry on aiming at the line across the path for hours, showing the greatest forbearance toward each other. But usually Anders couldn't resist teasing his little brother, and Hans was a gratifying victim who would work himself into an explosive state and then strike back as best he could. Fortunately, Hans was quite tall. According to his mother he looked like a fifteen-year-old when he was still only thirteen, and he quickly became a specialist in pithy remarks that struck Anders where he was most vulnerable. Occasionally things turned so rough when the brothers were arguing and fighting that the adults got frightened and physically had to keep them apart. One time a mirror in the boys' room got broken; it was most likely Hans who was the culprit, and even after he grew up, his fury could take its toll on the dishes and other objects at Bjerkebæk.

Undset tried as best she could to give her sons exactly the "growing soil" that they each required, whether it was sports equipment for Anders or theater costumes for Hans. Once she sewed a carnival outfit for her youngest, and she was particularly pleased with how it turned out. It had a red comb, white wings, and a long tail, so the boy could truly strut around like a rooster. She knew her son all too well.

Both boys received all the nice clothing and sports equipment that they needed, and of course they had a wealth of books. Undset read to them and told them stories. She taught them to play card games and solitaire, and she tried to interest them in plants and history and other topics that she herself enjoyed. When it was time for birthday parties, she took part in the preparations as well as the obligatory games, which could be anything from the Norwegian equivalent of "London Bridge is falling down" to "geographical names" – a game that involved writing down names that began with a specific letter of the alphabet, as many as possible in a couple of minutes. Undset always had the longest list with the strangest names, and when she was accused of cheating

Hans liked to dress up – here as a priest.

Anders among the priests and nuns at the consecration of St. Torfinn Chapel in 1924.

– "that's not a real place" – she would immediately tell the children all about that particular place.

Since Hans' birthday was in the summer, he was allowed to celebrate his name day instead, either on March 21 (Benedict) or June 24 (Johannes). During the week between Christmas and New Year's, the boys always invited their friends to a party in the hearth room, and their mother sent them to dancing school, which ended with the obligatory and rather snobbish "recital ball." She took them on drives with picnic baskets, and on vacations to visit family in Sweden and Denmark. She did all the right things, but she kept her distance. After a visit at Bjerkebæk in 1935, Nini Roll Anker wrote in her diary with amazement:

> She's actually completely unchanged from the time when we were young – her world is books, the sagas, legends, all of history written down through the ages, the history of humanity, specific families, the earth and the heavens. *That* is where she lives. And in spite of everything she knows of real life through experience and knowledge, she is removed from reality; she even

Anders airborne.

avoids talking about practical matters with those closest to her. She asked
me to find out from Anders about his travel plans – "it's not in my nature to
talk with the boys about such things."

Svarstad saw very little of his children for long periods of time, but occasionally
he would visit them at Bjerkebæk, and when the boys were older they had
contact with him in Oslo. In the summer they liked to visit their father's family
in Røyse. There they saw their half-siblings, went swimming in Tyrifjorden,
and roamed freely.

Anders became more and more like his paternal namesake, especially in
appearance, with his etched profile and distinctively shaped lips. Hans was
mostly interested in his father's status as an artist; in his childish way the boy
was determined to view Svarstad as the greatest person in the whole world, or
at least greater than his mother. The difference between the two boys became
even more evident from the way they reacted to their mother's conversion to
Catholicism. Anders was only ten when she started receiving instruction, and
during those first years Undset often took her son along to mass and other

church events, such as the consecration of St. Torfinn's Chapel in Hamar. A photo taken on that occasion shows Anders dressed in a sailor suit, the only child present among the priests and nuns wearing ankle-length robes and the matronly women with their big hats.

Like so many new converts, Sigrid Undset burned with religious zeal during the first years after she was accepted into the Catholic Church, and this was something that affected the entire household. In March 1925, Undset left Hans with the nuns in Hamar while she took Anders and her mother, Charlotte Undset, to Italy to celebrate her first Easter as a Catholic. It was her third visit to Italy. During her first stay there, she had met Svarstad and was struck by the sort of passionate love that breaks all the rules. Her second stay in Italy was when Anders was born; he turned out to be such a fragile little creature that she felt her whole body seized with maternal angst. Now on this third occasion she was a pilgrim following the monks on the road to Golgotha. It was almost as if she had her own trilogy in mind: *The Wreath*, *The Wife*, and *The Cross*.

Her stay with the Benedictine monks at the cloister on Monte Cassino was an emotional experience, as evidenced in the travel report that Undset wrote for the Norwegian Catholic publication *Kimer I Klokker*. When we read her private letters, we get the sense that it wasn't easy for her to deal with her two traveling companions. Another hardship was the fact that the Catholic Church was then celebrating one of its holy years, which meant that Italy was the destination for thousands of pilgrims, arriving from near and far. To Nils Anker, her neighbor and friend, Undset complained about how strenuous the trip was:

Here in Italy I've had very little time or opportunity to write – with my mother and son to attend to and with a good deal of socializing – more than in a whole year back home, and much more than I really care for. The rooms don't exactly lend themselves to peace and quiet either – the hotel hosts are lining their pockets because of the celebration of l'Anno Santo, all the rooms are booked. At the place where I stayed for Easter, I had to use the window-sill to write the cards for my mother; they were all I managed to send off. That was at Monte Cassino – the ancient Benedictine cloister up in Abruzzi. Anders and I were there from the Saturday before Palm Sunday until the day after Easter. We stayed in a little guesthouse for women outside the cloister gates, but we ate in the visitors' refectory and went to church both in the morning and afternoon... In the hours between services we went for walks in the garden.

Four siblings, two of them Catholic and two Protestant: Gunhild, Anders, Ebba, and Hans.

It may have been this first close contact with Catholicism that gave Anders such an overdose of religion that he refused to follow his mother any further along the path of faith. Perhaps he didn't find it much fun to accompany her from church to church and to pray for peace among the peoples of Europe, a "task" that she speaks of as a type of penance in her letter to Nils Anker.

After returning from Italy, Undset invited her family and friends to a mass at Bjerkebæk, and Nils Anker gathered everyone to be photographed out in the courtyard. First the entire group was photographed together, then just those who were Catholics: Hans, Ebba, Sigrid Undset, Father Bechaux, and a few others. But not Anders. He was retreating from his mother's sphere of influence. Over the years the distance between Undset and her elder son grew in other areas as well. He went his own way, was "off vagabonding," as she called it, keeping her out of his private life and rarely writing letters when he was away from home. In that sense, he became more and more like his father, who was also a wanderer and a rather uncommunicative person. Even so, those who knew them best noticed that a feeling of composure marked the relationship between Anders and his mother, which spoke of a shared sense of trust and security. Each understood where the other stood.

Things were different with Hans. The younger son observed his mother's religious life with curiosity; it appealed both to his imagination and his sense of drama. At one of his mother's "little breakfasts for the faithful" after the morning mass, Hans asked: "Father Lutz, what exactly happened with that snake in the Garden of Eden? Did it crawl on its belly or did it have tiny little feet to walk on?"

On another occasion, at St. Torfinn's Chapel in Hamar, the congregation could hear a boy's voice asking loudly in a broad Fåberg accent as the priest appeared in the choir: "Why does he have that hat on his head?"

The questions may have been naive, but at least his interest was genuine, and Sigrid Undset devoted all her efforts to making a good Catholic out of her younger son. "I'm trying to make it an offering of my own free will," she confided to Gösta. It was an offering for which Hans would end up paying a high price.

It's difficult to say what sort of discussions took place within the family regarding Undset's religious life. In the Lutheran church register for Mesna parish the following facts were entered:

"Author Sigrid Undset withdrawn October 30, 1924. To: Catholicism."

Then three years passed before any more information about the family at Bjerkebæk was entered:

"Anders C. Svarstad (child) withdrawn March 24, 1928. To: No religious community."

Anders was not confirmed, either as a Catholic or a Lutheran. He chose to go his own way, and that couldn't have been easy for him. Hans, on the other hand, followed his mother, and she preferred to give the impression that he was driven by his own motivations. To Astri, she wrote:

He no doubt intends to propose that all of your children should become Catholics, and it seems as if he's now taking the offensive. The worst of all was one time when we had strangers visiting, and the conversation shifted to religious intolerance and the persecution of heretics – and Hans piped up from the corner where he'd been listening: "Yes, I really think so too. They should *do something* with people who are dumb enough to be Lutherans!" You can bet that those visitors had something to gossip about afterwards regarding how that child was being brought up!

Very early on, Sigrid Undset devised a strict program of instruction for Hans, with secular as well as religious lessons. When he turned six, he became a pupil at Gudrun Ørn's school. Both there and at home he was constantly drawing pictures, and when he was not drawing, he showed himself to be quite a bookworm, devouring everything from fairy tales by Hans Christian Andersen to his mother's encyclopedias. When Anders started secondary school, Undset decided that her younger son also had a need for something other than the "old-lady education" offered by Gudrun Ørn, and so she sent him to study with Monsignor Kjelstrup in Hamar, who had a reputation for knowing how to handle unruly boys. In August 1926 Undset wrote to her sister Signe Thomas:

> Hans is in Hamar – I talked to him on the phone yesterday. He's very happy to be there, but is also looking forward to having me come and get him. I had a few words with Msgr. Kjelstrup: Hans eats his meals with him, and goes over there every day with him or Jens, the acolyte, or else he plays in the garden when he's not studying or in chapel. And Msgr. Kjelstrup is apparently quite pleased with his pupil.

Anders received a new suit and confirmation gifts even though he was not confirmed.

In spite of Undset's assurances that Hans was thriving in Hamar, Signe and Sigge Thomas were critical of her intense religious devotion and the effect it was having on the children. Perhaps they saw how domineering she could be and were unwilling to follow her. On the other hand, Undset's mother, who was living in the Thomas home, decided to follow her daughter into the Catholic Church. Others who did the same included Bjerkebæk's housekeeper Mathea Mortenstuen, Undset's stepdaughter Ebba, and her friends Gösta af Geijerstam and Helene Frøisland. All of them converted to Catholicism. Signe and Sigge Thomas chose to withdraw themselves and their daughters from the state church and – like Anders – were then listed as belonging to "no religious community." We can only guess what was behind all the withdrawals and conversions among those belonging to Sigrid Undset's circle, what sort of discussions and struggles for freedom went on, what kind of sincere faith and noble intentions reigned, and what type of religious fanaticism and psychological problems might have been present. For Sigrid Undset, her actions as a Catholic became a costly endeavor, and we can only speculate as to what extent she consciously allowed herself to be used. Was it from a position of strength or from weakness? For

Hans, his mother's religious involvement had severe consequences. In January 1927 he was sent to a Catholic school, Sta. Sunniva's in Oslo and became a boarder at the St. Joseph Institute. This was something for which he would never forgive his mother.

As far as Mosse was concerned, things were a bit simpler. She was the secret centerpoint of the family, and no one made any unreasonable demands on her. Hans displayed a touching concern for his sister and tried to help her whenever she had an attack of epilepsy. Anders paid less attention to her and kept his friends away. Whenever there were strangers visiting Bjerkebæk, Mosse was kept out of sight. Other children were afraid of her and stayed a safe distance away, because she had a tendency to pinch and scream horribly. But punishment and patience were of no use in teaching Mosse anything; she lived in her own world.

In the autumn of 1922, Sigrid Undset made a last attempt to find out what was really the matter with her daughter by taking her to Kristiania. In the household archives there is a piece of paper that testifies to the girl's tragic condition. On December 20, 1922, the Pediatric Clinic at Pilestredet 77 sent a bill to Undset for a stay of 36 days, costing 25 kroner per day. This was quite a lengthy hospital stay for a seven-year-old girl, and yet it was a luxury for that time, when examinations and treatment were reserved for those who could afford to pay. But Mosse could not be helped. Even today no one is able to say for sure what ailed her. "Rett syndrome" has been mentioned, as well as multiple sclerosis – and perhaps she suffered from a combination of illnesses. The doctors at the pediatric clinic could offer Undset no hope of improvement. On the contrary, they advised her to send the girl to De Kellerske Anstalter in Jutland, Denmark; it was one of the best institutions of its kind in Scandinavia.

Undset realized that Mosse would always be "severely retarded," which was the phrase that she used, and now she had to make a decision as to her daughter's future fate. She contacted the institution in Denmark and made an appointment to visit, because she wanted to see the place for herself. To her sister Ragnhild Wiberg she wrote: "Tomorrow I'm going out to buy a gramophone! I'm a little embarrassed about purchasing such a thing, but I'll put it upstairs in the bedroom. It's for poor little Mosse – I want her to have all the joys that I can give her, and I know that she'll be delighted."

Undset thought that Ebba would also benefit from going to Denmark, so she wrote to a well-respected school in Jutland, the Askov Folk College, to

Mosse in the garden with her beloved "Abba," Mary Andersen.

apply for a place for her stepdaughter. She was greatly concerned about Ebba's future, and when the acceptance letter arrived from Askov, she was both happy and relieved:

Dear Signe!

A letter from Mrs. Appel at Askov today – Ebba has been accepted. Hurray! I can't tell you how happy I am to have this matter settled at last. And she's going to stay in the home of Mrs. Appel's brother, Mr. Schrøder, B.A., who's the son of "old Schrøder," the founder of Askov. The young girls are given lodging with the teachers' families, so Ebba will be living with 14 other girls – in the very thick of things – and Mrs. Appel promises personally and with great kindness that she and her brother and sister-in-law will look after her, so that she'll get the most possible benefit from the experience.

As for clothes, I've asked Ebba to contact you at once. A windbreaker and skirt made of windproof fabric are essential in that eternal Danish gale, a good traveling suit that is extra-thick and a winter sports outfit, preferably made to measure; I was thinking two dresses for school, for example a blue one for church and a knit dress (so she won't be tempted to wear out the skirt of her suit on the school bench), 1 little taffeta or silk jersey dress for parties. A couple of blouses, stockings, underwear, and towels – the latter for Mother should be bought right away. We'll take the money from my account at Aschehoug – you have carte blanche, and I'm confident that if I leave it all to you, it will cost at least 1/3 less than if I took care of matters myself.

That's all I have time for today. I'll write to Aschehoug about financing the enterprise, and to Mrs. Appel, telling her that I'd like to shake her hand a million times. I'm inexpressibly happy that this has been settled, at any rate...

Give my greetings to Mama, Sigge, and your children.

Your Sigrid.

Ebba enjoyed a wonderful year at Askov, which was one of Denmark's most desirable folk colleges. But De Kellerske Anstalter was never again mentioned as a possible home for Mosse. Nor was any other institution. After her visit, Undset decided that her daughter should be allowed to stay at home for as long as she lived. And that was what happened. Every evening the maids would put Mosse to bed and go to tell Undset that her daughter was waiting. Then she would immediately get up from her desk in the alcove and walk through the hearth room along the long, red-painted corridor that connected the two houses. She would cross through the living room and climb the narrow staircase to the second floor. A thud could be heard when Undset fell to her knees next to Mosse's bed, and the household help would know that at this moment she was saying a prayer for her daughter.

Over the years Sigrid Undset brooded a great deal over the relationship between "fortunate" and "unfortunate" individuals. Caring for her helpless daughter left its mark on both her writing and her political opinions. In her novel *Ida Elisabeth* from 1932, Undset has the main character ask what will become of the poor wretches whom strong and healthy people view merely as flotsam. In the story Dr. Sommervold toys with the idea of mercy killing as a possible way out and says that we should take it with composure "if the practice of throwing oneself off a cliff as our ancestors once did should become accepted again, in one form or another." He tries to convince Ida Elisabeth that it's unreasonable to expect those who are strong and healthy, those who are "motor vehicles," to squander their strength on the weak, those who are merely "trailers without engines." But for Ida Elisabeth, compassion is her guiding star, and she comes to the conclusion that a person's worth is anchored in his status as God's inviolable creation, not in his ability to work or produce. By the time Hitler and Stalin began spreading their propaganda, making an individual's worth a variable factor dependent on how much the person could contribute to the community, Sigrid Undset had long since established her own view on the matter. She was convinced that Mosse was one of God's children, an *enfant de dieu*, and therefore inviolable.

Undset's stepdaughter Ebba caused her a great deal of worry over the years, even after her stay at Askov. She just couldn't manage very well on her own, although for certain periods of time she did hold various jobs, but she was always dependent on support from the family. Things went better for her sister Gunhild. She married when she was only eighteen, and then settled in England with her husband and their two children. Gunhild's husband was an engineer on one of Thomas Frederik Olsen's ships that sailed between Norway and Newcastle, and he was able to help Gunhild's family obtain reasonably priced transport across the North Sea. For a time Ebba lived with her sister and brother-in-law outside of Newcastle. In the spring of 1928, she converted to Catholicism, and Sigrid Undset went to England to be present for the solemn event. But Ebba longed for home in Norway and for "Mother," so Undset let her come back to Bjerkebæk, giving her the task of translating a book by the English author G.K. Chesterton. Her Norwegian translation of *The Catholic*

Anders Svarstad, junior and senior, visiting Trond at Brøttum.

Church and Conversion was published by Aschehoug in 1929, at Undset's expense. But this assignment did not lead to a professional career for Ebba.

The children of Undset's sisters came to Bjerkebæk even more often than her stepchildren. They felt like it was their second home, and so they came to Lillehammer at Christmastime and during school vacations, staying for short visits or occasionally for extended periods. Once it was Ragnhild Wiberg who needed help, and Undset told Gösta in a letter:

> My sister who lives in Stockholm has been deathly ill for six months – now she's at Balberg Sanatorium to get her strength back (God willing, as my paternal grandmother used to say – she's still far from fully recovered). And her two children, mentioned above, have been here since May, and they'll stay until their mother is well enough to go back home to all the housekeeping and work, which means for an indefinite amount of time. They're 4 and 18 months. So there's not much peace and quiet for working here.

The lack of quiet was a genuine torment to Undset, because she had a great need to be alone and to enter into her own world. Solitude and the peace to concentrate were essential for her to be able to write, and she was painfully aware of her own impatience whenever she was disturbed at her work. "For as long as I live, I don't suppose I'll ever be quit of the desire to tell all unwelcome people and matters to go to hell," she concluded. And she admitted to Gösta that even having Ragnhild visiting was a trial. "She chatters endlessly... I've always had a great fondness for her, which has enabled me to do a good deal for her, but I can't listen to her for two minutes in a row without snapping at her."

In another lament to her old friend, Undset writes, "Sometimes I think I know exactly what that little tugboat on Lake Mjøsa feels like when it's towing logs..."

Her youngest stepchild, Trond, was one of the heaviest "logs," because he was slow-witted and never able to hold a job. It was Mary Andersen, Abba, who became Trond's anchor in life. With great interest, Mary had watched Sigrid Undset's progress along the path of faith, and for a while she weighed whether she should follow her employer and convert to Catholicism. Undset encouraged her with gifts of saint figurines and prayer books. But then Mary fell in love, and in February 1928 she married Hans Stendahl and went to live on a farm called Thorstad Nordre in Brøttum, about 20 kilometers south of Lillehammer. Mary was allowed to choose between a vacuum cleaner and a dinner set for a wedding present and chose the latter. According to the receipt, the set consisted of 86 pieces and cost 142.10 kroner, so it must have filled up a good deal of space on the gift table.

Sigrid Undset missed her warm-hearted Danish housekeeper, and in a letter written several months after the wedding, she sounded a bit hurt, saying that she hadn't seen anything of Mary since her marriage. But the contact between them did not come to an end, and a steady stream of packages was exchanged over the years between Bjerkebæk and Thorstad, usually furnishings for the house in one direction and farm produce in the other. What made the bonds between the two families especially strong was the fact that Mary and her husband became Trond Svarstad's salvation. When Undset's stepson was eighteen, she started gathering information about agricultural schools in eastern Norway, with the boy's future in mind. To her friend Ingeborg Møller, who was herself the mother of three boys, Undset reported that she was writing "to all the horticultural and small-farm schools in the Oppland region for their brochures – for a stepson, whose future I've agreed to secure. Since he's not entirely normal, it's not exactly easy. But there must be a solution." Svarstad kept hinting that he wanted to send Trond to sea, but Undset couldn't stand the thought of what would happen to him among strangers. Abba wanted to earn some extra money, so in October 1928, the boy moved out to Thorstad, and there he settled in. Undset paid for Trond's food and lodging through one of the stipends that she had established with her Nobel Prize money. Other expenses she paid directly out of her own pocket, as revealed in the following letter to Mary Stendahl:

> With regard to Trond's clothes, I think it would be best if *you* buy whatever he needs the next time you come into town, and have them send me the bill. If it's impossible to have him measured properly, you can at least get a general idea, or take along one of his items of clothing, much better than I could do by sheer guesswork. And at the same time you should buy underwear and socks or whatever else he needs. It's no good bothering his father with this, and besides, I don't know where he is right now.

From 1919 until 1928 Mary Andersen was the one who bore one of Sigrid Undset's greatest burdens by taking care of Mosse. After that she cared for Trond in her own home in such a way that Undset could feel assured that the boy was happy. The other household help who offered Undset great support was Mathea Mortenstuen from Tretten. When she was hired, a new era began at Bjerkebæk, but of course that was not something they could know on that day in 1925 when the young woman appeared on the doorstep for the first time.

Mathea Mortenstuen

Sigrid Undset's godmother, Mathea Bådstø, was for many years in charge of the lending library in Tretten. One of the most frequent borrowers was Mathea Mortenstuen, a young woman who got on well with her older namesake. She was to become a very important person in the daily life at Bjerkebæk.

Mathea Mortenstuen was born in 1903 and grew up on a small farm on the banks of Gudbrandsdalslågen. After the obligatory school years, she went on to study at the School for Continuing Education, and her graduation certificate testifies to a bright and diligent pupil who received top marks in all subjects. When she was seventeen and eighteen she attended the Northern Gudbrandsdal School of Agriculture and Domestic Science, where she once again received good grades in all her subjects – from cooking and botany to social studies and Norwegian. Miss Mortenstuen did best in household bookkeeping and dressmaking, while she seemed to show least interest in "kitchen work."

It's impossible to know whether Mathea Bådstø was thinking about her younger namesake's spiritual welfare and wanted to secure a Catholic employer for her, or whether she was thinking about Sigrid Undset's physical welfare and wanted to furnish her with skilled domestic help. In any case, she was the one who put the two in touch with each other, and in 1925 Mathea Mortenstuen arrived at Bjerkebæk. She immediately established a good relationship with the Mistress and the other household help, Mary Andersen, the children's dear

Mathea Mortenstuen (1903–1964), as a young woman.

Avgangsvidnesbyrd

fra

fortsættelsesskolen i Øier.

Mathea Mortenstuen.

født den *14. 1. 03* har vinteren *1917-18* gjennemgaat et seks maaneders kursus ved Øier fortsættelsesskole. *Hun* har vist *meget* flid og gjort *meget* fremgang. *Hendes* forhold har været ¹⁾ *meget godt.* Ved avgangsprøven har *hun* faat følgende enkelte karakterer:

Kirkehistorie . . . . *Særdeles godt.*
Norsk skriftlig . . . . . . *Særdeles godt.*
Norsk mundtlig . . . . . *Særdeles godt.*
Regning . . . . *Særdeles godt.*
Naturkundskap . . . . . . *Særdeles godt.*
Historie . . . . *Særdeles godt.*
Geografi . . . . *Særdeles godt.*
Tegning . . . .
Skrivning . . . .
Orden i skriftlige arbeider . *Særdeles godt.*

Øier den *1 mai. 1918*

Martens Bøhler.

lærer.

¹) Bedste karakter for forh. er meget godt.

Abba. The new housemaid was clever and took her responsibilities very seriously. Even though she was only 22, she was not alarmed by the disabled daughter in the house; she tended to Mosse's needs with consideration and authority. Nor was she frightened off by the Catholic visitors who came to Bjerkebæk; on the contrary, through her contact with Mathea Bådstø she herself had developed an interest in Catholicism.

Class picture from the Nordre Gudbrandsdal School of Agriculture and Domestic Science.

It's clear that from the very start Mathea Mortenstuen was entrusted with far more than just the cooking and cleaning. Mathea, or Thea, as the children called her, quickly became an assistant to whom Undset could relinquish complete responsibility for the daily chores and housekeeping at Bjerkebæk. It was Mathea who guarded access to the house, it was she who took the calls whenever the "telephone beast" became too intrusive, and it was she who ensured that the Mistress had peace to write and at least a measure of much-needed freedom. She also looked after the boys, although with varying degrees of success. In the fall of 1926 she took part in making all the arrangements for a celebration honoring Hans Benedikt, because on October 10 of that year it was his turn to kneel before the altar in St. Torfinn Chapel for his first communion. "May the blessings of the Holy Family descend upon your soul and bring you peace and true happiness," it said on the card that was sent to friends and acquaintances to mark the occasion.

Mathea saw to it that spiritual nourishment was not the only thing that visitors to Bjerkebæk received. She was a marvelous cook, and the well-equipped kitchen gave her plenty of opportunities to display her skills. Undset appreciated Mathea's expertise and gave her high praise when she mentioned her to friends. There was just one thing that caused her some concern, and that was the young woman's mercurial temperament. The Mistress and Abba took it in stride, but Nora Sollien, who was the third domestic servant at the time, did not. She threatened to quit.

"Maid trouble" was a subject that nearly all housewives complained about, and Sigrid Undset was no exception. In a lament to her sister Signe Thomas, who was herself struggling with an unhappy maid, Undset wrote:

> The eternal discord between my maids has led to Nora Sollien giving notice yesterday. Sobs, tears, explanations – I felt as if I were inside a meat grinder. Nora and Mathea are both willing to give up their positions and leave. Both agree that it doesn't work with 3, both agree that with Abba alone, things would be fine, but... (They both admire her.) Well, I don't dare send Mathea away, I don't know what might happen to her, with that temper of hers – that was what N. also pointed out, that when she is utterly desperate, she threatens to do harm to herself. So I asked Nora whether she might like to work for you if she was to be parted from Mosse, and she said that was her most fervent wish – she's terrified of ending up in a strife-filled home. So, if you want to fire your "horrid creature," who is unhappy working for you and hire Miss Sollien instead, let me know at once.

In the end, the situation was resolved with Mathea's departure from Bjerkebæk. Like her benefactress, Miss Bådstø, she had a desire to see more of the world, although not as far away as the United States. Mathea Mortenstuen went to the capital to stay with the Geist family; where she received food and lodging in return for helping with the housework. Her host, Josef Geist, was the head of one of the large Catholic families in Oslo. Like numerous other families in the congregation, he was a descendant of German craftsmen, many of whom had come to Norway in the nineteenth century. In her novel of conversion, *Gymnadenia*, from 1929, Sigrid Undset describes the Gotaas family, who clearly come from a similar background.

Most likely it was Mathea Bådstø who found Thea the position with the Geist family, although it might have been Undset too, because by now she was a famous – not to mention notorious – convert, and she had quickly developed a large network of contacts among the Catholics. She was especially familiar

The maids hanging the laundry behind the house at Bjerkebæk.

with everyone connected to Sta. Sunniva School in Oslo after Hans was accepted as a student in January 1927. Occasionally Hans would run into Mathea Mortenstuen in St. Olav Church, because she had started receiving instruction in the Catholic faith. After mass Hans would pour out his heart to Thea, telling her all of his feelings. He was a boarder at the St. Joseph Institute right near his school, and only a couple of weeks after his arrival, he bravely wrote home: "I'm doing well in school, yesterday I went to confession at the church, tomorrow I'm going to be an acolyte, I'm supposed to send you greetings from Mother Scholastica and from Mother Zoé and from Father Augustine. Please tell everyone at home hello from me. Thank you so much for the rosary."

It may have been school policy to restrict contact between students and their parents, at any rate until the children had gotten settled in their new environment. But Hans longed for home, and he was miserably unhappy. Naturally he was teased, because he was an awkward boy and because he spoke with a rural Gudbrandsdal accent. He was vain and arrogant to an almost comical degree, and during classes he sometimes worked with such fierce intensity that he would suddenly get a cramp in his writing hand, and the other boys would then gawk as he started carrying on like a madman, dancing around and waving his arms about. After a while Hans' talents came to light, and his classmates discovered that he was a wizard at drawing caricatures of the teachers. His exercise books were filled with funny figures, and in a few subjects, especially history, he impressed everyone with his knowledge. More important was the fact that he showed himself to be an unusually fearless and generous friend, and this prompted the other boys to regard him with respect.

As the son of Sigrid Undset, Hans enjoyed many privileges at the St. Joseph Institute. He was exempt from washing dishes and helping with the cleaning and other practical chores that were taken in turn by the other boys. He was also exempt from corporal punishment, which the others ran the risk of incurring if they broke the school rules. Hans kept a careful eye on his position in the hierarchy and carried out his duties as acolyte with much gravity. In general he had a great sense for anything that smacked of drama, and after a short time his Fåberg dialect disappeared for good and was replaced by a formal and old-fashioned standard Norwegian. His new environment no doubt had a stimulating effect on him in many ways, but neither the special privileges nor the exciting surroundings could erase the feeling that he was far from home.

After a while the boy was allowed to visit his maternal grandmother and the Thomas family in Ullevål Haveby on the weekends. Whenever Uncle Sigge and little cousin Signe would come to "sign out" Hans from the boarding school, the two children would race along the sidewalk like calves newly released in the spring.

When Hans and Thea met at church they probably discussed a topic that was of the greatest interest to everyone in the congregation: the approaching anniversary celebration at Stiklestad where the Christian king, Olav Haraldsson, had met his death at the hands of a heathen army in the year 1030. The Catholic Church had established a building committee in charge of erecting an Olav chapel on the site where the holy king fell, and Sigrid Undset was a key member of the group. Hans had also been assigned a role in the celebration and was eagerly looking forward to taking part along with his mother. There was a great deal of anticipation, because the 900th anniversary of the battle at Stiklestad was planned as a national event. As a martyred king, St. Olav held a special place in Norwegian history; he was the one, after all, who had put a definite end to the Viking customs and introduced Christian laws. According to Undset, Olav was the king who led Norway into the fold of civilized Europe and established a new, humane standard for his countrymen.

The anniversary was a welcome opportunity for the Norwegian authorities to display their pride in the nation's historical and cultural roots. The union with Denmark, which was dissolved in 1814, and the subsequent union with Sweden, which ended in 1905, had led to a pressing need to show Norway as an independent nation with a long and noble history. Of course the parliamentary committee in charge of the celebration preferred to ignore the fact that Olav Haraldsson did not belong to the Lutheran Church, for the purposes of Catholic propaganda, on the other hand, it was a plus that he was one of the great heroes of the mother church.

Thea was undoubtedly aware of the tug-of-war taking place, and she listened to Hans' interpretations of all the stupid things the Lutherans concocted. For her own part, Thea was not very happy with her present situation, because her big dream was to learn a more refined style of cooking. But that would mean giving up her position with the Geist family, and she wouldn't be able to sup-

Hans Benedikt Hugh Pius Svarstad was sent to a boarding school before he was eight years old.

Hans writes home.

port herself with her earnings. Hoping to be accepted as an apprentice in the kitchen of the Hotel Continental, she wrote to Sigrid Undset in the summer of 1927, asking to borrow some money. Undset, who at the time had Hans home for summer vacation, immediately answered in the affirmative. "Dear Mathea, Of course I'll lend you the sum that you mention, but please write and tell me whether I should send the money to you in Oslo or whether you'll pick it up when you come north. You're most welcome to visit us when you're in Lillehammer, but come soon if you can – Hans and I are going to join the pilgrims heading for Stiklestad."

A grateful Mathea started her cooking apprenticeship at the elegant hotel, and at Christmastime she sent presents to Bjerkebæk: an embroidered cushion for the dining room and a huge lobster claw that Hans kept with his most precious treasures. Mathea had assumed that eventually she would receive wages for her apprenticeship at the Continental, but that didn't happen. So she sent another letter to Lillehammer in which she asked two important questions: Would Sigrid Undset consider being her godmother, and could she come back to Bjerkebæk as household help? "You must know that it would be a great joy for me to be your godmother," replied Undset warmly. She also gave a positive response to the second request because Mary Andersen had now married and moved to Thorstad, so Undset needed reinforcements in the house. On March 6, 1928, Mathea Mortenstuen was accepted into the St. Olav congregation of the Catholic Church, and a couple of weeks later Undset wrote:

My dear Goddaughter,

Thank you for your letter which made me very happy – happy that you are happy. So often we don't *feel* what it is we are receiving when we first begin to live in the gracious treasures of the church...

Here things are the same as always, and tomorrow Msgr. Kjelstrup will come to pray with Hans. He'll stay until Wednesday and hold mass, then travel back south with the first train. I don't know whether Mathea Bådstø will come – but I have at least told her about it, so I hope she will. I'm not supposed to send greetings from Hans because he wants to write to you himself – it may be quite an odd letter. Sometimes he gets a spasm when he writes, and then he writes the strangest letters...

I haven't seen anything of Mary since she got married, but she must have her hands full with all the new things she has to get used to out there at Torstad.

I'll be in Oslo for a quick visit on Saturday and will go to St. Dominikus Sunday morning; perhaps we'll see each other there? Many greetings, also to the Geists, from your devoted godmother,

Sigrid Undset

After the eventful winter of 1927–28 when Mathea was learning to be both a cook and a Catholic, she returned to Bjerkebæk and swiftly took over the management of the household. She shopped for groceries and ordered supplies, she cooked, found extra help for the house when needed, answered the phone, turned away unwanted guests, took care of Mosse, and kept a tight rein on the boys whenever the Mistress was not at home. It was Mathea's efforts that made it possible for Undset to travel, both in Norway and abroad, whether it was to meetings of the Authors Union or to take time to visit a health spa or enjoy a vacation. And when the Mistress was away from home, the letters flowed between them.

During and after the Second World War, Mathea's loyalty and endurance were put to new tests, and with warm praise and countless gifts, Sigrid Undset sought to express her gratitude.

Most important was that Mathea took care of Mosse, both day and night.

Anders and Hans slept on the second floor of the house with the hearth room, in their room next to their mother's big bedroom. But Mosse had always had her bed upstairs in the house with the kitchen, at first next to Mary's bed and later next to Mathea's. On the second story there was no connection between the bedrooms in the two buildings, so in many ways they were two separate worlds. Only Undset herself and whoever was acting as her maid moved between the two regions on a regular basis, and even then it was always in accordance with established routines. The housekeeper's place was primarily in the kitchen building, but there she was indispensable. Mathea, who over time began having problems with her weight and with sciatica, plodded several times a day up and down the narrow stairs between the lower floor, with the living room and kitchen, and the upper floor, with the bedrooms and bath. Mosse, who became increasingly helpless, had to be maneuvered the same way. When Mosse had to sit on "the throne," as her specially made toilet was called, it was Mathea who handled the unpleasant part of the job. The same was true when Mosse suffered an epileptic fit and when she needed to be bathed.

Through her tireless caring for the afflicted daughter, Mathea acquired an authority at Bjerkebæk that Undset respected. She presents a glimpse of the situation in the book *Lykkelige dager* (translated as *Happy Times in Norway*). Of course this is a work of fiction, and no doubt an embellished portrait as well, written as it was during Undset's exile in the United States during World War II – with homesickness clutching like a claw at her heart. But the narrative is also marked by the clarity and perspective of distance. Sigrid Undset knew quite well how much she owed to Mathea Mortenstuen. She once wrote, "A child's welfare requires that someone is willing, continuously and alertly, to turn their attention downward – towards the little child growing up." She herself lacked the patience "every day to see her work disturbed and her plans crossed." Thea never tried to shirk her responsibility for Mosse, and it was undoubtedly her indefatigable attentiveness that made it possible for Undset to keep her daughter at home all her life. With the boys Thea had much less patience. She could get sick and tired of waiting on them and being ordered around, and she tried to the best of her ability to keep them in line. For their part, the boys wanted to show that they were above her in rank, and that in spite of everything there really was a difference between the masters and the servants.

The food that was served in Bjerkebæk's heyday was a story unto itself; everyone who was familiar with life inside the gate agreed about that. Undset usually kept out of the kitchen, but she was interested in the finer points of

During the Independence Day celebration on May 17th, Fredrik Bøe and Mathea took charge and saw to it that Mosse was also allowed to take part in whatever she would find most enjoyable.

cooking and liked to discuss them with Thea. That she valued domestic expertise is apparent from countless situations portrayed in her writings.

Kristin Lavransdatter is without doubt Undset's most ambitious housewife. Even in the throes of childbirth during her first winter at Husaby, she worries over what will be served to the neighbor women who are coming to assist her with the birth. In between the terrible labor pangs, Kristin thinks desperately: "They mustn't be allowed to taste the dried fish that Erlend had brought home in the fall, spoiled and full of mites that it was." But Kristin is strong-willed and quick to learn, and she becomes a superb mistress of her estate. She wins the heart of the priest on the neighboring property with "grouse on a spit, wrapped in the best bacon" and "reindeer tongues in French wine and honey."

On the other hand, poor Ingunn of Hestviken struggles to make cheese and to brew ale that is adequate enough that Olav Audunssøn can serve it to his neighbors without shame. Ingunn is bewildered and slow, and things don't go well for her. That is what usually happens with those who are poor housewives in the works of Sigrid Undset. It's the skillful ones who have the strength to succeed, such as Kristin Lavransdatter with her spirited sons, and Beate with her marvelous modern kitchen where meals could be eaten in a cosily furnished corner – she is the one who wins the battle for the engineer's favor in the short story "Selma Brøter."

It's not surprising that Mathea Mortenstuen, with her domestic training and apprenticeship at the Hotel Continental, would have ambitions within her profession. But one might wonder how Sigrid Undset had acquired an interest in housework and cooking. The garden was supposed to be bountiful, and the house had to be orderly and beautiful. In addition all of the food, both the simple meals and the special dinners, was marked by a fastidious choice of raw materials, great skill in their preparation, an ample budget, and an openness to new trends.

Things were not always this way for Sigrid Undset. In her autobiographical sketch *Twelve Years*, she recounts how she and her sisters loved to visit the homes of their friends, where the food was plentiful and delicious. In their own home with "Anine," as the mother of the story is called, the cooking was absolutely basic.

> The key principle behind Anine's concept of frugality was that any econo-mizing should involve the food. If the children had enough to eat three times a day, then all was well – as long as the milk and food was boiled or fried so thoroughly that not a single bacterium could survive the test of fire. Milk and porridge for breakfast, bread slices in boiled milk for supper, and for the midday meal something that was cheap.

For the three Undset sisters, Denmark was the land that flowed with milk and honey; it was there that they experienced a hint of luxury. In Kalundborg they were all served their favorite dishes: coral-red shrimps and scarlet radishes for their mother, while the children ate fried eggs and dark rye bread with drip-pings, and savored their aunt's spicy meat rolls. As a child, Sigrid definitely preferred the generous Danish fare to the simple food that she was served at the home of her father's pietistic family in Trondhjem.

Given the amount of porridge and bread eaten in Undset's childhood home, Sigrid developed a great craving for fresh vegetables and essential vitamins, especially in the spring. As a girl she learned from a friend how to dig up cara-way sprouts with a knife so the roots stayed with the plant. In May when the weather was good, they would set off with baskets and an old table knife to gather greens to make soup. Forty years later the young maid at Bjerkebæk,

Sigrid Bøe, was taught the same art by the Mistress herself, because caraway sprouts were plentiful on the grassy slopes around Lillehammer. Using a curved knife with a handle on each end, the herbs were finely diced before being tossed into Thea's soup pot. The nettles that grew in the thickets at Bjerkebæk could also be used, as long as they were new and light green. If they were going to prepare an especially fine meal, for example for Independence Day on May 17th, or for Undset's birthday on May 20th, they always picked fresh herbs, which had much more flavor than plants grown in greenhouses.

During World War II, when Sigrid Undset lived in New York, she discovered to her joy that caraway sprouts grew out in the country not far away, and when she vacationed in the Berkshires in Massachusetts and in Oneida County, she found great quantities of the herb everywhere. Perhaps it was the familiar and beloved taste of caraway soup, cooked in a tiny kitchen in Brooklyn, that helped her recall those long-gone days when she had to describe the month of May back home in Lillehammer for her memoir *Happy Times in Norway*.

The cooking at Bjerkebæk was marked not only by traditions from Sigrid Undset's childhood but also by her travels abroad. Her first lengthy trip had taken her to Italy in 1909, and there all her senses came to life. She was intoxicated by experiences and impressions, by the floral splendor and exotic smells – and by the wine. She went to trattorias and cafés, to tavernas and markets; she trudged along the banks of the Tiber River and out into the country, either alone or with some of her new artist friends. With delight she wrote home about "the ungodly marvelous wine here," describing nighttime carousing that ended with "fried eggs at the local café frequented by street workers at 4 a.m." For Undset, who was used to plain Norwegian food with little access to fresh ingredients in the winter, Italian cuisine came as a joyous shock. Olives and salads, artichokes and calamari, risotto and saltimbocca, stuffed cabbage (or *cavoli ripieni*, as it's called in Italian), and leg of mutton laced with garlic – all of these became Undset's favorites for the rest of her life. And they left their mark on the Bjerkebæk kitchen.

It was not just the food, wine, and floral splendor of Italy that stirred Undset's senses, it was also the fact that it was there she met Anders Castus Svarstad and fell passionately in love. Right after their first meeting, she wrote to her sister Signe that the painter was living in a pension on Piazza Colonna. There he sits, "frozen and starving, wrapped in a blanket in the middle of the room with a stone floor and no stove. He's remarkably impractical, even for a man." From the very beginning Svarstad aroused a maternal and nest-building instinct in Undset, and she immediately began putting away a trousseau in her chest of drawers. For her, as for all women at the time, marriage meant not only an obligation to love and honor but also to wash and cook.

When the newlyweds went to London and rented rooms from Mrs. Tanner in Hammersmith, Undset began teaching herself to cook in earnest. She collected English recipes, which she clipped out of newspapers, and she made her first tentative attempts at the culinary arts, because Svarstad couldn't abide English food. Undset had to agree that Mrs. Tanner's menu was not very adventurous, even though she was otherwise so enamored of everything English. "I *am* starting to grow tired of roast mutton – warm for dinner and cold for supper four times a week," she wrote to her sister Ragnhild. To break the monotony she bought *Mrs. Beeton's Cookery Book*, and on the title page she inscribed her new name: "Sigrid Undset Svarstad – London 1912."

So the meal preparation at Bjerkebæk was not based solely on the traditional foods of eastern Norway that Undset and Mathea were accustomed to from Kristiania and Tretten. It also drew inspiration from trends in Denmark, Italy, and England, as well as from continental cuisine, thanks to Mathea's apprenticeship at the Hotel Continental. The author Regine Normann was one of the people who witnessed at close hand her friend's development as the mistress of Bjerkebæk. In 1915 she visited Undset shortly after Mosse's birth, and in honor of Regine Normann, who was the child's godmother, grouse was on the menu. But the household help was inexperienced and the new mother was worn out, so the meal did not turn out to be the culinary delight that Undset had planned. In contrast, Regine writes of her visit to Lillehammer several years later. She had spent the morning paying calls on mutual friends in town, and when she returned to Bjerkebæk for the noon meal, she witnessed Undset's glowing joy at serving Italian food that she had cooked herself. This meal made such a strong impression on Regine that she wrote about it in the magazine *Urd* in November 1928, as a tribute to the newly celebrated Nobel Prize winner:

When I came back from my visits, a wonderful aroma met me and awakened every olfactory and sensory cell in my body. The entryway was filled with it, the rooms were filled with it, and the table was set with flowers and beautiful glasses on a snow-white cloth.

Then the mistress of the house appeared, hot and flushed after two long hours spent in the heat, and with a smile she invited me to the table. Standing there, she and her children said grace, while I too stood with my hands clasped.

FISH.

MRS. BEETON'S
COOKERY BOOK

ALL ABOUT
COOKERY, HOUSEHOLD WORK,
MARKETING, TRUSSING,
CARVING, Etc

*FULLY ILLUSTRATED WITH COLOURED
AND PHOTOGRAPHIC PLATES*

NEW EDITION

SIGRID UNDSETS BOKSAMLING
BJERKEBÆK

WARD, LOCK & CO., LIMITED
LONDON AND MELBOURNE
1912

1—Scallops. 2—Red Mullet. 3—Turbot. 4—Cod Steak. 5—Fried Sole.
6—Mayonnaise of Salmon. 7—Salmon, boiled. 8—Brown Trout. 9—Smelts.

Mrs. Beeton's Cookery Book – fully illustrated.

Then we sat down, and the older son filled the appropriate glass with red wine, and icy clear water in another. The bread basket was passed around, and the maid set warm plates in front of us. And then came the bowl of risotto! It was piping hot, steaming and lovely to look at, even lovelier to taste.

There was no hint of embarrassment in the mistress's eye when she invited me to help myself from the dish. She knew that this time the dream and the hand had worked together to create perfection.

For Regine's part, it may not have been something she consciously emphasized, but it's easy to see the similarity between Kristin Lavransdatter and Sigrid Undset as mistress of the home. Pleasure and ambition, piety and familial concord – they both loved to preside over a well-set table, surrounded by their sons.

Hundreds of household receipts have survived, showing what goods were delivered to Bjerkebæk's kitchen over the years. They reveal a great deal about how Sigrid Undset managed the household. Since most of them date from after

1926, we have to assume that Mathea Mortenstuen was the person responsible for putting them in files. In that way she was able to document what the ample outpouring of funds was used to purchase, because it was Mathea who placed the orders with the shops in town. She was a customer at the Fagstad, Avlangrud, and Bergseng grocery stores, the Ottesen butcher shop, the Myhre bakery, the Raabe greengrocer, Erik Skerven's dairy store, and the state-owned Lillehammer Wine Co-Op.

The receipts display many odd details. For instance, they seem to verify the anecdote that the Nobel Prize was celebrated with a glass of sherry on November 13, 1928, when the telegram from the Swedish Academy arrived. We can even confirm that it was Sherry Bonita that Undset and Svarstad were drinking when they toasted her prize, because the bottle had been bought a few days earlier at the wine co-op. In general the household archives contain a great deal of information that make daily life at Bjerkebæk seem much closer – so close, in fact, that we can practically smell what's cooking on the stove. We see that caraway sprouts were delivered from Ottesen's butcher shop in May 1924, so we can assume that Sigrid Undset once again had caraway soup on her birthday. But why hadn't they picked the sprouts themselves? Didn't Undset or her maids have time to dig up the herbs that spring when the work on the Dalseg house was at its height? Or was it the big royalties from *Kristin Lavransdatter* that had prompted new and more luxurious habits? Another small detail: we see that "Ova Maltine" recurs on countless receipts, year after year. When we read in *A Woman's Point of View* how warmly Sigrid Undset recommends malted milk for insomnia, we have some idea what sort of maladies the women at Bjerkebæk must have struggled with.

We also know a good deal about the physical appearance of the kitchen and where all the raw materials were prepared, even though there isn't a single photo from that part of the house. Naturally only the rooms meant for entertaining were photographed – never the private rooms, and certainly not the work areas used by the domestic help. During the first years, the kitchen was slightly smaller than it is today. It was remodeled in 1925 when Undset was on her pilgrimage in Rome and again in 1930 when the property was connected to the public water and sewer network. A counter was set up with space underneath so that a high chair could be pushed in, a detail that was considered very modern. Another modern addition was the dishwashing counter in stainless steel with two sinks, one for washing and one for rinsing. The cupboards and walls were painted the traditional blue-green, so the kitchen was a nice blend of old style and the latest of practical innovations.

One tradition that both Sigrid Undset and Mathea Mortenstuen stubbornly clung to was the use of wood fires for cooking. A big electric stove did make an appearance, but it was advertised for sale again in 1930. Instead a small electrical roasting oven was purchased and placed on the counter, to be used for small baked goods. A fine, old-fashioned wood stove with a steam hood dominated the kitchen, because a roast needed a wood fire if it was to be succulent; both Undset and Mathea agreed on that. After the war it turned out to be a plus to have a wood stove, since electricity was rationed, and for long periods of time there was no power at all. For many years the old way of cooking proved the most reliable.

As far as church-going was concerned, Mathea was not nearly as zealous as she was in the kitchen. Only during her first years as a new convert to Catholicism did she attend the masses that were held in the hearth room. Later she made do with ensuring that a hearty breakfast table stood ready when the service was finished. It was the custom to attend mass in the morning on an empty stomach, so everyone was hungry when it was over. At times Mathea grumbled a bit over these "breakfast Catholics," as she called them, muttering something about them attending more for the sake of the food than for the mass.

Sigrid Undset knew full well that she had Thea to thank for the daily pleasures of the table and for providing her with peace and quiet to work, so she paid her accordingly. For her part, Thea took pride in being able to put some savings aside, and eventually she became a relatively well-to-do woman. No doubt she also thrived as the boss of her own department and enjoyed being able to play an independent role. But as temperamental as she and Undset were, both of them occasionally resorted to slamming doors. Thea had her little tricks to maintain a sense of balance between them. "Didn't the Mistress say that she'd like to have trout for dinner today?" she might ask at breakfast, and then Undset wouldn't object. Or she might point sternly at Undset's dirty shoes when she came in from the garden, and say that there was a broom right next to the door, and she should see about using it. Mathea was even known to joke with the others in the house about how the Mistress had fallen for the new, spirited head doctor at the hospital, or how she was infatuated with the adroit skier who had won the Birkebeiner race. She might even start to lose patience if Undset let ten or twenty minutes go by before she came up from her study and took pity on whoever the poor soul was on the telephone. But no one else was permitted to say anything derogatory about the Mistress, and the young maids were firmly informed that they were to stand up whenever Undset came into the room. If they weren't aware of it before, Mathea would inform them that their employer was a world-class artist and a splendid person, and they should show her the proper respect!

The letters from Sigrid Undset that Mathea kept until she died show that the two women shared many interests besides cooking and caring for children. Or perhaps Thea, who was Undset's daily co-worker for a total of eighteen years, was influenced by her employer and adopted some of her eccentricities. She too took a passionate interest in newspapers and plants, photography and dogs, and in some areas it seems as if Thea even became "more Catholic than the Pope." For instance, Sigrid Undset writes bluntly in a letter to Mathea that it was "too bad about the camellia – but it's no good grieving over it – and truth be told, we have so many flowers at home that there's hardly any space anyway."

It couldn't have been easy for Mathea to have any sort of personal life, given the situation with Mosse, but around 1930 she acquired a sweetheart. His name was Fredrik Bøe, and he was one of the drivers who was summoned whenever Undset needed a car. He was a dapper fellow, employed by Iversen's Taxi Central in Lillehammer and known for his shrewd methods of handling money. When a call came in from Bjerkebæk, Bøe was quick to report for duty, and Mathea liked to invite him in for a cup of coffee in the kitchen if the opportunity presented itself. After the driver and the housekeeper had known each other for a few years, Mathea was invited to Løten to meet Fredrik Bøe's family, and there she met his sister Sigrid. She was the same age as Mosse, and at Mathea's request, Sigrid Bøe was hired at Bjerkebæk to take care of the disabled girl. She held the job for two and a half years.

With her acute memory and lively narrative talent, Sigrid Bøe (later Sigrid Nordby, after her marriage) has been an important source for describing what daily life was like inside the gate at Bjerkebæk. She remembers down to the smallest detail the day she arrived, on February 13, 1934:

> Thea met me at the station wearing a lambskin coat and with Njård on the leash, and my brother drove us up to Bjerkebæk. The coffee table in the dining room was set for three, with tea and rolls and pastries, and I thought with dread: Who is the third person? Soon we heard footsteps come tapping down the corridor. The Mistress always wore shoes with a low heel that clacked a bit when she walked, and she had a very recognizable gait because it was light and brisk even though she actually had a stout body. "The Mistress is coming," said Thea. And then the Mistress appeared, smiling, and

Fredrik Bøe in 1929 with his Essex Super Six.

said in the doorway, "I could tell from the dogs that you had arrived." Then she held out both hands and said, "You are most cordially welcome to Bjerkebæk! Now there will be two Sigrids camping out here, and when my niece comes from Oslo, there will be three. I wonder how that will go." "Oh, I think we'll have an easy time telling the two of you apart," I replied. Afterwards I asked my mother whether that was a stupid thing to say, but she said it was an excellent reply because it showed at once that I was aware of the great distance between us, and that was good.

Sigrid Bøe was very pleased with the conditions at her new workplace. She had her own cozy room above the kitchen, and the wages were good: 60 kroner a month was almost double the usual rate. In addition, the food was marvelous, and she thought the kitchen was very modern. She was a bit surprised that they used a wood stove but soon discovered that this was not due to a concern for the budget. Thea proclaimed that an electric stove was worthless if the food was to be any good. The work itself was all right, but Miss Bøe found the house terribly quiet, with little outside contact, so she was glad to do the errands in town. Almost on a daily basis she would be sent to the post office, because there was always a steady stream of letters and packages, both to and from Bjerkebæk. Her other duties included making the beds, lighting the stoves, setting the table, washing the dishes, and lending Thea a hand. Every day she took a walk with Mosse – out in the garden if the weather permitted, or otherwise on a set route through the living room, pantry, kitchen, and hallway, around and around. Sigrid would walk backwards as she sang to Mosse, holding both of the girl's hands in her own. In that way the ailing Mosse got a little exercise and had some variety in her monotonous and sedentary existence. Usually she stayed in the pantry, patient and remote, sitting in an armchair with a scarf tied from one armrest to the other so that she wouldn't fall out. Sometimes the children in the house would come in to see Mosse, cranking up the gramophone to play "Homecoming of the America Ship," or one of the other marches that she loved. But otherwise they kept away from that part of the house.

Sigrid Bøe did not have to do the heavy work, such as carrying wood or doing the laundry; Oscar Mikkelsen and Mari Moen took care of those chores. So all in all the girl felt that she had an easy job. The only tasks that she disliked were certain indelicate duties regarding Mosse, but here Thea would step in and Sigrid merely had to assist. After they had cleaned Mosse up, Sigrid was sternly reminded to wash her hands extra thoroughly, especially if the patient had one of her epileptic attacks. They probably thought this was necessary to avoid infection.

Sigrid received her instructions from Thea, not just in terms of hygiene but also regarding etiquette. She learned to set the table with the cutlery used for fish on the outside, and the knives and forks used for meat closest to the plate. She learned to position four glasses at each place-setting for special occasions, and if they were going to have a big party, which happened once in a while, Thea would go over the menu and explain what dishes were to be served and which wine was to be poured when – and from which side.

Miss Bøe quickly became familiar with Bjerkebæk's exotic specialties. One of the boys' favorites was spaghetti with tomato sauce, which was something she'd hardly even heard of, much less tasted. She learned to make French fries in the big frying pan and looked forward to Thea's homemade ice cream. But Mosse was the person who cheered the loudest when the lights in the dining room were turned off and Mathea struck a match to serve the crêpes flambées.

Although things could be quite fancy for parties, the daily routines were very simple. The boys were the first ones up in the morning, and they would find their breakfast under a domed plate on the kitchen counter. After four years at the Catholic boarding school in Oslo, Hans came home to Lillehammer. But as a student at the secondary school and then the Gymnasium, he was always out late, and he never managed to remember his books or mittens or lunch packet or anything else he was supposed to take care of himself. Especially after Anders had left home, there were many rushed mornings and numerous demerits in the school records for forgetting things, as well as complaints that showed up on Hans' report card.

Thea, the maid, and Mosse usually started their day around nine o'clock, while the Mistress often stayed in her own room until lunchtime. When Undset finally came downstairs, she would sit at the dining table with a pot of strong coffee and a couple of slices of bread while the maid went up to clean her bedroom. One important detail that they had to remember for the Mistress's first meal of the day was to set out clean ashtrays, both on the dining table and on the coffee table in the corner near the stove where the daily mail and newspapers were placed. And it never took long for both ashtrays to be filled.

Undset might spend about an hour in the dining room in the morning while she drank coffee, read the papers, and discussed with Thea the day's main meal, the grocery shopping, and other tasks. Mosse also had her regular time with her mother, who took the girl on her lap, caressing her and chatting with her. Then Undset would go to her study and did not want to be disturbed by phone calls or visitors for the next couple of hours. The only person who had free access, even if he arrived without an appointment, was the attorney Eilif Moe, who was Undset's business manager and good friend. If other guests arrived or if there was an important phone call, the maid had to go over to the alcove and knock, but it might take five or ten minutes before Undset appeared to pick up the phone. Sometimes the maid would have to remind Undset two or three times before she would get up and go to the pantry to answer the "telephone beast." The maids were horrified and thought she was certainly pushing the limits of polite behavior, because the phone was used only for important messages, after all, and it wasn't every day that someone called.

Dinner was served at three o'clock, and everyone, even guests of the house, were sternly advised to be prompt. Occasionally Undset would be the last to arrive. One day when she came in late and everyone else were already seated at the table, she said, "You all look like you're waiting for the king!" "That's exactly what we're doing. Even though you're not wearing a crown," replied Hans with a grin. His mother took her usual place, sitting in the armchair at the head of the table and said with a smile, "No, I won't get that until I'm in heaven."

The three "Thomas girls": Charlotte, Signe, and Sigrid.

Mosse always sat on the bench across from Undset, with the maids on either side of her. She had to be fed with a spoon, and when she was full, she'd announce it by biting on the spoon and clamping her mouth shut. If there were strangers visiting, Mosse and the maids would eat in the pantry or the kitchen. Some guests at Bjerkebæk said that they actually never saw Mosse, even though they made several visits. After dinner Sigrid Undset would go back to her study to work.

Supper was for the most part a simple repast, with a pot of tea for the Mistress and a plate of sandwiches. On some evenings Undset would sit for a while in the dining room with the others. Then they played cards – usually whist or Old Maid or Solitaire, or they would read or do needlework. But usually Undset retreated to her workroom. For the longest time she refused to get a radio because she didn't want to be disturbed by the noise.

Around midnight, after Thea and the household help had gone to bed, they might hear the clacking of footsteps as the Mistress walked across from her alcove to the pantry. Then they knew that it was time for her regular nightcap.

While Sigrid Bøe worked at Bjerkebæk, it was a glass of Italian fortified wine. The Marsala bottle fit perfectly on the bottom shelf to the right inside the big cupboard in the pantry, and next to it stood the Mistress's wine glass, which was washed only occasionally. After a few days when the bottle was empty, it was replaced by another from the wine stocked in the cellar. Now and then Undset also liked a glass of whisky, but that was something she kept to herself.

During fasting periods at Bjerkebæk the food was almost spartan, because meat and wine and desserts were not to be consumed. The days leading up to Easter marked a quiet time with a minimum of socializing or luxury. Thea compensated for this by serving delicious homemade fish courses and wonderful vegetable dishes with parsley butter, and on Sundays she might surprise the household by getting up early so she could serve fresh-baked rolls for breakfast. On the other hand, they feasted on Easter day. For breakfast Undset herself would decorate the Easter eggs and put them in a porcelain chicken that was placed on the table. For dinner the table was set with a white cloth and candles in tall candelabra. The good china, a set of hand-painted dishes from France, was brought out, along with crystal glasses and newly polished silver. Before the Mistress sat down at the table, she would always cross herself.

There weren't many parties over the course of a year because Undset was much too involved with her work to spend time on planning and socializing. But once she did tear herself away from her desk, she wanted everything to be superbly prepared, plentiful, and served with finesse. She would show up for memorable dinners that were given for both children and grownups, but she undoubtedly breathed a sigh of relief once the guests had finally left the house.

During the 1930s Undset began having trouble with her health. She was often worn out and complained that she felt "tired to death." Of course this put a damper on any social life. Mathea tried to help by serving a healthier and less fattening diet, which was something that she could also benefit from herself, because she had grown quite stout over the years. A new type of cookbook now appeared at Bjerkebæk: health-conscious cookbooks and recipes for specific diets. A reliable scale was put in Undset's bathroom, but she never did win the battle with her weight; it continued to fluctuate with temporary victories and regular defeats. She had a hard time resisting the temptations of the table, and at times she drank more than was good for her.

In spite of the difference in their position and social class, in temperament and matters of faith, in intellect and experience, the relationship between

Mathea and her employer was marked by a mutual respect and devotion. During the years before World War II, all the letters from Undset are addressed: "Dear Mathea." But after the war, she uses the slightly more familiar: "Dear Thea." Yet she always signs the letters with the formal phrase: "Your devoted Sigrid Undset." For her part, Thea begins the only known letter to her employer with "Honorable Mrs. Undset." She always spoke of the Mistress with pride, and all her life she took the greatest care of the books, photographs, and every other memento that she had from Bjerkebæk.

When Sigrid Bøe was at Bjerkebæk, she tried to give Thea some time to herself so that she could go out and meet her sweetheart. Even so, Fredrik Bøe must have been an incredibly patient suitor. The couple didn't marry until Undset left Norway when war broke out in 1940, and they stayed at Bjerkebæk for as long as the Gestapo allowed. In July 1949, shortly after Sigrid Undset's death, Hans wrote to Thea, thanking her warmly for everything she had done for his mother:

> You meant so much to my mother during all those years you spent together at Bjerkebæk. She had good reason to be extremely grateful for your caring and self-sacrificing spirit with regard to everything concerning Mosse's welfare... She thought of Mosse as her guardian angel from God; and you were certainly her guardian angel with regards to people. During the years that she was away, you looked after and brought to safety the things that she held most dear in her home, and you helped and supported all of her family members... Thank you for everything, dear Thea, for your generous spirit and your enormous heart – in many ways so amazingly similar to her own. During all those years you were her best and closest friend; and as far as character and emotional disposition, you were the closest relative she ever had.

After gaining some distance from his mother's death, Hans probably viewed the matter of kinship a bit differently, because at Bjerkebæk a clear distinction was made between social classes. He himself was highly conscious of this. Bjerkebæk had gradually changed from a place where everyone lived in close quarters and shared the work as need and occasion dictated, to a household with specialized functions and a clear hierarchy – with a housekeeper, nursemaid, laundress, gardener, and chauffeur, as well as other hired help ranging from various craftsmen to young maids from the neighborhood. In its heyday, Bjerkebæk was run more like a patrician household from earlier days than an ordinary home in a small town, and Sigrid Undset took her role as Mistress very seriously and made a point of maintaining her dignity. She allowed herself to smile a bit at Mathea's attempts to raise her own social status, such as when she celebrated her sons' birthday "in the grand style." After Undset's death, Mathea and Fredrik Bøe wanted to buy Bjerkebæk, but the heirs were offended by such an idea. Certain boundaries could not be crossed.

Miniature theaters and other sorts of drama

It's well known that problems can crop up in the best of families, even royal ones. When the wedding of the polar bear King Valemon and the troll's daughter was to be held in the castle "east of the sun and west of the moon," the bride's mother was unfortunate in her choice of hired help for the kitchen:

THE TROLL QUEEN
(Enters from outside, to the right)

You must forgive me, my dear Sigaros, but I had to see to the food. Just imagine, the new cook had put viper fat in the wedding cake, and she used the toad spit that I told her to whisk and put on top of the cake for frying the badger instead – she boiled the cowbane in the worm soup, and she's supposed to be a trained cook. She served for two hundred years with Old Man Hedal in Hedalsmuen, and yet that's the best she can do!

FIRST TROLL WOMAN

Maids these days... But you know, it's almost impossible to find any help other than wood nymphs, and they're half-human at that and no good as servants. They have to have every Thursday evening free, along with two or three other times during the week to fly off and gad about with the sons of Christians from the parish. And they sleep late and dawdle around at home in the mountain.

The Moe family's miniature theater.

Attorney Eilif Moe, sketched by Hans.

THE TROLL QUEEN

Yes, you can say that again. It's been impossible to find a decent cook for troll banquets ever since Old Granny from Witch Mountain stopped going out.

The trolls' wedding feast didn't turn out very well, in fact, the entire celebration was canceled, because as everyone knows, there is always a happy ending for good people in Norwegian fairy tales, while the troll rabble get such a thrashing that their long noses quiver. And it was just on Norwegian folk tales Sigrid Undset based her two comedies. In the autumn of 1926 she wrote the first one, *East of the Sun and West of the Moon*, for a homemade stage: "Moe's Miniature Theater," as it was called. At the time she was in the middle of writing her four-part epic *The Master of Hestviken*. Perhaps she had a need for some "comic relief," as it's called in English tragedies, or perhaps the Moe family's enthusiasm for the theater was contagious and prompted an acute case of playfulness – although it actually marked a return to one of her former interests. In her childhood, Sigrid had staged countless plays of her own devising for her sisters and friends – in the nursery and on several tiny, hand-painted stage sets that she made from matchboxes. Now she suddenly had a desire to try her hand at writing a play again.

Attorney Eilif Moe, who was Undset's business manager, lived on Einar Bues Vei just below Bjerkebæk with his wife Louise and their three children. One day he came home with a miniature theater cut out of paper, with ready-made stage sets, cardboard figures, and accompanying scripts. The slogan "Not Merely for Amusement" was written in elegant letters above the stage, just as it was over the proscenium of the Royal Theater in Copenhagen. Many of the town's citizens who were theater-lovers found it diverting to perform plays such as *Around the World in 80 Days*, *Aladdin and the Magic Lamp*, and *The Tinderbox* on similar miniature stages for their children. Undset watched a couple of these shows at the Moes' house and then eagerly suggested that they ought to try to put on a play of their own production.

Sigrid Undset and Hans were both at Maihaugen for the Håballsvaka festival in 1927.

Several weeks later she slapped a script down on the attorney's desk. After he had read it, he decided that the present stage needed improving – the store-bought miniature theater wasn't good enough.

Artist friends were summoned to lend a hand, and they set to work hammering and painting and sewing. Einar Fagstad and Alf Lundeby cut out the stage sets and figures from cardboard. Then they unrolled a piece of canvas 14 meters long on the floor of the Moe family's dining room and painted a backdrop showing one hazy blue ridge behind another. When the canvas was set up at the back of the stage and rolled across from one spool to the other, it looked as if the figures in the foreground were moving, as if they really were wandering through the mountains. The effect was amazing! Another neighbor, Lars Jorde, came over to help with the painting, summoning forth pillars and balustrades with a few brisk strokes of the brush. A blacksmith was asked to make runners so that the cardboard figures could be moved in and out of the wings. The attorney himself hammered together the theater, while his wife sewed curtains out of velvet with tassels and pull-cords. To top it all off, the town composer, Reidar Brøgger, got out some piano music that he had lying around and began reworking these fragments. This was how Sigrid Undset's script ended up having an accompanying musical score, with a number of short pieces intended for each scene. It was a well-composed and charming fairy-tale suite.

The premier of *East of the Sun and West of the Moon* took place on Ole Henrik Moe's seventh birthday in January 1927. Everyone who had helped make the theater was assigned a role, while Reidar Brøgger himself played the piano. There was great rejoicing, both in front of the stage and behind it, because the participants enjoyed themselves at least as much as the audience did. For Undset's part, she may have thought of the project as a theatrical amusement linked to the celebration of Epiphany, when the Christmas season was ushered out with fun and games. At any rate, the play was performed again the following year on January 6th. Later it was staged in the big hearth room at Bjerkebæk, with the main room serving as the audience area and Undset's workroom as the backdrop for the stage, which was placed in the doorway. All of her papers and writing materials had to be moved aside, and afterwards Undset complained that it took her several months to find *The Master of Hestviken* again.

The sanatoriums in the area were visited a couple of times by the celebrated troupe, and even Sigrid Undset participated in a few of the performances, usually playing the part of the troll woman. But theater director Moe claimed that she tended to say her lines when she inhaled rather than when she exhaled and preferred to limit her contribution to making pounding and stomping sounds.

Undset thoroughly enjoyed being part of the Moe theater project and allowed herself to be persuaded to join another of his pet enterprises: Maihaugen's procession during Håballsvaka, the summer festival celebrated in Lillehammer between the spring farm work and autumn harvest. In order to bring in extra income for the museum, a procession through the town was organized, with short performances at the museum itself. Merry citizens would don costumes and take part with great spirit, and Sigrid Undset dressed up as the wife of

Gudbrand i Lia, while Hans walked barefoot in the procession in spite of his grandmother's horrified objections.

Rumors of the festive theater performances soon spread, and the newspapers printed rather pompous remarks. "It's only natural that a work such as *East of the Sun and West of the Moon*, which has sprouted from Lillehammer soil, so to speak, and which has emerged entirely from conditions here, within the artist colony and its closest circles, would be welcomed with lively interest by Lillehammer residents," wrote the local paper. Before long Eilif Moe had to put a damper on expectations for larger productions of the play:

> Public performances are difficult due to the intimate nature of the theater. However, we do have plans to perform the piece this winter, when the right occasion presents itself. For that reason I have rebuilt the theater, expanding its size a bit, and Mrs. Sigrid Undset has now written another new fairy-tale comedy: *The King's Three Daughters in the Mountain Blue*. Brøgger has composed music for this play too, and Alf Lundeby has made all the scenery.

Two months after this notice appeared, the telegram arrived from the Swedish Academy, notifying Undset that she had been awarded the Nobel Prize in Literature, and after that she had neither time or opportunity for more theater performances for quite a while.

Reidar Brøgger was not as busy, so he continued to work on his fairy-tale suite, arranging the music for piano, violin, and cello. The concert version was well received, and the composer's ambitions grew. But Undset started getting uneasy when she heard that he wanted the play to be performed for children at the National Theater in Oslo. She had never imagined that her frivolous little play would be performed on a full-scale stage. The composer was in need of money, so he became more insistent, and in the end she gave her consent.

After a good deal of discussion it was decided that the New Theater and not the National Theater would stage the play. This was probably more to Undset's liking, since the head of the New Theater was Ingolf Schancke, whom she had admired in her youth. In addition, she had once long ago submitted a one-act play to the National Theater, and she'd barely even received a reply, much less ever seen the work performed. A slight like that was not something Undset would easily forget.

The fairy-tale comedy at the New Theater was planned as a Christmas performance with ballet dancers and a thirteen-piece orchestra, and the music was adapted by the renowned composer, Bjarne Brustad. In the meantime, Sigrid

Undset had been to Stockholm and received the Nobel Prize, so expectations had soared sky-high. There were predictions of a literary sensation: "Soon – hopefully very soon – *East of the Sun and West of the Moon* will appear on a number of foreign stages and testify to what can be created up here in the peaceful little town of Lillehammer," wrote the local paper, bursting with pride.

The première took place on December 20, 1929. It did not go well. The critic for *Tidens Tegn* wrote that the play "was performed for an overwhelmingly adult and quite disoriented audience. The best part of the performance was definitely the music by Reidar Brøgger and Bjarne Brustad. Second was Zaitzow's fairy-tale sets as well as Sonja Mjøen's lovely and natural performance as Cinderella. Last was the comedy itself." A few other reviews were less critical, and Kristian Elster, who was Undset's old friend and colleague, wrote with sympathy in *Nationen*:

> It's not meant to be a dramatic play, not even a children's comedy; it's exactly what it was originally intended to be: a subtext, as simple as possible, that follows the fairy tale's epic course and presents the events of the plot in bits of dialogue. The strength of the script is that in all its terseness, it conveys the tone of a genuine Norwegian fairy tale. But the character of the Norwegian fairy tale was something that the New Theater managed with great success to obliterate. The whole thing was given a pretentious air – a children's play in the guise of a full evening performance. Sigrid Undset's first dramatic work – who would have thought that this puppet-theater drama would end up sailing such a sea!

The reviewer for *Aftenposten* didn't mince words. "We see here to a persistent degree mere gestures instead of a bewitching mood. It borders on parody," he writes, adding however that the applause was both hearty and long. Sigrid Undset never heard the applause, because during the dress rehearsal she got up and left, snorting with indignation: "They never let me keep anything for myself!"

In spite of the harsh critique that the play garnered in the Oslo papers, the friends continued their theater performances in Lillehammer. Eventually the young people in the circle took over the work, as more of the adults, including Undset, withdrew to take their places in the audience. Anders always preferred to handle practical tasks. Once when he had to carry in an extra chair for a late-arriving guest, he was unlucky enough to step on his mother's foot in the dark. "Damn it!" slipped out of Undset's lips, to the horror of the audience, which that evening happened to consist of teachers and students from Gudrun Ørn's school.

In 1939 Ole Henrik Moe, only ten years old, took over Brøgger's place at the piano, and that contributed to his reputation as "the town's musical prodigy." Hans was one of the most eager actors whenever he had occasion to participate, and he always looked forward to "studying" for the theater performances. He loved visiting his friends on Erik Bues Vei and was especially fond of Louise Moe. More than once he suggested to Ole Henrik that they ought to switch mothers.

Hans must have viewed Ole Henrik's birthday celebration with mixed feelings, because as soon as it was over, his Christmas vacation inevitably came to an end and he had to go back to St. Joseph's Institute in Oslo. Even before he left he would start looking forward to the next holiday. But when Easter eventually arrived and the boys in Lillehammer all swarmed up Nordseterveien to the cabin of the Skiing Association, Hans had to be "at work" in St. Olav's Church, because Easter was of course the busy season for an acolyte. "It's sad not to have Hans here," his mother wrote to Gösta:

> He's probably longing for home again, the poor dear, but he's also enjoying himself immensely. I was with him all Easter. I have to tell you he is so sweet. I always arrive by a late train and then go to matins the next morning. Little Hans smiles like a sun as he walks up the church aisle, but he never casts even a glance at me. When I go up to the altar, he comes over and without a word kneels down at my side, and then I know that my little boy is praying only for *me* – when he leaves, he looks neither to the right or the left, but he waits outside the church door and flies into my arms as I come out. Then we go over to the institute and eat breakfast together in the parlatorium, and I hear about all the remarkable things that have happened to him since we last saw each other. For Easter he was an acolyte, and quite delighted with the role; children take a more active part in the service there, instead of just sitting still and listening. He admits quite honestly that sermons bore him, because he doesn't understand them, but there's no end to all the strange things he has thought about and prayed for when he kneels on the altar step behind the priest. But both of us are still looking forward to having him come home for summer vacation.

The element of theater inherent in the role of acolyte appealed to Hans, but completing his tasks in the church was often difficult for a boy who was clumsy

Sketches drawn by Hans.

and easily distracted. One Whitsunday, when full splendor was on display during the high mass in St. Olav Church, ten-year-old Hans was honored with the task of carrying Bishop Smit's long train during the procession. When the procession was supposed to start, the bishop couldn't budge because Hans had planted both feet on his Cappa Magna. When the other acolytes tried to pull him off, the boy vigorously objected, so the procession couldn't get started until one of the sisters came over to take Hans in hand.

Undset must have realized how hard it was for her son to be away from home, and she tried to prolong his vacations by occasionally sending him to Gudrun Ørn's school. But this compromise solution didn't work very well, because then he ended up being a stranger in two different school settings. The more recalcitrant the boy became, the more convinced his mother was that he needed discipline. And she had decided that both she and Hans would benefit from doing penance through self-denial. As she confided to Gösta:

> So I'm trying to make it a penance of my own free will, but I'm rather clumsy with that sort of act of faith – lack of practice, you know. Hans did his penance as sweetly as an angel – we said goodbye to each other in the chapel when I took him back to Oslo. He gave up all his amusements here at home, and all his good-night kisses, and everything else, though with two big tears in his eyes, which he did *not* let fall. But he undeniably needed to go back

there – partly because the school up here is so terrible, and for once Anders did his best to encourage his brother to protest – it's such an old-lady school, and both of the boys loathe the teacher.

It got increasingly difficult for Hans to return home after such long absences and resume his place among his friends. "He has a hard time getting along with others – here at home he doesn't get along with anyone, and no one gets along with him," wrote Sigrid Undset when the boy was home for Christmas. "He was invited to the Moes' house for Ole Henrik's birthday last week – was rather taken aback by the invitation and smiled in his mocking way. He and Ole Henrik haven't been on friendly terms for over a month because of some nonsense about a cap that Ole supposedly pulled off his head and tossed away."

Two years after Hans had started at Sta. Sunniva School, it was still no easier for him to commute between Lillehammer and Oslo, and Undset complained to Astri:

> I think it actually gets worse each time to take the boy back – the worst is seeing what a brave little boy he is, because he thinks it's awful but he's very aware that this is a sacrifice that we both have to make, and so he says good-bye like a brave fellow. Oh, Astri, be glad that your children are still so young – it won't be many years before I'll have to send Anders away, he wants to go to the college in Trondhjem, and little Hans is already out in the world.

The one person who was always home at Bjerkebæk was Mosse, but even she was growing and changing. When her lovely "bunad" dress got too small, Undset sent it to a girl at Sta. Sunniva, but Hans was so furious at seeing this stranger wearing his sister's clothes that he leaped at her and tore the blouse. The boy's violent outbursts were sometimes directed at his mother. Rolf Sand, who was in the same class as Hans, once said that Hans got so mad when his mother sent him a typed letter instead of one written by hand that he ripped it up without even reading it. Rolf and the other boys regarded Hans with a mixture of admiration and fear. Hans, in turn, kept his distance from most of his peers, both in Oslo and in Lillehammer. In general he became more and more of an outsider, and his mother was naturally worried.

Sigrid Undset was experiencing storm clouds in several areas during these years, both inside her own gate as well as outside. After visiting the cloister ruins on the island of Selja in Nordfjord with Gösta af Geijerstam in the summer of 1926, she started dreaming of having a summer house on the island, a peaceful place where she and her Catholic friends could retreat to enjoy the beautiful natural setting. She was fascinated by the historical background of the ruins of St. Albanus Church, because during the Middle Ages this was the site of a monastery built by Benedictine monks. It stood on the very spot where, according to legend, Sunniva, who was the daughter of an Irish king, had come ashore with her entourage and where she later suffered a martyr's death.

Of course, the clerics on Selja belonged to the Lutheran state church, and the parish pastor and council members were afraid that Undset and her Catholic friends might have a negative influence on the local populace. For this reason, they contacted the Norwegian government to prevent her from buying a small piece of land belonging to the parsonage as a building site. After much discussion within the bureaucracy and many letters to the editor, both pro and con, in the newspapers, the entire project came to a halt. The local paper in Lillehammer characterized the matter as "one of the worst attacks of bigotry ever committed in modern Norway" and couldn't understand why "the department hadn't rejected with abhorrence this attitude of fear, equally comical and sad, displayed by the island's elders."

An even worse controversy erupted the following year in connection with Marta Steinvik's anti-Catholic campaign. This energetic woman had studied at the conservative Menighetsfakultet, an independent institution educating theologians. She became convinced that "Catholicism was foreign and dangerous, and that the Jesuits had put together a sly strategy that allowed for the use of any means to make Norway Catholic again." The battle actually began several years earlier, in 1921, when the student association in Kristiania invited a Danish Jesuit to give a lecture titled "The Relationship of the Catholic Church to Modern Theology." A private individual reported the student group, referring to the so-called "Jesuit paragraph" in the constitution which forbade members of the Catholic mission from residing on Norwegian soil. A lively debate ensued in the newspapers. It ended with the Justice Department taking up the question of the legitimacy of the ban with the country's bishops and theological professors. The argument they presented was that it ran counter to spiritual freedom to exclude people from the kingdom of Norway because of their faith. At first the response was largely in favor of abolishing the legal paragraph, and a proposal was made for a revision. It was due to be considered in July of 1925, but before the matter reached that stage, Cardinal van Rossum made his visit to Norway and many well-known people had converted, including Sigrid Undset and Lars Eskeland, who was a highly respected educator and the principal of the folk college in Voss. More people were joining the Catholic congregations in Norway, and naturally this was of concern to the bishops of the state church.

The writer Marta Steinsvik was one of the most zealous in warning against this development. Shortly before the Storting, the Norwegian parliament, was to vote on the matter, Steinsvik was interviewed in *Aftenposten*, and her position was quite clear: "Send all the Norwegian Bolsheviks to Russia, close the borders to any more Jews than we already have, and keep the Jesuits out." The proposal to abolish the Jesuit paragraph was defeated, 99 votes to 33. It was actually not abolished until 1956.

Marta Steinsvik was not content with her victory in the parliament. She now went on the attack against Catholic priests' sexual sins in general, and the Catholic theologian Alfonso de Liguori, who wrote about moral issues, in particular. These were not trivial accusations that she leveled against Catholics regarding adultery, promiscuous activities, and the seduction of penitents. Her claims were so extreme that the Catholic parish priest in Kristiansand sued her for libel, and the Catholic women of Norway sent a protest to the Storting about her activities. Sigrid Undset was one of the signatories of this letter.

On Thursday, May 5, 1927, Marta Steinsvik came to Lillehammer, and Sigrid Undset showed up with two stenographers who wrote down every single word spoken from the podium. According to the report in *Gudbrandsdølen*, the speech was brilliantly delivered before a packed hall, but many were shocked by the heavy artillery the speaker used "about the idolatry that is called Church of Rome." To the journalist who was standing ready at the door afterwards, Undset remarked dryly that now people surely must understand why a woman like Marta Steinsvik was a Lutheran, while a man such as Lars Eskeland was a Catholic.

The heated controversy that arose in the wake of Steinsvik's lecture tour must have challenged both Undset's faith and her willingness to fight, because in March 1928 she was accepted as a Dominican lay sister of the third order and donned the name Sister Olave after her old hero, St. Olav. With that she took on new obligations, including praying at the canonical hours, which meant saying prayers at the same time as the nuns in the Dominican cloister did.

Marta Steinsvik lost the libel lawsuit in Kristiansand, but she won a large audience with the publication of her book *St. Peters Himmelnøkler* (*St. Peter's Keys to Heaven*) in 1928. That same year Sigrid Undset won the Nobel Prize in Literature.

The Nobel Prize comes to Lillehammer

The telegram from Stockholm couldn't have been more brief: "Swedish Academy awards you the Nobel Prize. Karlfeldt."

Sigrid Undset had refused to comment on the rumors that had been circulating for days, aware of the damage that had been done the year before when the Norwegian author Olav Duun was mistakenly proclaimed the winner of the literary prize in *Aftenposten*. That was why she hadn't set much store by the congratulations offered by the newspaper's editor, Frøis Frøisland, who called Bjerkebæk earlier that same Tuesday morning, on November 13, 1928. Not until she stood in the pantry and listened to the operator at the central switchboard reading aloud the telegram from the head of the Swedish Academy did she realize it was true.

She'd had good reason to be doubtful, even though she wasn't sure who her competitors were. But she assumed that Olav Duun would be a strong candidate if the choice was going to go to a Norwegian. It was highly unlikely that the prize would be given to a woman author because two years earlier, in 1926, it had been awarded to Grazia Deledda. Because the prize list since 1901 contained only two female names – the Swede Selma Lagerlöf and the Italian Grazia Deledda – a simple probability calculation seemed to indicate that the Nobel Prize in Literature would go to male writers for many years to come.

The official citation explaining why the Swedish Academy had chosen Sigrid

The Nobel Prize winner at home.

Undset was of course immediately analyzed and commented on in the press, but as for the internal discussions that went on before the decision was reached, they remained secret. Only in 2001, as part of the celebration of the 100th anniversary of the first Nobel Prize, did the Academy make its files public. What they revealed was extremely surprising.

In 1928 there were 36 candidates for the literary prize. The list included seven women writers, and four Norwegians. Undset was nominated by Helga Eng, a professor of pedagogy at the University of Oslo, and this was the fifth time that her name appeared on the list. She had made her "debut" as a candidate in 1922, the year in which her trilogy about Kristin Lavransdatter was completed. Back then it was Frederik Poulsen, director of the Ny Carlsberg Glyptotek museum in Copenhagen who submitted her name to the Swedish Academy.

The final decision about the prize was determined by "the eighteen" of the Academy, but the preparatory work and nominating procedures were handled by a committee of five individuals, including Professor Per Hallström, who acted as secretary, and Erik Axel Karlfeldt, head of the Swedish Academy and the "chairman," who was allowed two votes. According to the minutes of the meetings for 1928, the five members of the committee agreed that Olav Duun's use of Norwegian dialect caused them so much difficulty that he could stay on the waiting list for a while longer. The two Norwegian poets were summarily eliminated, and then one candidate from Norway still remained: Sigrid Undset. The question was to what degree she was qualified to receive the award. Alfred Nobel had written in his will that the literary prize should be given to the author who had produced "the best work of an idealistic bent," but no one really knew what Nobel meant by the word "idealistic." Most of the interpretations made use of key words such as "positive" or "humanistic" – and consequently neither Strindberg nor Ibsen was ever found worthy of the prize. The matter had been thoroughly discussed without reaching any unequivocal conclusion. But Nobel's foremost wish was that the prize should be given to the writer who "had made the greatest contribution to humanity," and this weighed heavily in the internal discussions, especially during the first decades of the history of the award.

As for Undset's qualifications, both positive and negative elements were presented. When her novels were first proposed for evaluation, the members of the Nobel Committee were largely positive. They focused on her debut novel *Mrs. Marta Oulie* and on *Kristin Lavransdatter*, praising the author for her extraordinary power and originality, both in her examination of the human soul and as a storyteller. The committee had only one major objection: her work was too much women's literature for their taste. That was the point, at least, although the phrase "women's literature" wasn't used, of course. "With great admiration for Sigrid Undset's indefatigable and rich narrative art, a man, at least, cannot help growing weary of the stormy and complicated stories of women's lives." That was the comment from the gentlemen, who agreed that "it would be possible to forgo without regret a good deal of the intimacy in the description." As for *Kristin Lavransdatter*, they found it disappointing "to see how little the women even back then, in the fourteenth century, had learned from life."

During the years following her first nomination for the prize, the four-part novel about Olav Audunssøn appeared, and then it was no longer possible for anyone to accuse Sigrid Undset of writing "only" women's literature, for in this weighty epic she impressed her readers with her portrayal of a man's experiences and psyche. This time it was the author's religious involvement that posed a problem, because Undset's conversion to Catholicism in 1924 – in between *Kristin Lavransdatter* and *The Master of Hestviken* – was something that many found difficult to accept, also east of the Norwegian border. It was considered a strike against her that she was Catholic, because a literary work that contradicted the state religion could not be considered "idealistic" – no matter how the word was interpreted. It was rumored that the king of Sweden, Gustav Adolf, who otherwise displayed little interest in literature, had expressed a negative opinion of Sigrid Undset's faith. The author herself didn't help matters by casting herself into a debate with the head of the Swedish state church.

In 1925 Archbishop Nathan Söderblom, who was a popular and respected man, issued invitations to a major ecumenical conference in Stockholm, and this was actually the first gathering of Christian religious communities in many centuries. The Catholics stayed away from the Stockholm conference, because they felt that their differences with the Lutherans were too great. But the delegates from the other religious communities discussed with even greater zeal how they could make the world more Christian. The archbishop summarized the entire debate in a book that was 926 pages long, and Sigrid Undset leveled her most biting criticism at this enormous tome in an article she wrote for the journal *Vor Verden*. In the article she wrote that the conference made her think of the time when the Molbo people of Denmark discussed how they should proceed in order to increase the stock of fish in their pond: "It was agreed that they would put in two salted herrings that could then propagate," she wrote, having dipped her pen in venom.

A zealous journalist saw to it that Undset's article was sent to Archbishop Söderblom, who gallantly and with a touch of condescension expressed his admiration for Undset's art and his own empathy for the newly converted Catholic's reference – "which risks being more royalist than the king himself." He was convinced that over time she would long to return to the church of the North. Undset retorted that she didn't have "a single sympathetically tinged memory from the Lutheran church service," and she regarded the entire state church as "a zealous declaration of prudence and materialistic ethics." One of the main points of her reply to Söderblom focused on the difference between the celibacy of the Catholic priests, which made them able to live modestly and devote all their efforts to their parishioners, and the Lutheran pastors who often had large families to support. She went so far as to state irreverently that in Denmark, Norway, and Sweden combined there were not even twenty theologians who would be willing to give up the wife and the family's Sunday dinners for the sake of the Lord. Sigrid Undset was certainly not trying to ingratiate herself with her Swedish neighbors – on the contrary!

In spite of the polemics that Undset exchanged with Nathan Söderblom, the heated discussion within the Swedish Academy's Nobel Committee was not primarily directed at her religious beliefs. Instead, they debated to what extent they could defend awarding the prize to her foremost rival, the Russian Maxim Gorky. This author had written in a shockingly open manner about the dispossessed at the bottom of Russian society – the poor, the outcast, the homeless. Gorky was first proposed for the prize in 1918, only a year after the Russian Revolution, and since then he had been nominated numerous times. Each time he was firmly rejected by a majority of committee members, but this time Professor Schück was supporting his nomination with extra vigor.

Schück had succeeded in promoting his favorite, Grazia Deledda, in 1926, and since no literary prize had been awarded in 1927, two winners could be chosen the following year – one for 1927 and one for 1928. So Schück saw some hope for Gorky and fervently discussed the author's gripping memoirs and his poetic depictions of the "Russian soul." Professor Hallström, the secretary in charge of the committee archives, objected that Gorky was best at depictions of brutality and "a picturesque squalor" and that the structure of his latest work was nothing but an "aimless muddle." For his part, Professor Karlgren feared most that awarding the prize to the favorite author of the Bolsheviks would be interpreted as offering "disquieting support" for their activities and provide fodder for the revolutionary forces. But Gorky had dissociated himself from the regime and moved to Italy! During the discussions the selection process became polarized. Should they give preference to a radical Marxist or to a reactionary Catholic? Or maybe even both?

Henrik Schück, who was a professor of literary history and the chancellor of Uppsala University, argued as forcefully *against* Sigrid Undset as he did *for* Maxim Gorky. He disagreed so strongly with both Hallström and Karlgren that he wrote a long "commentary" as an addendum to the minutes of the meetings. According to this "commentary," Undset had displayed great problems with the psychology of the historical novel. Schück finds it striking that in the Icelandic sagas, which he assumes are the literary models for her work, religion plays "almost no role." The sagas give short shrift to "minor sexual offenses," and even to murder. "In the work of Sigrid Undset, on the other hand, religion is a dominating factor," remarks the professor. He then comes to the extraordinary conclusion that the view of life as portrayed in her historical novels must be that of Undset herself! Another of his objections is that Undset has "no real narrative talent" – the plot proceeds too slowly, and there is so little dialogue in her novels that it causes the poor man "real effort to read her books to the end." Schück concludes with a prediction: "I venture to say that within a short time her novels will lack any readers." Indeed!

Another candidate for the literary prize who was only briefly mentioned in the minutes for 1928 was Henri Bergson. He was a French philosopher of Jewish origins and had been nominated several times, although his name didn't seem to be given high priority. In addition, his work didn't quite fit under the label of "literature," since he wrote nonfiction. Nor is he mentioned in Per Hallström's report, which he filed in Stockholm on September 27, 1928. Thomas Mann, on the other hand, did make an appearance as a dark horse in the committee's final deliberations: "The committee's very divided stand with regard to the prize nominees has resulted in 3 votes in favor of Sigrid Undset and 2 in favor of Maxim Gorky, while 1 vote rejected both candidates and 1 vote was in favor of Thomas Mann instead of Gorky."

During the course of the weeks preceding the day when "the eighteen" in a plenary session made their final decision, the discussion of candidates must have continued. In the end Gorky lost. His name was withdrawn as a nominee because they didn't think that they could vote for an author who had been so negatively discussed by several of the committee members. That same year Gorky signaled his position as an extreme leftist when he returned home from exile in Italy and offered his services as a dedicated supporter of the revolutionary regime. His politics then made him inviable for all future as a possible candidate for the prize. So from the right wing the uncontroversial Henri Bergson then entered the picture, and the following statement was issued:

The Nobel certificate.

The Swedish Academy decided on November 13, 1928, that the Nobel Prize in Literature for the year 1927 shall be awarded to Henri Bergson "to acknowledge his life-affirming ideas and the brilliant art with which they are presented"; and the Nobel Prize for the current year shall be awarded to Sigrid Undset "primarily for her powerful depictions of life during the Middle Ages in the North."

Fortunately, Undset was not aware of the Academy's heated discussions or of Professor Schück's highly vocal objections. Instead, she had her hands full receiving congratulations and flowers. When the telegram from Stockholm was read to her over the phone, Svarstad happened to be at Bjerkebæk visiting the children, so he was the first person to hear the news. "Well, I've been awarded the Nobel Prize," Undset told him. At Svarstad's suggestion, the occasion was celebrated with a glass of sherry. That evening a reporter from the Norwegian news service knocked on the door, but he received only the briefest of comments: "'Just say that I'm happily surprised,' she said, 'and by the way, I have a real dread of being interviewed, and now I've got to go up to say good-night to my children.' And with a friendly wave she disappeared up the stairs."

The first official delegation to show up at Bjerkebæk to deliver "a heartfelt thank you for the glory she has cast upon our country with her artistic achievements," included the chairman and vice-chairman of the Artists Association. They arrived by car from Oslo. "The gentlemen handed Mrs. Undset an enormous flower arrangement in the traditional golden brown colors of the Artists Association, and the chairman paid tribute to her with a few words and invited her to be the guest of honor at one of their next meetings."

Early Wednesday morning the flowers and telegrams began streaming in from near and far. The newspaper *Hamar Stiftstidende* reports:

> The rooms at Bjerkebæk almost look like one big hothouse with the most delightful flowers... Just with the noon mail delivery on Thursday she received 70 letters... Of course Mrs. Undset is keeping as far away as possible from the telephone, which is tended faithfully and vigilantly by two of the young women of the household, who are earning their full wages by answering the countless inquiries from both Norway and abroad, from journalists and other less intrusive individuals.

Undset's strong aversion to the press must have been well known, judging by all the comments on the subject. A cinematographer from the Norwegian Film Distribution Center and the Swedish Cinemas arrived in Lillehammer to film the prizewinner, but had to leave empty-handed. Undset had no desire to be immortalized in living pictures. The representative from *Tidens Tegn* had slightly better success. "Mrs. Undset's housekeeper answered the door. 'No, Mrs. Undset would not be available until five thirty in the evening.'" The journalist had to go off for a walk before the author would receive her, so she used the opportunity to find out how the big news was being celebrated in the neighborhood:

> We expected to find a town filled with jubilation and festivities, but we see that we were mistaken regarding the Gudbrandsdal mentality. Lillehammer is extremely proud of Sigrid Undset, but in a restrained way. The fact that Lillehammer has not put up the flags today does not mean that the honor bestowed on the town isn't appreciated – no doubt they are merely mustering their forces.

That was true. The Røros newspaper *Fjeld-Ljom* reported several days later that the town's leading citizens had considered a banquet celebration with a torchlight parade in the author's honor. Sigrid Undset graciously declined, however, saying that it would be better to show concern for the poor people of the town since Christmas was approaching. So they would have to think of some other plan.

The prize money, which was 156,000 Norwegian kroner, an amount comparable to 2.4 million kroner today, naturally aroused a great deal of interest. *Hamar Stiftstidende* reported that Undset was inundated with "letters from people pleading for money, more importunate and urgent than ever. And in unheard of quantities... Apparently people no longer have any compunctions, they practically throw themselves at the Nobel Prize winner like vultures, as if Mrs. Undset didn't already know how she is going to use the prize money. Oh yes, she has known for a long time and will undoubtedly tell us eventually." The announcement of what the money would be used for appeared in *Aftenposten* on November 26, under the bold headline:

> **Sigrid Undset to use all her Nobel money to establish various foundations.**
> *The first foundation of 80,000 kroner was established yesterday. The interest from this sum will be used to help parents caring at home for children who have moderate or severe developmental problems... Mrs. Undset will announce the other foundations after she returns from Stockholm.*

In this instance the reporter happened to be the paper's editor-in-chief, Frøis Frøisland, one of the few journalists who was allowed admittance to Bjerkebæk. In an article titled "Mrs. Undset in conversation with *Aftenposten*," Frøisland quotes her as saying: "With the establishment of this foundation of 80,000 kroner, my primary intention is to fight to preserve a home where there are one or more children with moderate or severe developmental problems. It is my wish to make a contribution to saving the child for the parents and the parents for the child." The news of the "Maren Charlotte Undset Svarstad Foundation," which would make an annual award on October 29, Mosse's birthday, was received with great enthusiasm and respect. "Mrs. Undset's marvelous plan does not surprise those who for many years have witnessed her warm heart, vigilant concern, and social consciousness. She has long demonstrated that she is as great a human being as she is an artist," wrote Ronald Fangen, chairman of the Authors' Union.

The announcement of her second project appeared on December 10, the very day of the Nobel celebration in Stockholm. It was then revealed that Undset had donated 15,000 kroner to the relief fund of the Authors' Union. With that contribution she more than repaid the grant that she had received from the union at the beginning of her career. This donation was also received with applause and admiration in the press, but it's possible that her family was not as enthusiastic. Anders was then fifteen years old and attending secondary school in Lillehammer, while Hans was nine and a pupil at the Catholic boarding school in Oslo. It's unlikely they were consulted. When Anders arrived at school after his mother had been to Stockholm to receive the prize, his teachers congratulated him, and jokingly hinted that the family's new wealth would surely bring many pleasures, also to him. Anders replied tersely that for his part, he hadn't seen even 25 øre of the prize money.

Frøis and Helene Frøisland.

Sigrid Undset's mother, the old "archduchess," didn't seem entirely pleased either. In 1997, in the linen closet at Bjerkebæk, among the tablecloths and bed linens, a letter was found that had been sent by Charlotte Undset to her daughter. It was written immediately after an announcement appeared in *Aftenposten* stating that all of the prize money had been designated for foundations. The letter draws a link between "the two beautiful little books" that Charlotte Undset had received and her daughter's lavish generosity toward strangers; there is also a reminder of her own situation when she became a widow with three little girls to support. All of which indicate that she may have wanted to caution her daughter to come to her senses:

My dear Sigrid,
　　Many thanks for the two beautiful little books that I received last night; I haven't yet had time to look at them much, but they look quite lovely, both outside and inside, when I leaf through them. Thank you so much.
　　It's awful that even now, after announcing that you will give the *whole* prize away to *foundations*, you are still plagued by these private entreaties. If you *hadn't* won the prize, they would have had to find some way to fend for themselves; so that's what they should do now! If things keep on this way, you're going to end up losing money!! [...]
　　I've bought a beautiful brown silk dress from Paulsson so that you'll have as elegant a mother as it's possible for me to be.
　　All this fuss is happening exactly 35 years after I watched you and Ragnhild leave the deathbed where Ingvald's body lay – with his hands clasped in front

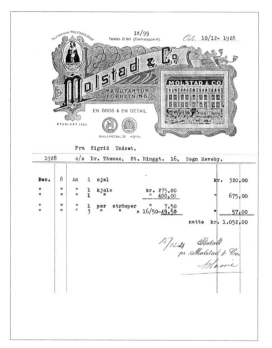

The Nobel Prize winner ordered a new outfit from the Molstad shop for the occasion.

of him. I can still see those two thin little backs clad in dark blue sweaters, with the long brown hair tumbling down – and I can hear Ragnhild's little voice in the doorway saying: "Sigrid, now we're fatherless!" Exactly 35 years have passed since then, when everything capsized for me... and now everything is fuss and festivities! Yes, life is strange!!!

Sigrid Undset left Lillehammer in good time as the birthday of Alfred Nobel and the award ceremony approached. Anders stayed home, but Eilif Moe went with her. Undset wanted to share the honor with her good friend and business manager, and she later gave him a deluxe edition of *Kristin Lavransdatter* with an inscription in memory of "when we were in Stockholm and received the Nobel Prize." The guest of honor had of course bought herself a new outfit, with Bally shoes, a new lambskin coat and matching hat, and a dress of shimmering velvet made by the ultra-fashionable Molstad shop in Oslo.

Then the real celebrating began. On Friday, December 7, the Authors Union and the Aschehoug Publishing Company invited 180 guests to a banquet at the Grand Hotel in Oslo. With publisher William Nygaard and Mrs. Hambro, the wife of the president of parliament, leading the way, the guests entered the Rococo Hall to the strains of a festive polonaise by Johan Svendsen. Twelve people were scheduled to speak, including Edvard Hambro, Prime Minister Johan Ludwig Mowinckel, the Swedish minister Torvald Magnusson Höjer, chairman of the Authors' Union Ronald Fangen, the author Barbra Ring, Frøis Frøisland, and Nini Roll Anker. "Then Mrs. Undset stood up, prompting silence and anticipation, and thanked everyone in a blessedly brief, natural, and beautiful manner." Her speech was received with a great deal of applause, and finally "Einar Lunde delivered a greeting from Lillehammer, which had more than just her tax returns to thank her for." Afterwards there was a "private party for Mrs. Undset and her closest friends at the lovely home of director Molstad on Nordstrand." And according to *Morgenposten*, that party went on until the wee hours of the morning.

The Nobel Prize winners in Stockholm's concert hall.

If Sigrid Undset celebrated as much as the others, it must have been quite exhausting for her, because the following day she had to give a speech entitled "The Change of Faith in Norway – From Heathendom to Christianity" in the university's auditorium. In her speech she pointed out that even learned Lutherans often understood very little about the Catholic past of Norway or about the psychology expressed in the religious writings from the high Middle Ages. She left no doubt that she herself was deeply knowledgeable about that period of Norwegian history between the saga era and the Reformation. Did this indicate that she had actually heard a bit about the Swedish Academy's internal discussions? It seems possible.

With young Miss Synnøve Anker from Lillehammer as her "chambermaid," Undset then continued by night train to Stockholm. In the gray light of Monday morning, at 7:05, the author was met at the station by official representatives and her sister Ragnhild Wiberg. At the Hotel Imperial, an entire suite had been reserved for the celebrated guest, and there, for once, she held a press conference. She used the occasion to pronounce a few stern remarks about the new medium of the day, the radio, which was raking in revenue from writers' works without paying them an øre.

On the afternoon of December 10, which was Alfred Nobel's birthday, Sigrid Undset took to the podium in the grand auditorium of the Concert Hall as one of the three prizewinners who were present. As the only woman among the honored guests, she sat in the front row between two German professors of chemistry, Heinrich Otto Wieland and Adolf Otto Reinhold Windaus. Every member of the royal family was in attendance, and the journalists noted with satisfaction that Princess Märtha's hemline was entirely proper on this occasion. She had recently shocked the press with her fashionable and highly daring short skirts.

Professor Schück gave the welcome speech, of course without saying a single word about his own objections to the prizewinner. Söderman's overture to "The Maid of Orleans" struck a heroic tone, which was further emphasized by "Siegfried's Rhine Journey" – German music by Richard Wagner. The work of the two chemists was praised "in the most eloquent German" – to the joy of some and the chagrin of others. The Frenchman Henri Bergson, who was awarded the prize in literature for 1927, was not present, but Debussy's "Petite Suite" was played in his honor.

Then the sound of Edvard Grieg's "Til våren" ("To the Spring") flowed over the hall, and the atmosphere became at once lighter and more Nordic. Dr. Hallström's speech honoring Undset was viewed as the high point of the ceremony, but to the disappointment of the audience, he spoke in such a low voice that only those closest to him could hear what he said. The rumor had spread that the Swedish king was not particularly enthused by the honor being shown to Sigrid Undset, and it was also noted that she did not make a very deep curtsey when she received the medal from King Gustaf. The reporter for the Swedish newspaper *Dagens Nyheter* speculated whether the old monarch might still harbor bitter feelings over the dissolution of the union between Sweden and Norway. Wearing a miniature of the Norwegian Order of St. Olav and "a dark gold dress, she descended the stairs of the podium and went over to His Majesty to receive her award... She made a moderate curtsey, for the time is past when the Bernadotte kings were also considered the fathers of the

Sigrid Undset and the Crown Prince at the Grand Hotel.

nation in Oslo, although she must have seen Oscar II in power. Perhaps she was one of the young conspirators in 1905?" In spite of this possibility, the applause for Sigrid Undset was conspicuously warm.

That evening there was a banquet at the Grand Hotel, and Undset was seated next to the Swedish Crown Prince – the king had declined to attend. But the Crown Prince was close in age to Undset, and he was both interested in art and well-traveled, so they undoubtedly enjoyed each other's company. The keynote speech honoring all three prizewinners was given in German, after first ascertaining that Undset understood the language. She could hardly deny it, since she had spent ten years as an employee of the Wisbech company, and as the boss's secretary she had typed all his correspondence with the Allgemeine Elektrizitäts-Gesellschaft. The party ended early, but the next day the celebration continued with 70 guests invited for dinner at Stockholm Palace. After that it was the turn of Undset's Swedish publisher, Nordstedt & Sons. They too wanted to pay tribute to the prizewinner, and then she had to pay calls on the St. Eugenia congregation and Concordia Catolica.

The festivities lasted two whole weeks, from the time Undset left Lillehammer until she was back home again. For the last stage, as she traveled north by train from Oslo, she was accompanied by Hans, who had Christmas vacation from Sta. Sunniva School. In Lillehammer the local residents had finally decided how they would celebrate the Nobel Prize winner, and on the evening of

December 18, the whole town turned out. It was a beautiful night, with no wind and a slightly overcast sky. The street from the train station and up to Storgatan was packed with people on both sides – 3,000 people according to *Lillehammer Tilskuer*. Among them was Anders, who along with his boy scout comrades had formed a guard of honor up the street. "When the train approached Lillehammer, the torches were lit, and a beautiful sight greeted Mrs. Undset as she stood at the window of the train compartment and looked up toward the town." Anders went on board to greet his mother, and then she came out onto the platform, flanked by her two sons. The local newspaper writes with emotion about what followed:

> When she arrived at the station gate, the teacher Stian Kristensen, who was in charge of the lovely arrangements, mounted an improvised podium to offer a few heartfelt words welcoming Mrs. Undset. He said something like this: "We welcome you home from your triumphal procession. With joy and pride we have followed your path. To thank you for what you have meant to our country and our people, we wish to pay tribute to you in this simple fashion."
>
> The teacher then gave three times three cheers for Mrs. Undset, and everyone else joined in with enthusiasm. Visibly moved, Mrs. Undset said: "This is the most beautiful greeting I've ever seen in my life. Thank you so much!"
>
> Accompanied by her children, Mrs. Undset then exited from the station and got into the sleigh pulled by two horses with gleaming harnesses. Slowly it made its way up the street, as the torchbearers and the rest of the crowd fell in behind and walked up to Storgaten. Cheers followed her.
>
> Then at Stortorget the remains of all the torches were put into a huge bonfire, and the flames cast a red glow over the darkness. It's doubtful that anyone has ever made a more beautiful entry in Lillehammer, nor has anyone ever received a more sincere tribute.

Many were fascinated by the glory that had been bestowed upon Bjerkebæk, and the tributes continued. Eystein Eggen wrote the poem "Dronningar" ("Queens") in which the historical and ruthless Queen Sigrid Storråde ends up faring poorly in comparison with the contemporary "Sigrid the mild-tempered" who had impressed so many by giving away her prize money. The same praise is offered in Frimann Clasen's poem "in honor of the queen of prose." Two of the verses are as follows:

In the proud dale a castle looms
not far from the waters of Gjendin,
it glows tonight from all its rooms
and the mistress in the portal stands
her gaze surveying the lands!

Quietly she lives inside the gates,
Gudbrandsdalen's queen of prose;
yet her heart is big and beats for those
who live in poor and dire straits.

The jubilation that surrounded the Nobel Prize winner gradually subsided, but
in early spring a second movement followed with dissonant chords. With the
memory of the Marta Steinsvik anti-Catholic propaganda fresh in everyone's
mind, Undset had waited to make her announcement about the third foundation she intended to establish. After visiting her fellow convert Lars Eskeland,
she was ready to make her last donation, and in late March the newspapers
reported:

New Foundation from Sigrid Undset

Mrs. Sigrid Undset has once again established a foundation. Named the St.
Gudmund's Foundation and endowed with 60.000 kroner, the interest on
the funds will be used to help educate children from Catholic homes in
Norway at Catholic schools. The interest amount will be distributed every
year on March 16, the anniversary of the death of St. Gudmund, who was
the bishop of Iceland from 1203 until 1237. He was known to be a man with
a particular interest in the education of poor children.

The criticism began the very next day. F. Stang Conradi, who was the head of
a government department, wrote an indignant article in *Morgenbladet* in which
he practically accused Undset of breaking the law:

Even in Sweden the state religion is Lutheranism... To put it mildly, it shows
both bad manners and ingratitude toward the Swedish donors when the
prizewinner misuses the gift in such a fashion that it indirectly benefits a
purpose that is diametrically opposed to the wishes of the donors... It is here
that Mrs. Undset wishes Papism to carry on its undermining work – in order
perhaps to win additional terrain. But Mrs. Undset is a Norwegian citizen,

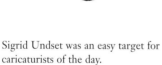

Sigrid Undset was an easy target for caricaturists of the day.

and she knows that according to our constitution, Lutheranism is the state religion. Yet she is doing her best to undermine it, to work against the constitution.

In a comment several days later Conradi shows that the Swedish newspapers had also leveled criticism at Undset's "Catholic foundation." But *Aftenposten* defends her by stating that there is no basis "for the assumption that she had necessarily created the endowment with funds from her Nobel Prize money." Neither Undset nor her attorney was available to comment on the issue "because they were away." The editors of *Morgenbladet* chose a different tack and pointed out that the prize money did not come from the Swedish government but rather from Alfred Nobel, and that there were no legal conditions that would determine how the money was spent.

The only stipulation with regard to the literary prize is that the recipients should be authors with an *idealistic* view of life – a proviso which, as is well known, put Henrik Ibsen out of the running for the honor. And there was no shortage of cases in which the prize money was used for purely propaganda purposes. We might mention, for instance, Anatole France who received the literary prize in 1921 and donated the entire sum to Communist endeavors.

Nevertheless, we assume that for Conradi the choice between communist propaganda and Catholic influence was a question of choosing between cholera and the plague.

Ebba, Mosse, and Thea wearing elegant fur coats.

The difficult thirties

Bjerkebæk, Lillehammer, December 13, 1929

Dear Aunt Kirsa,

Please forgive me for typing this letter to you, but at least you won't have to strain your eyes – I know that my handwriting isn't very easy to decipher...

I'm sitting here in the midst of my Christmas correspondence. If there were many people who wrote to me before to confide in me all manner of miseries, there certainly aren't any fewer of them now. I haven't received any requests to help anyone living on the moon, so now I know for certain that it is unoccupied; on the other hand, I've heard from Norwegians stranded in China, for example, and from people in Bulgaria and New Zealand – and I'm so tired of finding the same stack of letters every morning, most of them from complete strangers...

The children are fine. Ebba is here, as you may know; she's doing a little secretarial work for me. Anders is grown up now. He has even acquired a pipe and belongs to a bridge club for young gentlemen that meets once a week. He has turned out to be a handsome boy and a sweet and pleasant son, though he's not the talkative sort. Little Mosse is also grown up now, but she hasn't really developed at all – she does learn to say new things, but then she thinks it's so fun to say them that she repeats the phrases nonstop and

Sigrid Undset, Christmas 1935.

forgets the old ones, but she is almost always happy and content. Hans continues to be a sweet little lad – although even he isn't so little anymore; he's quite tall for his age.

Take good care of yourself and have a happy Christmas...

Much love, Your devoted

Sigrid Undset

The Christmas letters that Sigrid Undset sent to her aunt Kirsa in Copenhagen were probably warmer in tone than the ones she sent to the other aunt on her father's side of the family. Aunt Halma in Trondhjem was a very stern and critical spinster. When Undset made her literary debut, she received a letter from Aunt Halma saying that she ought to stick to her work as an office secretary. And when news of the Nobel Prize was announced Undset was told that she would have to watch herself so as not to become arrogant! Anders and Hans were very fond of their eccentric great-aunt and thought she deserved a three-star listing in the Baedeker travel guide for Trondhjem. It made a big impression on the boys that she would barge right out into Kongens Gate without looking either to the right or the left, fuming at the cars: "Get out of my way!"

As is evident in Undset's Christmas letter to Aunt Kirsa, the increasing prosperity at Bjerkebæk brought joy but other things as well. Even though she had used all the money from the Swedish Academy to set up foundations, the royalties she received from increasing book sales benefited both the family and the city treasurer. Rumor had it that if not for the large revenues from the author on Nordseterveien, the municipal tax rates would have been higher. Sigrid Undset felt embarrassed by all the curiosity about her private life, and she was annoyed by the intrusiveness of obtuse reporters. Busloads of tourists actually stopped outside the garden gate, making her maids feel like prisoners in their own home. The situation improved after Mikkelsen put up the high plank fence facing Nordseterveien, so that the courtyard was protected from view. After that, anyone who wanted to talk to someone in the house had to ring the bell and then submit to the critical questioning of the housemaids and the angry barking of the dogs before they were allowed in to see the Mistress.

On a more positive note, Sigrid Undset was looking forward to the plans to connect her property to the public water and sewer system. Ever since the family moved in, there had been problems with the well at the back of the house and with the water pipes in the basement. Once Bjerkebæk was hooked up to the municipal water and sewer lines, Undset took the opportunity to put in two bathrooms with toilets, one in each of the houses. They were equipped with specially ordered fittings from the United States and with lovely white tiles on the walls, which prompted these luxuries to be dubbed the "Hollywood baths" by Undset's nieces. To Mathea's great satisfaction, the kitchen was also modernized, because after the Nobel Prize medal entered the house, there were even greater expectations with regard to the meals served at Bjerkebæk.

Undset felt quite strongly that she was under constant scrutiny and did her best to keep at a distance the gawkers and those who wished to criticize her. She knew she was called Queen Sigrid Storråde and that even the most minor of missteps might release an avalanche of gleeful malice. Behind the plank fence surrounding Bjerkebæk, everything was certainly not idyllic, especially the relationship between her two sons. "I live in perpetual fear that Anders and Hans will end up seriously hurting each other – their fights are dreadful," she confided to Astri af Geijerstam. "Hans has a difficult time getting along with people – he doesn't get along with anyone outside our home, and no one gets along with him," she wrote to Signe Thomas.

No, Hans was no longer little and "sweet," either toward his mother or toward the others at Bjerkebæk. His rebellious streak cropped up often and was given free rein. "Thanks for the birthday greetings that I didn't get," he wrote sarcastically to Thea a few days after his birthday, while Anders received the following response as a thank you for a box of candy: "As you can see, I didn't eat myself to death." When introducing himself to strangers, the conceited youth would recite his full name, including the one given to him upon becoming a Catholic: "Hans Benedikt Hugh Pius Undset Svarstad." That sort of thing did not go unnoticed; people reacted with astonishment and sneers, causing his mother to feel an even greater need to protect herself and her family.

Fortunately, Sigrid Undset also received attention that was welcome. When she was awarded the Grand Cross of the Order of St. Olav, the honor couldn't have come at a better time. It occurred in 1930, in the midst of the preparations for the magnificent Olav celebration. Undset was involved in the building of the new Catholic chapel at Stiklestad, on the site where St. Olav met his death on July 29, nine centuries earlier. She had also made generous donations for the decoration of the chapel. As one of the most prominent Catholics in Norway, she was to participate in several processions and masses during the week-long celebration, both at the consecration of the chapel in Stiklestad and during the festivities in Trondhjem. With great anticipation, she was looking forward to the celebration in her father's home town and to being a guest at the newly restored Nidaros Cathedral, where Ingvald Undset had played archaeologist in his childhood.

Hans as an acolyte.

Then came the announcement that the invited Catholic guests of Norway were to be kept at arm's length from the most prestigious of all the events. It was to take place in Nidaros Cathedral on July 29 – on St. Olav's Day – with the king and government officials and all of Norway's cultural elite in attendance. However, the Catholic leaders were not welcome inside the cathedral for fear of the propaganda effect, so seats had been reserved for them outside the church. This prompted a great deal of press coverage, of course, along with a bitter debate, and in the midst of all the controversy came the announcement that Sigrid Undset had been named Knight of the Order of St. Olav.

She must have experienced the honor as a welcome pat on the back from the highest quarters. When Undset appeared at the royal palace to express her thanks for the honor, King Haakon gave her a big, heartfelt smile. "Well, Mrs. Undset," he said, speaking with an accent that revealed his Danish birth, "I see that we're both going to Trondhjem. And you will sit outside while I sit inside, and Bishop Berggrav will give a long sermon. Perhaps we should take along a lunch!" After her audience with the king, Undset went straight home to her mother and sister, and the king's remarks were repeated with great enthusiasm – and in Danish, of course!

Sigrid Undset said many times that she thought Trondhjem (which changed its name to Trondheim in 1931) was Norway's most beautiful city, but the reception she was given in 1930 couldn't have been particularly pleasant for her. She received a much warmer welcome in Iceland the year after the Olav celebration. Both boys accompanied her to the island of the sagas, and for Hans, who had now been permanently discharged from Sta. Sunniva School, the joy was especially great. Their visit to Iceland was a memorable one. In the fall of 1931, when Hans became a pupil at the Kringsjå School quite close to Bjerkebæk, he wrote an essay about the experience titled "A Trip Abroad," in which he describes with delight and in great detail the dramatic events of the summer.

His essay starts off rather cautiously: "It was on July 3 that our trip to Iceland was to begin. After eating breakfast, we took the train to Oslo. For our travel reading we had *Morgenbladet, Nationen, Allers, Hjemmet,* and *Njåls Saga*." The next stage was by train to Bergen, but their departure from that port city was delayed by a few days because Anders had developed a nasty abscess in his throat that had to be lanced. In Bergen he had to consult a doctor:

> When my brother came back, he was really miserable. He'd waited for two hours in the cramped waiting room until it was his turn. And having the boil in his throat lanced wasn't much fun either. After that he had to go back to the doctor, but my mother and I drove up to "Bellevue" and had dinner there. When my brother came back from the doctor we went to "Holbergs Hus" where we had something to drink and soft bread for my brother, and after that he had to go to the hospital. The boat left at 10 o'clock. It was called the *Nova*. The next day we went up on deck, but I was invited up to the bridge by the first officer.

It doesn't take much to read between the lines and realize what a luxury it must have been for a twelve-year-old boy who had spent four and a half years in a boarding school to have his mother all to himself. And the drama continued, to the great joy of Hans:

> The next day there was a thick fog. We were supposed to reach the Faeroe Islands by 8 o'clock in the morning, but then we ran aground right outside of Tórshavn, so we barely managed to get there by 8 o'clock at night! We stayed in Tórshavn for three days until the ship was repaired, and we saw things like the museum and the ruins of the cathedral at Kirkebøl. We also visited a Faeroese poet, Mr. Djurhuus.

While they were in Tórshavn, Sigrid Undset received a telegram from Mathea Mortenstuen, saying that Anders was better and that he wanted to take the steamboat *Lyra* to join them. Greatly relieved, Undset wrote back to say that a weight had been lifted from her heart at the good news. In Akureyri on the east coast of Iceland, Anders finally caught up with his mother and brother. But judging by his school essay, Hans was more interested in the attention they received from company directors and professors, and he writes enthusiastically about lava and hot springs and sightseeing trips to Thingvellir and Gullfoss. "On our last day on Iceland they gave a big party for Mother at Hotel Borg, and the government officials were present," he concludes proudly. Undset's own wry remarks about the same event were: "Well, here we sit, somewhere between

It was discouraging to read Hans' report card.

state prisoners and honored guests." She was certainly not an easy person to please.

In the spring of 1932, it was Mosse's turn to undergo a dramatic event. The farmer at Randgaard had taken a dislike to her huge cat Sisyphus with the bright yellow fur. The cat roamed the neighborhood and had killed some chickens owned by the farmer's wife. So one day he shot the cat, and Mosse was inconsolable. Undset thought they ought to have the animal skinned so that Mosse could at least have the pelt of Sisyphus to comfort her. And that's what they did. This anecdote would probably have been dismissed as pure fiction except that the bill for having the cat skinned still exists!

Other problems required other solutions. In May 1932 as Undset's fiftieth birthday approached, the attention from the press became so bothersome that the celebrant had to escape by hired car to Vadstena in Sweden. Anders was in the middle of graduation activities while Hans was struggling with his entrance exams for secondary school, so the boys couldn't go along. But to make up for this, their mother promised them a trip to the resort at Lyckorna on the west coast of Sweden later in the summer. When the time came, Hans and his mother made the trip together, while Mathea, as usual, had to stay home to take care of Mosse. After a few days Anders joined them at the seaside hotel, and Mathea received the following report:

> Anders didn't feel like waiting for the little local trains in Sweden but took a cab instead... He woke up the whole hotel at 3 a.m. and joined us at breakfast, penniless and grinning. He can spend an entire morning, as much time as he likes, in the sea, and otherwise there is tennis and dancing, so *he's* doing just fine. If only Hans would deign to make friends too, but for now he just trudges about, dressed as if it were midwinter, and as sullen as always when he's at his worst.

In the next letter it appears that Anders has left again, and his brother has finally stripped off his clothes and started to swim and soak up the sun. In the meantime Undset had mudbaths and massage treatments for the rheumatism that troubled her so much, and to Thea she complained that she was "brown and black and blue over my whole body from the iron claws of the woman bath attendant." The big news was that she had received a telegram from Anders, who had joined the military. He was already installed in a barracks out on the heath and was preparing for his first bivouac. His mother remarked wryly that "now it's a different sort of dance than staying home and playing the young gentleman – but it's what he himself wanted, and thank God for that."

The plans for Hans didn't go nearly as smoothly. In a third letter from Lyckorna, Undset sent discouraging news:

Mme. la duchesse (– avec mssgr. le duc)

The count and countess, as Hans depicted them.

Dear Mathea,

I've received some unhappy news from the school – Hans didn't pass the entrance exam! The letter was here when we came back from Gothenburg yesterday evening. The poor boy has been sobbing most of the night and has refused to eat anything either last night or this morning. It's very sad – but if this can just be a lesson for the boy so that he becomes a little less conceited and more willing to pull himself together, then it might be seen as serving some purpose. Otherwise he has been quite amenable – for Hans – and he's become a good swimmer. From Anders I received a few scribbles this morning. He's at Lahaugmoen, not Laholmoen as I wrote after my mother's account; he has 8 hours of exercises a day, is exhausted and heartily pleased with everything, from what I hear.

When Sigrid Undset returned to Lillehammer, she had a conversation with the principal, and so Hans was admitted to the secondary school after all. To keep up with the other students, he needed private tutoring in math, but that could be arranged. Discipline was a bigger problem, and in this case it did no good for his mother to plead his case. Hans constantly came to school late and unprepared, and when the teachers reprimanded him, he responded by resorting to his favorite phrase to pronounce them: "Untalented!" Undset was sometimes in such despair that the housemaids felt genuinely sorry for her. One day when they were sitting at the dinner table, Hans began carrying on as usual about the teachers with "no talent," and about the day's dose of trouble. Undset stared at him in disbelief. "Is that really true? did you really tell the teacher that he couldn't reprimand the son of a Nobel Prize winner?" she asked her son as a deep flush spread over her face and throat. Without even blinking, Hans confirmed this was indeed true. Oh yes, that was exactly what he had said.

Undset had more talks with the principal and with Hans – to no avail. Finally things got so bad that she sent her son to Hartmann's School in Asker, a private "reformatory" for difficult boys in need of discipline. It was there that Hans began swearing in such a fashion that he far surpassed his mother. His former teachers at St. Sunniva would have been stunned. "The Devil in all his glory, Hallelujah!" This was one of his milder epithets.

In both boys' defense, it must be said that of course it couldn't have been easy to handle the role of the "sons of a Nobel Prize winner." Hans tended to go overboard when given an audience and enjoyed being in the spotlight. At the same time, he began living a secret life in which he could develop the hidden sides of his personality. Anders, on the other hand, preferred to avoid any type of attention and did best when he was away from Bjerkebæk. The expectations of the outside world were burdensome enough, but the expectations of their mother were also something they had to face. Just after Anders came of age at 21, Undset wrote to her friend Ingeborg Møller:

> I've been reading the essays written by Anton Brøgger's youngest son. I couldn't help saying to my boys that I really ought to be mad that neither of them has published a single book as yet. Anders merely said: "Just imagine if we had, Mama! How angry you would have been *then*!" (They call me Mama whenever they want to irk me.)

Undset undoubtedly placed more importance on her demand for loyalty and self-sacrifice than on her sons' literary skills. When Anders was a boy, and before Hans was born, Undset wrote some lines that must have had a strong impact on the boys when they were older:

> I would rather know that my son lay torn to pieces and dead in the ground that still belonged to his people when he fell, than that he should be alive

and fighting in a subjugated land... And if I had a son who renounced me and said that he had no country – then I could only say that I do not know this person; death has taken my child from me – the other death that St. Francis speaks of, that which is damnation.

Sigrid Undset fumed at all politicians who spoke warmly of pacifism and neutrality as she held firmly to her own point of view. And when her boys were small, she often sat on the edge of their beds at night and sang to them: "Fight for all that you hold dear, die if that's what it takes." And they probably realized that she meant it.

Anders in uniform.

After making two attempts, Anders had to give up his plans to enter the technical college in Trond-heim. But since he was thriving in the military, he decided to go to officers' training school. When he was discharged in 1934, he had only achieved the rank of second lieutenant, the lowest ranking officer in the military. Yet this didn't hurt his self-esteem, especially after he got a motorcycle and could enjoy the speed and feeling of freedom that it gave him. More importantly, he was lucky with the ladies, at least with Gunvor Hjerkinn from the village of Kapp near Gjøvik. She was fair-haired and lovely, gentle and engaging, but fortunately she also possessed good sense and patience. At Whitsuntide in 1935 the young woman was invited to Bjerkebæk to meet Anders' mother. When the couple drove up to the house and the roar of the motorcycle had subsided, Sigrid Undset exclaimed that she couldn't understand why anyone would sit on the back of such a monster! But Gunvor was in love and simply laughed; she liked both the boy and his motor-bike.

It couldn't have been easy to be scrutinized as a future daughter-in-law by the critical and caustic Undset. Their first encounter wasn't lacking in feelings of constraint, but over the years Gunvor Hjerkinn received many demonstra-tions of Undset's concern and respect. In the fall of 1938, the two lovebirds temporarily had to say goodbye to each other because Anders was about to start his professional training – in England. His mother was clearly relieved. "Finally he was accepted as an apprentice at the Austin automobile factory in Birmingham. He's pleased as punch to be there, as I am that he has finally found work," she wrote to Ingeborg Møller.

Undset had her own problems to contend with, and one of them was financial. According to *Lillehammer Tilskuer*, in 1930 she paid the most taxes in Fåberg municipality, paying one third of her annual income. But the "difficult thirties" were affecting both book sales and many of her closest friends, and this meant that their income was dropping while expenses were on the rise. One of her friends who constantly needed financial help was Gösta af Geijerstam; others who received a gift of 100 kroner each for Christmas were old seamstresses and poor relatives – 35 individuals in all, according to Nini Roll Anker. The household help at Bjerkebæk was told that economizing was necessary, and when the autobiographical book *The Longest Years* arrived from the printer, Undset unwrapped it and said with a sigh, "Well, let's hope that people are interested in reading about this girl so that we can straighten out our finances here at Bjerkebæk."

Poor health was another recurrent problem. Rheumatism and eczema, a bad back and excess weight, sinus trouble and toothaches often plagued Undset. In addition, her consumption of alcohol was at times greater than it ought to be, and the bills from the Lillehammer Wine Co-Op grew perilously high. It didn't help matters that Helene Frøisland, who was also a good customer at the Wine Co-Op, had moved into the neighborhood. She had been widowed in 1930 when Frøis Frøisland died from cancer at a far too young age. Undset wrote to her sister about her old friend, saying that "she always goes to such extremes with whatever she does – and now she has a garden. She comes and goes, wet as a crow from a garden hose that she and the children use to water the garden and themselves, and is given cuttings from one plant or another."

A broken arm made it difficult for Undset to write, and her work wasn't going well. She felt caught in a vicious circle and began seriously talking about moving to Oslo, but once again she mustered her strong will and self-discipline. Nini Roll Anker, who visited Bjerkebæk in November 1935, was very worried about her friend's state of health and wrote in her diary: "She won't finish her book this year – she has been very depressed these past few years and used too many stimulants. But since her stay at Montebello this summer, she no longer drinks whisky – she has also lost weight, but she's extremely listless and tired."

An enormous use of tobacco didn't make her health any better. For many years Undset smoked the mildly perfumed Milo cigarettes all day long. In January 1936 she even posed for a photograph that was used to advertise

Sigrid Undset posed for an advertisement photo in January 1936.

Tiedemann's Tobacco, sitting in her hearth room with a cigarette between her fingers and a smile on her lips. Perhaps she was paid in kind. Undset's confessor tried to get her to stop smoking; he thought it would be a suitable penance for her sins, but she merely blew off that prohibition, literally speaking.

The time that she'd spent away from home in the summer, which Nini mentioned in her diary, was one of several trips Undset made to the fashionable Danish health spa Montebello on Sjælland. There she was put on a diet and received massage treatments. Judging by her letters to Mathea, her health and her mood were both suffering; it almost sounds as if she were having hallucinations:

> So I've started a treatment again... But it's almost too hot to go for walks until evening. Mostly I sit in the park and read or sew. There are black grass snakes here, and even though I know they're harmless, they look so disgusting... I had to give one of them a swat with my sewing. I flung it at a baby toad that was hopping for dear life across the road near where I was sitting. There are also revolting numbers of rats over by the ponds; they've eaten almost all the ducklings. And mosquitoes are swarming everywhere. I was advised to rub on lavender water, and you should do the same for yourself and for Mosse – there's some lavender water on my dressing table. But whether it actually helps is another matter – to be blunt, I have the impres-

sion that the mosquitoes around here practically think of it as some sort of delicate condiment on their food. But perhaps they're too sophisticated. They also say that eucalyptus oil from the pharmacy is good. (Everyone here discusses remedies to combat the mosquitoes.)

Trivial torments such as mosquitoes were no doubt unpleasant enough, but it was primarily the political situation in Europe that was taking its toll on Undset's health. In her novel *Ida Elisabeth*, published in 1932, she had already taken a stand against Nazism and its contempt for the weakest individuals in society. It was with the deepest distrust that she observed the Fascists' worship of those who were strong and productive, and she expressed her uneasiness at the growing anti-Semitism and the blind glorification of the Aryan race in an article titled "Fortschritt, Rasse und Religion" ("Progress, Race, and Religion"), which appeared in a Swiss publication. This article ended up costing her enormous sums in lost royalties from Germany, where her books had been extremely popular. As of 1932, a total of 700,000 copies of her novels had been printed in German, while in English there were only 400,000 copies in print. But Undset gave no consideration to sales or royalties when she expressed her views, and the result was financial woes, as Nini wrote in her diary:

> Her income has shrunk considerably, also in Germany, where she had many readers. With the greatest difficulty her lawyer has managed to recoup 18,000 kroner that her publisher owed her. And for her latest book, no publisher can be found, ever since she went on the attack in Catholic journals about Hitler's new religion. In addition she is – and has been – generous to an overwhelming degree. She may be a great artist, but she is equally as great a human being. And yet – helpless and lonely.

In the fall of 1935 Sigrid Undset was nominated to be the new head of the Authors' Union, and a short time later, when the German pacifist Carl von Ossietzky was proposed as a candidate for the Nobel Peace Prize, the spotlight became focused on her in earnest. The Peace Prize is the only Nobel prize that is not awarded in Sweden, but rather in Norway. The Norwegian writer Knut Hamsun, who had won the Nobel Prize in literature in 1920, publicly criticized the Norwegian Nobel committee for having taken Ossietzky under its protection. After all, he was a concentration camp prisoner who had revealed secret German rearmament! That was treason against Norway's German friends! Along with 32 other members of the Authors Union, Undset formulated a protest against Hamsun, and the

```
i    4

          1    stålvisp                                       ...
          I    melsigt                                        2.8
     18   I    glasskål    Nordlys       smaragd,             2.0
          I      "            "             "                 1.3
          I      "            "             "                 0.8
          I2   blomsterpotter        no. Io.          0/22    2.6
          I2   skåler                                 0/25    3.0
     6    leie av: 94    kopper                       0/09    8.4
          "    "    96   asjetter                     0/08    7.6
          "    "     3   fløtestell                   0/I6    0.4
          "    "     4   sukkerklyper                 0/I5    0.6
          "    "    5o   theskjeer                    0/03    1.5
          "    "     4   thekanner                    0/4o    1.6
          manco v/retur: 2 overkopper                0/6o    1.2
          I    suppeøse                                       2.5
          2    siler                                  0/35    0.7
          I    citronpresse                                   0.5
.    15   6    gulvkluter         sv.                 0/7o    4.2

     18
```

Whenever large delegations came to Bjerkebæk, Undset would rent place settings and serving dishes from a shop in town. Such was the case when the Nordic booksellers' assistants were invited to her home.

following year Ossietzky was awarded the Peace Prize in absentia. The newspaper *Westdeutscher Beobachter* reported that Undset's works immediately landed on the list of banned books, and it became increasingly difficult for Attorney Moe to get remittances from Germany transferred to Norway.

The Spanish Civil War was the next shock. Undset's niece Signe Ollendorff recounts:

> There was no radio at Bjerkebæk. Aunt Sigrid got her news from the morning paper. During the summers of '36 and '37 I stayed at Bjerkebæk for lengthy periods of time, and I remember Aunt Sigrid's reaction to the news of the Spanish Civil War. The articles made a strong impression on her – also physically. Her eyes grew tremendously somber, she turned very pale, put the paper aside, but then took it along with her, saying that she wanted to read it alone. I think she had a premonition of what was to come.

Undset didn't carry out her plan to move away from Lillehammer because the thirties brought a steady stream of new and serious worries, and in spite of everything, Bjerkebæk was a protected and peaceful place. But it was a busy period when Undset often had to leave home, both for personal reasons and on behalf of the Authors' Union. Some of the trips were even quite pleasurable.

Undset was playing around with writing plans that took her to northern Norway to track down family roots on her mother's side, and along the Helgeland coast she found descendants of her ancestors who had emigrated from Scotland in the eighteenth century. "Keith" had been the family's surname as long as they lived in Scotland, but they changed it to "Gyth" when some of them settled in Nordland, while others headed farther south to Vestfold and Denmark. She became deeply interested in her mother's genealogy, and in the previous epoch of her family history. She cultivated her literary interests in the highly exclusive "Golden-Age Club" – which consisted of only two members: Sigrid Undset and Ingeborg Møller. In this "club" the focus was on the rational ideas of the Enlightenment and the orphic raptures of Romanticism. The learned ladies read the works of Goethe and Oehlenschläger, Holberg and Wergeland, taking turns in the role of chairperson and rank-and-file member. Undset felt no urge to write any more contemporary novels, but she was planning a trilogy of historical novels, this time set in the eighteenth century, with her mother's ancestors serving as the basis for the story.

As usual, however, the problem was finding enough peace and quiet to work. In 1935 Undset traveled to Finland on behalf of the Authors' Union; in 1936 she went to Stockholm on a similar errand, and in 1937 to Copenhagen. Her sons made their own plans and chose their own traveling companions, and she worried about them – from a proper distance. In April 1937 she headed for England, both to visit Anders and to see more of the country that she had loved ever since she had discovered William Shakespeare when she was only fourteen years old.

Her first thought as the ship docked at Newcastle-on-Tyne was meeting her son, but he was busy and kept her waiting. "I'm going to Birmingham on Saturday – had word from Anders that he's terribly busy Thursday and Friday, so it would suit him better if I came on Saturday," she wrote a bit disconsolately to Mathea. Her mood improved when she got out of the city and saw the orchards in full bloom; they looked like hills of rime-covered forests. In North-field she took lodgings at a hotel situated in an old garden:

> [It] must have *once* been simply magnificent, and yet the wilderness is full of flowers and birds and rabbits, and the building was *once* the sort of elegant old English home that you read about in books – but now factories and the like have been built across the whole region, and no one wants the expense of keeping it up – everything is unbelievably grimy and horrid. But it's only five minutes from where Anders lives, and he doesn't have much time to devote to me. But we've spent two whole Sundays together, and otherwise a little time in the evenings, even went to the theater one night. He looks good, is very interested in his work, and likes the people he works with, and the lads who share his apartment. They each have their own bedroom and

Gunvor Hjerkinn and Anders announce their engagement.

share the living room, so it's good that they get along so well. I'm to send you many greetings from him... Anders is coming home in the summer, but he'll have only a month altogether, and I see that he'll have lots of places to go. But in any case I'm glad that I've seen him now.

Undset could tell that Anders was busy with his own life, and she understood that in the future she would have to get by without his help and support. After several weeks in England, she reported to Thea that "Anders went to Germany today, to meet the girl from Gjøvik. They're apparently going to 'make things public' when he comes home this summer, so we may not see much of him at home. But he's thrilled, so..." She bravely made the best of the situation, and during the course of those two months she explored the British Isles, from Winchester in the south and Glastonbury in the west, and then she traveled north all the way to Kirkwall on the Orkney Islands. Along the way she searched for traces of her mother's family, trying to find out where the Keiths had lived.

During the summer Gunvor and Anders announced their engagement, and after a brief stay at Bjerkebæk, they left to visit her family. Sigrid Undset experienced the truth of the words that "a daughter is your daughter all your life, while a son is yours till he gets a wife." Now only Hans was at home, both to

Hans and Tippa.

his mother's joy and her eternal consternation. He started at a new school, Lillehammer Gymnasium, but the old problems followed him, and soon his report card was filled with remarks such as: "Hans has detention again Thursday and Friday until 6 o'clock. He has been late several times this week and didn't show up at all for early morning inspection." The mood in the house would be tense for a few days, but then Signe's daughters might turn up, and laughter would be heard again as the young people ran in and out. Undset was particularly pleased whenever little Signe came to visit, because she was quieter than her twin sisters, and Hans and little Signe were very close.

Authors' Union business took up a great deal of her time. There were thirteen or fourteen board meetings in Oslo each year, and as chairperson, Sigrid Undset had to be present at all anniversaries and funerals. For this reason, she worked mostly on essays and articles and similar writing projects that demanded less concentration than fiction. After her big trip to England, she wrote an essay about D. H. Lawrence, whom she greatly admired, and about the medieval mystic Margery Kempe. She also wrote about her visit to Glastonbury where according to legend her old hero, King Arthur, lay buried. These articles were put together with other pieces she had written earlier, and in the summer of 1938 they were published under the title *Selvportretter og landskapsbilder* (Self-Portraits and Landscape Pictures).

Occasionally Undset's old passion for botany would flare up, and then she would set off on day expeditions to collect plants, which she identified and pressed in her herbarium. Although her will was strong, her flesh was still frail, and in July 1938 she again went to the health spa at Montebello in Denmark. This time she stayed for almost two months. In addition to a special diet and massage treatments, she was given bromide and phenobarbital, which gave her a rash and terrible itching. When she went to bed she would have nightmares about Mosse and about two little boys that she failed to save from drowning. To Thea she confessed that she wished she was home and in the mountains "instead of at this sorry place where half of all the guests are rolled around in wheelchairs or hobble about on crutches."

There was a striking number of Jews at the health spa, and their difficult situation made a strong impression on Undset. "They can't even get the children of their relatives out of Germany, even if they guarantee to provide for their education and find them jobs in their own businesses – so many have come to Denmark that the Danes say they can't take in any more." After returning home, Undset wrote to Ingeborg Møller that she was "worn out from trying to gain admittance into the country for a German Jew – a former publisher." All the same, she did contribute to getting Max Tau out of Germany and to Norway. Undset's niece Signe Ollendorff explains:

> I remember Max Tau from a party at Bjerkebæk in the late '30s. "Und wenn ich Norwegen sage, dann sage ich Sigrid Undset – und wenn ich Danke sage, dann sage ich Sigrid Undset." ("Whenever I say Norway, I mean Sigrid Undset – and whenever I say thank you, I mean Sigrid Undset.") She looked up at him – extremely touched. It was the sort of situation that she had a hard time taking – but she admired Max Tau.

In spite of the political turmoil and her poor health, Undset started on her historical novel. It was going to be a trilogy that began in 1793, with the contrast between "enlightened" Lutheranism and "romantic" Catholicism as the backdrop. In the foreground would be the relationship between two brothers, Vilhelm and Claus. Her work on this novel, titled *Madame Dorthea*, was inspired by the Danish-Norwegian ancestry of her mother, and Undset knew that if Charlotte Undset was to see the book finished, she needed to hurry.

Her mother's health had caused much concern for many years, and now Charlotte was feeling dejected and nervous and fretful. As a child she had fallen down the cellar stairs, and the old back injury became worse the older she got. "The old tigress," as the boys called her, had lost most of her eyesight and most of her claws. Undset confided her worries in a letter to Mary Stendahl of Thorstad Farm, who was Mosse's old nursemaid Abba and now served as foster mother for Undset's stepson Trond. Mary knew both Undset's mother and her sister, Signe Thomas, from her time at Bjerkebæk.

> It's pitiful to see her now – and almost as bad to see my sister, who is so worn out from nursing Mama, who as you might imagine is not a particularly pliable patient and demands constant care. At times she's completely lucid, but I don't know whether you remember that she has always been plagued by bad dreams – she screamed so horribly in the night when she was here

that Marguerite hardly dared sleep in the room next door to her. It has gotten even worse, and now she can no longer distinguish between what she's dreaming and what is real, so the nights are awful.

Christmas 1938 was a difficult time at Bjerkebæk. Hans insisted on inviting his classmates to a dance party, and his mother reluctantly agreed. "Even *that* she begrudged me," complained the offended boy to his friends. He chose to ignore the struggles his mother was going through, even though he must have known that both Mathea and Mosse were bedridden, one with sciatica and the other with a bad cold. His guests, on the other hand, noticed that Undset seemed even more formal and remote than usual when she received them.

Two weeks later Mosse died. The girl's old nursemaid was one of the first to be informed:

Lillehammer, January 13, 1939

Dear Mary,
Mosse died peacefully yesterday morning. I'm writing this to you because otherwise we're not going to announce it; there are so few who even knew her. She will be buried on Monday morning at the little cemetery in Mesnali – she'll be taken up there today, after Svarstad has seen her. He's supposedly arriving by the noon train. And it's likely that he'll come out to Thorstad as well. Mosse looks so lovely as she lies in the casket, adorned like a bride, in a white dress with veil and a myrtle wreath, for St. John says that such are the ones who follow the Lamb wherever it goes.
    Many greetings,
    Your devoted
    Sigrid Undset

Undset had made arrangements for a double gravesite at the cemetery in Mesnali, and that was where Mosse was buried. Perhaps she chose this particular church because it resembled the church in Sollia to which her forefathers had belonged. Both were small, sun-scorched timbered buildings with an expansive view of green forests and blue mountains. Or perhaps she was thinking about all the wonderful car trips that she and Mathea and Fredrik Bøe had taken with Mosse in these regions. But there's no doubt that one important factor was that the sympathetic pastor at Mesnali had no objections to having a Catholic priest

Charlotte Undset was 84 when she died in 1939.

officiate at Mosse's funeral, and that was not something that could be taken for granted. The peaceful setting probably also played a role in the choice of gravesite, for Undset must have thought about the fact that someday she too would be laid to rest in this place.

The house seemed inexpressibly empty without Mosse, and yet Undset was relieved, because she had often worried about what would happen to Mosse if the girl outlived her mother. Now at any rate she no longer needed to worry about that.

Life went on, and spring came. Hans graduated from school and celebrated his freedom with friends, and a new report found its way to Mary Stendahl:

> Hans is at Maribu right now visiting the Moe family at their cabin. Naturally I was happy that he passed his exams, but now it's a matter of what he's going to do with himself. I haven't heard from Anders in a while, but if things remain relatively peaceful in the world, he'll probably stay in England until October 1. That's when his four-year training period is over. If only he finds something to do when he gets home so that he can marry.

During that fall, the page proofs for *Madame Dorthea* were sent back and forth between Oslo and Lillehammer. The novel was based on an unsolved mystery concerning Sigrid Undset's great-great-grandfather, Peter Flor Worsøe. In 1800 he disappeared without a trace from the family history, and there was no record of his death. "This presented many possibilities, most likely an unsolved accident," said Signe Thomas when a curious student asked her about the background for the novel a few years after Undset's death. "It's only recently that one of the archivists has solved the mystery – and purely by chance," she reported. Undset knew very little about her great-great-grandfather when she wrote her novel – only that he had been manager of the Nøstetangen glassworks in Norway, and that he had sent his son to stay with relatives in Jutland in Denmark so he could study to become a pastor. There the son later married and had many children, including Clara Petrea Severine, who became Undset's maternal grandmother. What Undset didn't know was that in 1800, when the pastor was done with his studies, Worsøe went to Jutland to attend his son's ordination. But instead he ended up attending a funeral – his own. Perhaps his death was caused by a sudden heart attack or a stroke. At any rate, Worsøe did not return to Norway, and his death was listed in the church register in Låstrup in Denmark, but it was never recorded in Norway.

And yet it was not the manager's mysterious fate that was of primary interest

Mosse's illness eventually robbed her of all strength.

to Undset, even though she used his disappearance as the dramatic prelude to her novel. Her focus was on how Madame Dorthea handled the situation when she was left alone with the responsibility for her half-grown children when tragedy suddenly struck the family. She was particularly interested in how the relationship between the two brothers would develop. Vilhelm Adolf was the responsible firstborn son to whom his mother always turned whenever she needed support, whereas Claus Hartvig was the lanky and lively youth who was always getting into trouble.

"Dear, dear children – be friends always, stick together!" their mother urges them in the novel. Madame Dorthea no doubt sees that her boys are "much less children" than she had imagined. Vilhelm experiences his first painful love, while Claus discovers the temptations of liquor. They are already beyond her control, and the only thing she can ask of them is that they should forgive each other all thoughtless offenses and stick together, because "in spite of all its imperfections, the bond of blood, the bond of kinship is the most sacred, the strongest tie that binds us together as human beings in this imperfect world."

A few weeks before the book about Madame Dorthea was printed, Charlotte Undset died. The date was August 23, 1939, and on the following day her sister, Agnes Gyth, died in Kalundborg. Sigrid Undset feared that more blows and even greater calamities were waiting in the wings.

"Fight for all that you hold dear"

When Anders realized that his grandmother was dying, he decided to postpone his departure for England. The day after he attended her funeral, German armies invaded Poland, which meant that England was at war. It was impossible for him to return there. "So now I don't know what he'll end up doing – maybe he'll be called up for military service, since he's a non-commissioned officer, after all, and he has applied to be transferred to the mechanized infantry where he thinks he might do some good," wrote Sigrid Undset to Ingeborg Møller. On the day that the world war broke out, Hans matriculated as a student at the University of Oslo. "What a strange day for that to happen," commented Undset. She was heartsick with worry about the fate of Finland and her own country's lack of mobilization, and she prayed to God that He might "release us from the chains of sin that we in our weakness have allowed to bind us."

But all doors were not closed. Now Undset had neither Mosse nor her mother to take care of, and so she was eyeing the possibility of realizing her old dream to visit America. Back in 1922 she had signed a contract with Alfred A. Knopf to publish her books in English, and since then she had received many personal letters and invitations from the dynamic publisher and his wife. With great zeal and diligence the couple had worked to make Sigrid Undset's novels well known in the United States, and one winter day in 1932 the publisher himself had even come to Lillehammer to pay a visit. The local newspaper was impressed by this

Anders on duty in the army.

attention; no doubt the editors didn't realize that the Mistress of Bjerkebæk was regarded as "the greatest living woman novelist" in the States. Some years later, when Undset was staying at a health spa in Denmark, Blanche Knopf turned up for a visit, and the author was once again asked: When would her next novel be ready? And when was she finally going to come to the United States?

Now that her familial burdens were lifted, Sigrid Undset at last allowed herself to be persuaded, and during the winter of 1939–40, concrete plans were made for an extensive author tour under the auspices of Nordmannsforbundet and the Knopf publishing company. The theme for Undset's lectures was to be both literary and political, because she felt that she ought to make an attempt to arouse American opinion to fight against Nazism in Europe. She received staunch support from the Knopfs, who were Jewish and well-informed about the monstrous activities going on behind the barbed-wire fences in Germany.

Anders was having problems getting his papers sent over from England. Strictly speaking, he was still a couple of months short of finishing his training, and it was uncertain what sort of job he'd be able to find. He took what he could get – a temporary job at a car repair shop in Oslo, cramped lodgings in the city – and then he signed up as an instructor for volunteers who needed rifle training. Sigrid Undset was in despair over the fact that the Norwegian military was making no serious efforts to mobilize: "We have disarmed ourselves, both spiritually and militarily," she raged.

Her own war efforts were initially directed at Finland, which was at war with the Soviet Union. She asked for a large advance from Aschehoug, borrowed money using Bjerkebæk as security, and sold her Nobel medal for 25,000 kroner. The buyer was Johan Andresen, the wealthy owner of Tiedemann's Tobacco Factory. Undset donated the money to aid Finland, but Andresen was gallant enough to send the medal back to her. Several years later Knut Hamsun gave his Nobel medal to Hitler's propaganda minister, Joseph Goebbels. That was Hamsun's response to her appeal.

Undset's assistance didn't stop at just sending money. Three Finnish siblings were taken in at Bjerkebæk during the last winter before the war came to Norway. Elmi, Toimi, and Eira were evacuated from their native country so they would be safe in a free and neutral land. They were "happy, compliant, gentle, and sweet – and so lovely that it's a joy to see them. They're so tiny – from 2 ½ years old to not quite 5, and they don't know a word of any language but Finnish, yet it doesn't matter. They chatter on and on without really caring whether we answer or not," Undset reported.

Elmi, Toimi, and Eira.

Then came April 9, 1940, and the Nazi invasion of Norway. Sigrid Undset and both of her sons were in Oslo when the air-raid sirens sounded, but they made their way home as fast as possible. The Finnish children were hastily sent off to Ingeborg Møller, who lived in Gausdal, around 20 kilometers north of Lille-hammer. Undset wanted the children to be kept a safe distance away from the dangerous main roads, and she didn't want them to experience any acts of war at close range. Anders immediately reported for duty at the Jørstadmoen mil-itary camp, just outside Lillehammer, and barely managed to stop by Bjerkebæk before he disappeared with his rifle over his shoulder. At first he was sent south to Hadeland, where attempts were being made to stop the progress of the invading soldiers, but with each day that passed, Norwegian forces on both sides of Lake Mjøsa were compelled to retreat farther north. Hans and Ole Henrik, Eilif Moe's son, reported as volunteers for the medical corps at Jørstad-moen and tried to make themselves useful at the field hospitals that were set up. They cheered when they heard that a plane full of German paratroopers, that had been hit by anti-aircraft fire, had to make an emergency landing in a field right across from Bjerkebæk. The pilot shot himself in the wreckage, but a gang of Lillehammer boys helped the Norwegian home guard capture the others on board. The victory was short-lived.

Sigrid Undset also reported for duty. She was assigned to help with censoring the mail, but she didn't have a chance to do much work because on April 19 a long column of German military vehicles was reported on its way, only 25 kilometers south of Lillehammer. Undset realized that she had to evacuate, but she couldn't leave without money. Fortunately, Mathea had a hundred-kroner bill, so Undset stuck it in her handbag and bade her housekeeper a hasty farewell. Then she climbed into a car that drove up the valley, past Tretten to the village of Hundorp. She left in the nick of time, because the following day German tanks rolled through the streets of Lillehammer and continued northward without stopping. By April 23 the Norwegian and British forces had to retreat from Tretten, which they had viewed as a natural "stronghold" for defending the valley.

At the Hundorp folk college, the principal and his wife had offered shelter to a small group of resistance fighters who had to seek safety in order not to be taken hostage by the occupying forces. There Sigrid Undset got a foretaste of what was to be her mission for the next five years: working for the liberation of Norway. In an improvised studio at the Otta train station, she gave a speech that was recorded on a lacquer disk, which was then smuggled out of the country and broadcast on the BBC. The response from Goebbels' propaganda ministry was immediate: Henceforth it was forbidden to sell Sigrid Undset's books in all regions under German control. Two days later, on April 25, a new edict was issued: Henceforth it was even forbidden to mention her name in the press.

The hardest blow to strike Sigrid Undset came on April 27 in Gausdal. More than 3,000 men under the leadership of Colonel Dahl had gathered in this small side valley and in the center near Segalstad bridge – they were all that remained of several battalions and companies that were in retreat. One of the soldiers was Anders. The men were spread out in smaller groups, unable to join forces to form an effective unit. The German troops rolled in along the country roads, from Tretten in the east, from Lillehammer and Saksumdal in the south. The Norwegians were virtually surrounded; farms were burned, and civilians from the area were driven in front of the advancing troops as human shields.

The home of the great Norwegian writer Bjørnstjerne Bjørnson was spared because the author's son, who ran the farm, was a prominent member of the Norwegian Nazi party, known as National Unity. The farmer had evacuated the estate along with all the members of his household, and a Norwegian machine gun corps took up position at the bottom of the garden in an attempt to stop the Germans. When the leader of the corps tried to go up to the deserted main buildings, he was hit by a sniper's bullet.

To create new obstacles, Segalstad bridge was blown up, and a retreat was considered via a mountain road to the northwest. But the Germans would be able to block the narrow valley from the north, so this plan was abandoned. On April 27, around 9 o'clock in the evening, second Lieutenant Anders Undset Svarstad and Sverre Tom Simensen were on reconnaissance at Segalstad bridge. A German soldier on a motorcycle with a comrade in the sidecar came driving along the road. Anders had orders to stay under cover, but he ventured forward to get within shooting range. That cost him his life.

Two days later Colonel Dahl and his men surrendered, and the battle for Gausdal was over. Some of the soldiers managed to make their way home through the woods, hiding away their uniforms and military equipment, but most were taken prisoner and interned at Jørstadmoen and in Lillehammer. For a small country and an even smaller army, the losses were heavy. In Gausdal seven civilians were killed, as well as 39 soldiers; and 87 buildings were burned to the ground.

Poor little Elmi, Toimi, and Eira had been sent from the frying pan into the fire, for while Gausdal was in flames, there was almost no action in Lillehammer. To avoid the destruction of major cultural treasures, the military leadership had decided that Lillehammer should be declared an "open city," which meant that it would not be defended militarily. Both the Allies and the Germans wished to spare the city because of the Sandvig Collections at Maihaugen. This was just a foretaste of the difficult situation that many cultural institutions would experience during the entire war, a position that demanded a delicate balancing act by both military and civilian leaders.

In the chaos that resulted as groups of German, English, and Norwegian soldiers advanced without clear front lines, Hans and Ole Henrik Moe had managed to make their way north to Otta in an attempt to catch up with Sigrid Undset and her companions. The boys arrived too late and decided to go back to Lillehammer on skis. At the winter resort at Høvringen they made contact with Allied officers. "We met many Englishmen who were wearing street shoes – in the springtime thaw," Moe recounts, shaking his head.

As they continued home, the boys were asked to map the movements of the German troops, but this too turned out to be a hopeless endeavor. They talked to some of the local sheriffs as they went south down the valley but soon discovered that many of them had their party membership in order – in National Unity. The boys ended up staying in the heights where it was still possible to move on skis, and then they headed south over the mountains. In the magnificent Easter weather Ole Henrik became snow-blind, and when they reached the mountain pastures of Goppollen, which Hans knew so well from many vacations, they broke into a farmhouse to find food and shelter.

Sigrid Undset and her companions were escorted via Romsdalen down to the fjord, through the tiny town of Åndalsnes, which had been torched, and out to the bay of Hustadvika. There they boarded a cutter that stole northward – in marvelously beautiful spring nights without a breath of wind. Undset lay on the deck each night, soaking in the lovely images, as if storing them up for an uncertain future. From Mo i Rana in Nordland the refugees made their way eastward toward the Swedish border, first by truck, then by sleigh. They took the last stretch on foot. On May 10 an exhausted Sigrid Undset was met at the Stockholm train station by her friends Alice and Yngve Lyttkens. They had just received word that Anders had been killed.

After the battles around Lake Mjøsa subsided, Gunvor Hjerkinn bicycled the 50 or 60 kilometers from the village of Kapp near Gjøvik to Lillehammer. When she arrived in the town, she asked people if they'd heard any news about Anders. The rumors warned of the worst, and as soon as the housemaid at Bjerkebæk opened the door, Gunvor realized the rumors were true. Without a word she collapsed in the doorway. Only a few weeks earlier, at Easter, Anders had been a guest of her family, and they had discussed their wedding plans.

Signe Thomas managed to come from Oslo to make arrangements for Anders' funeral. It was to take place at Mesnali on May 8, a little more than a year since she had last been at the small cemetery. That time Frederik Bøe had led the procession, lighting the way with a lantern in the winter darkness, and there had been deep snowdrifts along the paths. This time the white anemones gleamed along the edge of the woods. No headstone had been put up over Mosse as yet, and the simple grave was opened so that her brother's coffin could be lowered into it. Signe Thomas asked Pastor Hauge to sing "Fight for all that you hold dear," and the small group of mourners joined in as best they could. The coffin was adorned with white anemones that Gunvor had picked in the woods and a bouquet of blue squill that Mathea had brought from the garden at Bjerkebæk.

Hans had made it home and was present at his brother's funeral, but as soon as the ceremony was over, he went back to Oslo with Signe Thomas. After spending a whole night discussing the matter with his aunt and his cousin Signe, he decided to go to Sweden. We can only wonder what the boy felt when he arrived in Stockholm and found out what his mother's first words were when

The journey to the United States went via Japan.

she learned the news of Anders' death. She had said that she was proud of her son who had fallen for his country. Apparently she said not a word about her grief, nor did she question the necessity of his death. She pulled herself together, held herself erect, and went on fighting.

On July 13, 1940, Undset and her only remaining child set off on the long journey through Russia and Japan to cross the Pacific Ocean to the United States. In 1942 Undset's diary from this journey was published in English under the title *Return to the Future*. After the war it was supposed to come out in Norwegian, but due to protests from the Soviet ambassador in Norway, it was withdrawn by the publisher. The Norwegian edition was finally published posthumously in 1949 (*Tilbake til fremtiden*). The book is a propaganda treatise in which Undset uses her vast historical knowledge for a clear political purpose. "Her clarity of vision and perspective are impressive. As a political agitator she is so one-sided that the message explodes," writes the scholar Astrid Sæther about the book. Behind her controlled facade Undset harbored burning emotions, and the fire of hatred and bitterness that she felt regarding the invasion by the Nazis flared up with ferocious power in her political statements.

Undset realized that her career as a fiction writer was over. Before she left Stockholm, she told Alice Lyttkens that she didn't plan to write the sequel to her novel about Madame Dorthea and her sons. The conflict between the two brothers was not a theme that interested her anymore. The new world presented entirely new challenges, and the first thing she needed to do was find some sort of foothold for herself.

In Lillehammer, life soon resumed its calm routines. The interned soldiers from the battles at Gausdal were released after less than two weeks, and before summer arrived, all military action in Norway had ceased. At Bjerkebæk, it was now Mathea Mortenstuen who was responsible for daily matters, ably assisted by Fredrik Bøe. Mosse and Charlotte Undset were gone, the bedrooms belonging to the Mistress and her sons stood empty; only the dogs were left. But the spring chores in the garden demanded attention, and food had to be produced and stored, because no one knew how long the war would last, not to mention who would win. When Fredrik Bøe proposed marriage, Mathea said yes, and on the very day that Sigrid Undset and Hans began their long journey eastward toward the United States, the couple at Bjerkebæk published their marriage banns. On the Eve of St. Olav's Day they went to the pastor's office to be married, with Fredrik's older sister Petra and her husband Einar Bækkevold as witnesses. Petra has written extensively about the wedding in her autobiography:

Wedding at Bjerkebæk

We arrived at Lillehammer on schedule. We could see Fredrik standing on the platform waiting for us. He had his own car since he was both a car dealer and cab owner. So we drove up behind the tall fence at Bjerkebæk and were met by Thea herself. She said that the "Mistress" – she always called her simply the "Mistress" – had just left for America, so as not to be arrested by the Germans.

Thea had been left with the responsibility for the whole house – and could use all the rooms – she was welcome to have guests so that it wouldn't seem empty and deserted, the Mistress had said. At any rate, it was far from quiet in the house because Thea had 2 maids and there were 5 or 6 barking dogs, mostly inside, and in the kitchen their food bowls were lined up in a row.

In Sigrid Undset's bed

When it was finally bedtime, we were glad to escape from all the barking and to have Thea accompany us upstairs to the second floor. "Petra, you must sleep in the Mistress's bed." "Oh, I don't think so," I said at once. On the second floor of Bjerkebæk there are several large rooms, and when she opened the door to the Mistress's room, I felt like someone who didn't have an admission ticket.

So many curiosities and antiques were inside. Thea also opened the door to the elegant bathroom. "Here you are – have a look around and sleep well. And don't make the bed in the morning, it's best if the room looks like it's occupied." The bathroom was lovely, as was the Mistress's bed. But the mattress was so soft that I felt as if I disappeared in all the feathers. On the bedside table were several costly objects. I admired in particular a strange old clock. Thea told me that it was the poet Henrik Wergeland's mantelpiece clock. Einar was given another large room, all to himself.

Then the wedding day dawned. I saw that Thea had prepared most of the dinner. She offered me a taste of the gravy. Good gracious! I didn't think I'd ever tasted anything like it. And such an enormous pot! She had contacts on the black market, as well as family and friends up the valley, so the pantry at Bjerkebæk was not lacking a thing.

But there was something that worried Thea. It had to do with their wedding. Both pastors in Lillehammer had closed their offices under the German occupation. And the one who had been assigned the job was a man that Thea didn't like, but she had to settle for him because there was no one else. I seem to recall that his last name was Sæter. And the reason I remember him was because the first thing he said as the wedding was about to begin was that he didn't sing. So he asked the rest of us to sing. We were only four people, the bridal couple, Einar, and myself. Einar doesn't sing. He says that he can't find the proper note. Fredrik has never been much of a singer, but I think that this time he tried to hum a bit. Thea had no singing voice at all. So I had to sing all alone, first "Love from God," all three verses, and after the vows I was told to sing "Love Is the Source of Light." At dinner Thea and I joked about my solo performance at their wedding. The other guests were a couple of neighbors and two relatives from up in the valley.

While Mr. and Mrs. Bøe took care of the houses and garden at Bjerkebæk, it fell to Attorney Eilif Moe to manage Sigrid Undset's finances. When she fled the country she left behind large debts, but also large assets. These were immediately confiscated by the German Security Police, or the "Liquidation Committee for Confiscated Property," as it was called. By May 3, Alfred Knopf informed Attorney Moe that he was going to hold back Undset's royalties from book sales in the United States so that the money would be at her disposal if she should come to America. But Moe was in need of funds to pay Undset's taxes and asked Knopf to send as much as he could to Norway.

Even worse, Moe received a letter from the tax authorities in Oppland, informing him that the Finance Department would no longer pay the artist stipend to Undset. Yet the bills kept pouring in, for everything from membership fees and insurance premiums to taxes and the annual lease payment on the land. Other queries came in, and Moe answered them all as best he could. Mrs. Tilley in Hamar wrote to ask whether she could access a savings account that her son had been given as a christening gift by Sigrid Undset. The parish priest at St. Torfinn Chapel wondered whether Moe knew what had happened to the church silver that was stored at Bjerkebæk. And from Gaustad Asylum, a woman reported that she was part of God's World Plan; she wanted to appeal to Sigrid Undset for 10,000 kroner in order to finish a radio play that would prevent the dead astral worlds from waking up! It was no doubt much easier for Moe to acquiesce to a request from a sheriff who asked Mrs. Undset to donate two woolen blankets, clean and in good condition, for the use of the German military. "Refusal, evasion, or failure to comply may be punishable in accordance with German law."

A new letter arrived from the taxman, who was an ardent adherent of the new Quisling government in Norway. He warned Attorney Moe that a forced sale would take place at Bjerkebæk if the remaining taxes were not immediately paid. It was hard to know what to do, but Eilif Moe was a highly respected man with a large network of contacts, and he knew how to make use of them. In the autumn of 1940 he wrote to Harald Grieg, head of the publishing company Gyldendal Norsk Forlag, to explore the possibility of obtaining funds through the sale of Undset's shares in the company, but the price that Grieg offered was not acceptable. Moe had to find other means for fending off the tax authorities. On October 18, 1941, a new warning letter arrived from the sheriff, threatening to bring the tax matter before the Finance Department if the debt wasn't paid. Eilif Moe wrote back at once:

> In as much as I herewith remit the remaining federal taxes due for 1939/40, I wish to inform you of the following with regard to the payment of federal taxes for 1940/41: Shortly after war broke out, Mrs. Undset left for the United States, where she has been engaged to give lectures in accordance with a contract signed prior to the war. As a consequence, her income from literary activities has completely ceased, and for all of 1940 and 1941 I have received on her behalf only a couple of minor royalty payments from abroad, while the income from Norwegian sales has thus far been used to defray previously existing advances from the publisher H. Aschehoug & Co. Payment of her author stipends has ceased. In the meantime, I am hoping gradually to effect the liquidation of some of her assets, and the resultant incoming funds will be used to cover her back taxes.

Significant sums were needed, because for the fiscal year 1940–41 alone, Sigrid Undset had been assessed over 20,000 kroner in federal and local taxes. Bjerkebæk had already been mortgaged, so the solution was a new loan, using the property as security, this time from the Anders Sandvig Foundation, which Attorney Moe had access to by virtue of his position as chairman of the board at Maihaugen. The search for liquid funds continued, and in the next round Sigrid Undset's previous patron, factory owner Johan H. Andresen, came to the rescue. He bought her six Gyldendal shares for 10,800 kroner, and after that some of her taxes could be paid. The sale of shares came in the nick of time, because shortly after the transaction was completed, the Nazis took over the publishing house, and both Andresen and the other Gyldendal board members were sent to the prison camp at Grini.

At Bjerkebæk Mathea and Fredrik Bøe were busy keeping the wheels turning, in a literal sense. Bøe's access to a means of transport was worth its weight in gold during such times. By making use of his contacts in the region, the couple was able to provide the Mistress's relatives in Oslo with many welcome packages of provisions. With great care they started smuggling out the most valuable items in the house, because they realized that Bjerkebæk had come under the spotlight of the German secret police. The Gestapo had installed itself in the villa of Tra14 south of town, and the Nazis were constantly requisitioning houses for their own use.

Sigrid Undset was now in New York, and Hans had begun studying history at Harvard. They were aware in general terms of what was happening back home at Bjerkebæk, and Undset wrote to her son that she hoped Bøe and Thea could "gradually slip away some of the things that we love the most and that are irreplaceable, because it probably won't be long before they seize 'my properties' too." The fact that she put quotation marks around "my properties" may be because Bjerkebæk had been mortgaged to the hilt. It's unclear how much more she knew about the situation back home, because it seems as though Attorney Moe and Sigrid Undset were not in direct contact with each other. No doubt that would have been too risky. On the other hand, she regularly corresponded with her sister Ragnhild Wiberg in Stockholm, and a great deal of information was exchanged through this channel. The letters they wrote to each other were sometimes written in English and were often in code. Undset often signed her letters "Berit Heyerdahl-Hansen" in "Pohjola."

Ingeborg Møller was afraid that Undset's possessions would be spread to the winds and wrote to her friend via Stockholm: "Signe and I have talked a good deal about the silverware and paintings – I gave her back what I had borrowed. She and Mrs. Bøe are the closest heirs, after all, so they probably divided up these items. But they will of course bestow most of it on the painter's son when he becomes an adult one day. He is the only one who can carry on the family now." The reply from Sigrid Undset is dated two months later. "Perhaps the Bøes won't be allowed to stay at Bjerkeli much longer, but from what I hear, they do have somewhere to move to, and the fact that they've inherited from the old folks makes sense; I'm very pleased."

Undset doesn't seem to have lost any sleep over the uncertain fate of Bjerke-bæk. She worked hard to support Hans and herself with her writing and endeavored to win over the Americans to the cause of the Allies. She traveled a good deal, giving lectures and speeches and wrote even more articles and reports. This took all the energy she could muster; the lectures, in particular, were a strain because she never felt comfortable standing in the spotlight. In front of large audiences she was practically helpless, even though she'd been given lessons in how to deliver a speech. The written word was and remained her

Sigrid Undset in her room at the Hotel Margaret.

medium. Even so, in many ways she was thriving in her new life, living in a cozy apartment at the Hotel Margaret in Brooklyn, with a small but exclusive circle of friends. She felt a spiritual kinship with the American writers Hope Emily Allen, Marjorie Kinnan Rawlings, and Willa Cather. As she wrote, "people who are interested in the same things always find each other in some way." The natural beauty of the vast and varied country also captivated her, and the everyday friendliness of Americans did her good, whether it came from the newspaper seller on the corner or the little boy named Harvey in the park, who offered to give her a tiny snake in a milk bottle.

At Bjerkebæk Mathea and Fredrik Bøe invited Undset's family to a Christmas party during that first winter of the war, with good food and drink and a big Christmas tree, almost like in the old days. They were certain that the Mistress would have wanted it that way, and besides, they had good news to share. They were expecting twins. "Thea is unbelievably kind and sweet, and her husband is too. They are in good health, and their business is apparently going extremely well. They're both so clever," Signe Thomas reported to her sister in the States. In the summer of 1941 Mathea gave birth to two fine, healthy boys, and once again there was celebrating at Bjerkebæk. Gunvor Hjerkinn was godmother to one of the boys who was baptized Arne Gunnar – taking the first initials from both her name and Anders'. His twin brother was baptized Fredrik Magnus, using the initials of his parents' names.

The boys grew and thrived, and when the second winter of the war arrived, the Bøe family once again celebrated Christmas at Bjerkebæk – with resourcefulness and whatever good food they'd managed to "conjure up" under the circumstances. Perhaps some people thought that they were doing *too* well. At any rate, in late January 1942 they received a registered letter from SS-Untersturmführer Max Krüger at Gestapo headquarters in the villa Trararo: "Kündigung Ihrer Wohnung. Die von Ihnen in dem ehemaligen Grundstück der Sigrid Undset bewohnte Wohnung wird hiermit zum 28.2.42 gekündigt." ("Foreclosure on your dwelling. The dwelling occupied by you at the former property of Sigrid Undset is hereby foreclosed as of February 28, 1942.") This was the notice they had been fearing.

They had four weeks to move, and there were many eyes watching to see what they took from the house over to the tiny apartment they had rented in town. It was extremely cold that winter in Lillehammer, but when the twins were rolled out the gate, there was often more than blankets and mattresses hiding in the bottom of the big baby carriage. The old family silver was rescued in this way, but larger conveyances were required for other household items.

Bjerkebæk in winter garb.

The family in Oslo was alerted, and transport was somehow miraculously procured. When the car arrived in Lillehammer on a bitterly cold February day, Thea had finished packing up most of the valuables into crates. Paintings by I. C. Dahl and by Munthe, old pattern illustrations for the Flora Danica china, along with rare books, antiques, and family treasures were all ready to be moved.

Among the most costly possessions were Sigrid Undset's handwritten manuscripts. Under cover of the winter darkness, everything was piled into the car, and then they immediately set off south for Oslo – with their hearts in their throats. That same evening Signe Thomas smuggled the manuscripts via a side entrance into the wardrobe area of the University Library, where she was employed. The next day she packed everything into two metal boxes with padlocks, and these boxes were then given fake labels with false names and dates and put in storage. There they remained in safety until many years after the war.

The Gestapo undoubtedly had plans for Bjerkebæk, but because of Undset's status as a famous author, they proceeded cautiously. Eilif Moe, who was chairman of the board for the Sandvig Collections at Maihaugen, saw an opportunity for securing the home's valuables via the museum. He set about the task, which required the greatest possible finesse. In March the Norwegian "Minister Dr. Gulbrand, Department of Public Information and Culture" received a letter from his German superior, "The Reichskommissar for the Occupied Norwegian Regions." The letter claimed that selling the requisitioned property would not be advisable since it contained an extremely valuable collection of Norwegian cultural objects. On the other hand, it would not be desirable to establish a museum that might attract a cult following and become a center for political resistance. It was the opinion of the Reichskommissar that a third option be considered, which involved transferring the contents of the home to an existing museum and using the buildings as an *Erholungsheim*. What sort of "convalescent home" the buildings at Bjerkebæk could be used for, and for whom, was not specified in the letter.

The Department replied that they would be happy to take over the property and recommended that the Sandvig Collections at Maihaugen should be given the administrative responsibility. The letter was signed with the proper Nazi salutation: "Oslo, 29 June 1942. Sieg Heil. Gulbrand Lunde." Even so, trouble erupted. The Reichskommissar's man refused to go along with such an arrangement because according to his sources Maihaugen was a center of the resistance movement for the district. "Director Sandvig and his entire family are known to be outspoken opponents of National Unity." Not only were the Sandvig Collections a gathering place for those who were dissatisfied with the "new order" but Attorney Moe was also under suspicion and known to be a representative of the resistance movement. The conclusion was that Undset's property had to be secured, but the Sandvig Collections were not to play any role in the arrangements.

Eilif Moe, the lawyer who had one son in the English RAF and another who was carrying out illegal activities in Oslo, and was himself in daily contact with the active resistance fighters Haakon Thallaug and Anna Henriksen at his office, was now in a difficult situation. He had to try to convince the authorities of his own and Maihaugen's Nazi sympathies:

> The Sandvig Collections have at all times, as I have also pointed out, observed a strictly neutral position, and to my knowledge no incident has occurred that would justify the characterization that has been made. As for Sandvig himself, I know that he has been extremely concerned that he either personally or in his capacity as manager might act in such a way as to damage the museum with regard to the present Norwegian or German authorities. [...]

As for S.U., no one here is aware of any cult. In general there has been absolutely no mention of her name. As for me personally, it is flattering to be shown such attention, but I think I can say that my actions have always been professional and correct.

Guldbrand Lunde supported Moe's description of the Sandvig Collections and hurried to tell the German Reichskommissar that "3 of the board's 7 members belong to National Unity." What he didn't mention was that these had been named to the board by the Nazi authorities. Lunde concluded by stating a desire to undertake an inventory of the contents of the house, including the book collection.

Attorney Moe was now prevented from intervening, because in the fall of 1942 he was arrested. This occurred shortly after his youngest son, Ole Henrik Moe, was caught in Oslo with microfilms in his possession. Father and son were both imprisoned at Møllergaten 19, but the senior Moe was released after a couple of months. The son suffered a crueler fate. He was denounced by an informer and taken to Grini prison, and from there to Sachsenhausen concentration camp in Germany, while his apartment in Oslo was taken over by agents of the German security police, Sipo. Eilif Moe's colleague Haakon Thallaug was also arrested and sent to Sachsenhausen, possibly because he had visited Ole Henrik's apartment, and a short time later two of the Sipo agents were liquidated there. Ole Henrik spent a long time in the concentration camp in Germany, returning home with the "white buses" in the spring of 1945. His brother, Tycho Moe, who was a pilot, never came back. He lost his life in a sortie over Normandy. It was a terrible time for their mother.

After the Bøe family left Bjerkebæk, the Gestapo allowed one of its functionaries to move in, a Mrs. Neeraal, along with her mother and son. The attorney then received one bill after another, via the Gestapo, for repairs to the roof, windows, stoves and doors, as well as for fixing burst pipes – that old problem – and even for the repair of mattresses. In November 1943 he actually received a bill for "work on an air-raid shelter at Mrs. Undseth's Villa" from a local contractor. The contractor had first sent the bill to the German security police, who forwarded it to "das Konto von Frau Undseth." The attorney had to pay all the bills from Sigrid Undset's own income, in spite of the fact that her resources were considerably diminished. One time Moe pulled off the trick of having her publisher in Potsdam send him royalties with the permission of the authorities, and another time he managed to get several thousand kroner from a publisher in Amsterdam. Whenever he needed money from Aschehoug, he would ask them to transfer funds, but never more than was actually necessary. At the same time he was careful to inform the Gestapo that there was very little money in Sigrid Undset's bank account; there was a limit to how many bills they could send him. In this way he managed to walk a fine line from one year to the next.

As long as Mrs. Neeraal lived at Bjerkebæk, everything was kept nice and neat, but when she moved out, the property was used as a residence for "German tarts," meaning young Norwegian girls who had sweethearts on the wrong side. Soon there were several baby carriages standing outside the living-room windows, and the girls let their friends, Germans as well as Norwegians, do whatever they pleased. Sigrid Undset was furious when she heard about the butcher who had shown up as an "observer" and simply helped himself:

> He even drove off with a truckload of perennials from the garden. In a closet Thea found some scraps of fabric with my monogram that had been snipped off the corners of the towels; that was all that was left of them. But they didn't touch most of the furniture. "Mrs. Undset has nothing but old junk," said the tarts, who lived there in the end... But you know – as one of the Gestapo members said somewhere, as he took part in confiscating the books: It's not that we don't have our own culture, you shouldn't think that, but we stick to the German. Yet we read both Goethe and Beethoven. What he had read of Beethoven he couldn't recall, but Beethoven was an excellent author.

Head librarian Wilhelm Munthe from the University Library in Oslo was the person who came to Undset's rescue and made sure that most of her library, which was her pride and joy, was saved. Working with Attorney Moe and librarian John Ansteinsson from the Royal Norwegian Society of Science in Trondheim, Munthe saved 7,000 volumes of her book collection from being spread to the winds. As early as the autumn of 1941, Munthe wrote to the Reichskommissar's cultural division to point out that Sigrid Undset's library, in addition to works of fiction, consisted of "an extraordinarily valuable collection of historical and archaeological works of a purely scholarly nature." He explained that the books had been catalogued with the intention of one day being donated to the library of the Society of Science in Trondheim. Munthe referred to Ingvald Undset's valuable work and to Sigrid Undset's generous donations to this library, which specialized in her father's field of interest, meaning archaeology. He concluded by writing: "It would be most lamentable if this book collection should be lost or dispersed. Therefore permit me to direct your

The bust of St. Bruno in the alcove that was Sigrid Undset's workroom.

attention to the matter in the hope that you might see to it that the library of our great medieval author will end up with the venerable cultural institution for which it was intended."

Wilhelm Munthe sent a copy of his letter to Eilif Moe, but for a long time nothing much happened. In December 1942, Moe, who had just been released from imprisonment at Møllergaten 19, paid a visit to the Reichskommissar and pressed for a resolution, but without success. Four months later, Munthe writes that he has been given verbal permission to move the books and that he is counting on the fact that he and Moe together will be able to solve the problem of transport. John Ansteinsson received this message too and immediately went to Lillehammer. When he arrived, it turned out that there had been a miscommunication between the parties involved, and the Gestapo refused to release the books.

More time passed with nothing happening. Moe got worried and sent a letter to Ansteinsson: "Have you heard anything from the Security Police? I've heard nothing, nor have I wanted to inquire. It's possible that it's less urgent now and that the library may be allowed to remain where it is for the time being, but it's not a satisfactory solution. Best would be to have it stored down here somewhere. I ask you to drop me a few lines." Moe had good reason to worry, because now everyone could both see and hear that things were getting lively up at Bjerkebæk. Finally the security police relented, and the Røros newspaper *Fjell-Ljom* describes what happened:

> Twice librarian Ansteinsson traveled to Lillehammer without being allowed inside. But then in January 1944 he was told that he could come and get the books. He was given one day to pack them up – by 5 o'clock on that day 7,000 volumes had to be out of the house! Many good helpers set to work. Even though the task had to be carried out under the supervision of the notorious Gestapo officer Såtveit, they put their hearts and souls into it. The books were taken to a place in Lillehammer where they were packed into crates made by Lillehammer Dampsag & Høvleri. The entire book collection was then sent to Romedal Church in Hedmark, a stone church used by the National Archives for storing its evacuated collections.

When the war was over, Attorney Moe wrote to Ansteinsson: "I think it was just in the nick of time that we got the books out, because right after New Year's some Nazi tarts moved in, and the place was heavily vandalized."

Sigrid Undset knew little about what had happened to her library, but a few rumors did reach her. The books were her greatest treasures – maybe not the volumes that were the most valuable or rare, but rather those books she'd had from her childhood and youth which meant something to her personally. She talks about this in an article that she wrote for the Christmas issue of *The New York Times Book Review* in December 1943:

THE BOOKS THAT LAST FOREVER

Among the things I shall miss the most, when someday I return to Norway, will be a small pile of books – some of which were given to me as a small child, all of them guarded jealously over more than fifty years. My whole family was bookish. All of us were given many books on Christmas and birthdays. Of course, most of these volumes were lost or soiled or torn – or were lent to someone and never returned. But I kept that small, personal collection of mine intact.

Friends may have saved some of the more valuable books from my library in Norway: seventeenth-century editions of the Sagas, rare volumes I used to show visitors, editions of English and Scottish ballads which I bought in

London with money that came to me from my first English translation. My friends in Norway, of course, would know that these volumes cannot be replaced. But they would know nothing of that other shelf – where I kept the books of my childhood.

One final episode of the story took place after the war. When she was back home, Undset asked for a summary of all the expenses the Society of Science had incurred from the rescue operation, and she paid back the entire sum of 1,452 kroner and 56 øre. Another part of the story is that after Undset's death, Hans made sure that the books that were of interest to the Society of Science actually were sent to Trondheim – a total of 1,282 volumes. The personal treasures and the fiction collection consisting of signed copies from Undset's author colleagues (more than 1,000 volumes) remained with Frederik and Mathea Bøe, but their heirs ensured that this part of the book collection was kept intact and that the volumes eventually were returned to Bjerkebæk, where they belong.

While her friends were conspiring to rescue as many things as possible from Bjerkebæk, Sigrid Undset was sitting in her apartment in Brooklyn, writing all sorts of essays and articles, many on commission. Not everything was of equally high literary quality. The memoirs that she wrote during these years are what have been read the most after her death, especially the story of her life at Bjerkebæk in the 1920s. She wrote *Happy Times in Norway* when Eleanor Roosevelt asked all the authors who were living in exile in the United States to describe what the daily life of children was like in their native countries. The Norwegian edition, titled *Lykkelige Dager*, was not published until after the war. In the foreword to the book, Undset quotes her son Hans: "You know, Mother, if we get our country back from the Germans, nothing else matters. If we don't, and if you and I still have to go on living, we have to realize that Anders was the only lucky one in our family."

In spite of long periods of ill health, Undset did her utmost to help fight against the occupiers. She produced articles and speeches, fairy tales and little songs for Norwegian Christmas booklets, contributions for anthologies and reports, and she got involved in social and political issues. She was a member of an organization called "The Society for Prevention of World War III" and contributed her views to their monthly publication. She was the vice-chairperson of "The Emergency Committee to Save the Jewish People of Europe," and she lashed out at anti-Semitism wherever this pestilence popped up. For instance, she raged at a Catholic priest in Detroit who had spoken out against the Jews. Undset agitated strongly for an independent state for this hard-pressed people.

Sigrid Undset engaged in propaganda in the United States.

Every day she followed every detail of the news about the progress of the war and greedily collected information from her homeland. The Norwegian authorities asked her to draw up a list of the cultural treasures that should be spared if a violent conclusion of the war should take place in Norway. As to the legal settlement after the war was ended, she expressed her opinion regarding the

Moscow agreement, which involved an obligation to punish war criminals severely when the time came. That was a promise that she hoped would be kept. And she wrote letters. Sometimes she worked so many hours at the typewriter that her nails split and her fingertips bled.

Many of the letters were to Hans. After only a year he had given up his studies at Harvard and gone to England, where he was assigned a modest position in the administration of the Norwegian exile government. The tone of his mother's letters is one of tenderness and warmth, but at the same time she tries to get him to view their situation realistically, especially when it concerns their finances.

A botanical friend from Massachusetts.

> You must be prepared for the fact that I won't have much to spare when we come home. I myself have gotten used to living a sort of bachelor life over here, doing most things myself, washing my clothes and ironing them and cooking my own food, and living as frugally as I can... My friends belong to "the quiet ones of the country," not making much of themselves, with little outward influence, or rather none at all; they have their work and their loved ones, and they detest vulgarity and hubbub and noise and any sort of advertising.

Hans was not as good as his mother at putting thrift before expenses, and he asked to borrow money. For once his mother had to say no. She told him that she had been doing so much work for free that "I simply don't have the pounds that you want to borrow from me. The income from my old books gives me just enough to live on if I'm careful and, as I said, over the past year I've done little but unpaid work, and I've been ill."

In the fall of 1943, Sigrid Undset received word that Svarstad had died. She wrote to her son that, in spite of everything, she was glad that his father had died a natural death in a hospital and that there was nothing secret or particularly unpleasant about the way he died. There were many other deaths that could not be described as positively.

Like so many times when she was going through a difficult period, Undset sought solace in nature. She took great pleasure in traveling around in the United States, either in carrying out her speaking obligations or on vacation.

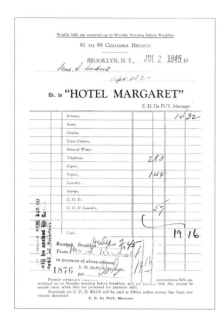

Bill from the Hotel Margaret.

She bought herself a sketchbook like the one she'd had in her youth to record some of her impressions on paper, bushes and trees in particular. She played with the idea of taking back to Norway some of the new plants that she had come to know. Perhaps she could have an "American garden" at Bjerkebæk. Her sense for drama sometimes led her to imagine that life back home was much worse than the routine gray existence that most people, in spite of everything, were actually experiencing. But she still harbored bright dreams of the future, especially when it came to her beloved garden. In May 1944 she wrote in *Harper's Bazaar:*

I have a mind to try and plant some dogwood in Norway. It may never come to pass – who can tell if any of us who are going to return to a devastated country will ever get the leisure, or the means, to make pleasure gardens? – but it has been a kind of game to me and some dear American friends, to plan the "Little America" I want to plant, when I am back in my own country. They have promised to send me trees and shrubs and tubers and seeds, and in the middle of the plot there should be a flagstaff to fly the Stars and Stripes from, when my friends come over to visit me and see the flowers of Norway. It may never materialize. But we have had no end of fun in planning.

When peace finally came, Sigrid Undset wanted to return home as soon as possible, but she was unsure what she would find there. She wrote about her dilemma to Marjorie Kinnan Rawlings: "As to returning to my old home, I don't think I want to. It is not just that those Gestapo men and their tarts lived there; at present it is used as a refuge for a number of the people from the north of Norway who were forcibly driven south when the Germans burnt down all the houses and villages in Finnmark, so it has been cleansed, as it were, by being inhabited by decent folk afterwards." Even though it was a form of redemption in Undset's eyes that refugees from Finnmark had lived at Bjerkebæk during the spring and thus "cleansed" the house after the Nazi occupation, she was still prepared for the worst. She was certain that all the furniture was gone and that there wouldn't be a tree or shrub left in the garden. In addition, she had grown accustomed to living alone, and she no longer needed such a big house. Nor did she have the finances to maintain the property.

Nevertheless, Undset threw herself with great zeal into making preparations for her return home. She thought of everything that her closest family and friends had done without during the five long years of the war. A couple of crates were filled with tea and coffee, sewing materials and underwear, nice soap and silk stockings – goods that could give them a touch of luxury again. But the big van filled with everything that she had collected in her apartment at the Hotel Margaret could wait; her possessions would be sent to Norway when there was more available transport across the Atlantic. On May 19, 1945, Undset sent the following telegram to England:

Second Lieutenant Hans Svarstad, Norwegian Dept. of Justice, Kingdom House, Princessgate, London SW7.
DEAREST WOULD LOVE TO MEET YOU IN LONDON HOME-WARD BOUND EXPECTING LEAVING SECOND HALF JUNE THANKS FOR BOTH TELEGRAMS MUCH LOVE MOTHER SIGRID UNDSET

It took longer than she had hoped to make her departure because arrangements for passenger traffic were not yet fully operational. In the meantime she got vaccinations for typhus and typhoid, measles and diphtheria. Finally – on July 21, 1945 – Sigrid Undset boarded the freighter *Montevideo*, registered as an "assistant crew member." She was now on her way home to Norway.

The curtain falls

The stories I have heard of those who have been tortured and killed by the Gestapo – some of them boys, and girls too, I have known since they were toddlers, children of my friends at home – make me sick and crazy with hatred. And I cannot understand how the mothers and wives and children of these victims can bear to know their nearest ones [are] in the Gestapo prisons.

Sigrid Undset wrote these words to Marjorie Kinnan Rawlings just before she left the United States in 1945. After five years in exile her command of written English was excellent, though not perfect. In the first letter that she wrote to the American author after coming home to Norway, it's evident that Rawlings had sent along a sum of money to be used for the rebuilding efforts in the war-ravaged country. Undset reported that she had given most of the money, along with a sum under her own name, to a foundation that provided for the education of children who had lost their parents during the war. The rest she gave to northern Norway, "where the Germans destroyed everything with true German thoroughness – some 60,000 people are living in the basements of their burnt-out houses, in caves and old mines." The need for charitable work was greater than ever, and even though she was exhausted and alone, Undset was ready to do her part.

Arne and Fred help out in the garden.

At Bjerkebæk things were much better than she had expected. Upon arriving home she reported that "it's unbelievable what Thea and Bøe, her husband, have managed to do – most of the valuables and things with sentimental value have been saved." Best of all was that Thea herself was back at Bjerkebæk and had settled into her old role as the housekeeper. She had brought her family with her, which was a blessing to the lonesome Undset. "The Bøes have moved into the old house, and I live in the new one – meaning the oldest building to the south – and I will have my meals with them. The arrangement couldn't be better, and their twins are the nicest and sweetest little boys imaginable, nothing but a pleasure to have them in the house," Undset reported with relief. The arrangement was advantageous to both parties, since they each had their own house, after all. And with Undset's income, Mathea's cooking skills, and Frederik Bøe's expertise in dealing on the black market, they could live in relative comfort, even during a time of shortages and rationing.

Most of the furniture, paintings, and antiques were once again in their proper places, and even the most beautiful of the potted plants, a crown-of-thorns, had been saved. Almost all the bed linens and kitchen equipment were gone, and the book collection that had been rescued was still hidden away in the basement of Romedal Church. Undset's dog Tippa was still alive, but she was no longer the fiery creature who had been named after Xantippe, the hot-tempered wife of Socrates. Tippa had grown old and quiet and complacent. The garden was a sorry sight, as it was overgrown and untended, and many of the finest perennials had been stolen. All the same, a relieved Sigrid Undset wrote to Marjorie Kinnan Rawlings:

> It was my luck that this house lacked central heating and really comfortable furniture (according to German ideas). So they just put in some of their females – some interpreters of the Gestapo to begin with, afterwards their tarts. Pictures, books and valuables were saved by friends of mine, and most of my furniture my "lodgers" threw out in the yards or in basements and attics, because it was "just old junk" – pieces of old Norwegian handicraft of the eighteenth and early nineteenth century. But of bedclothes, linen, household goods and so on nothing is left – I had to beg licence from Sweden to get bedclothes for two beds for myself and Hans – who now lives in Oslo and studies at the university, but of course goes home for a visit sometimes. My former housekeeper and husband, very nice people, and their twin boys of four have moved in and taken over part of the house – nobody is permitted to have more than a few rooms, the housing situation being as it is. But

Mathea Bøe and the twins.

this is an excellent arrangement for me, because Mrs. Bøe, as her name is now, takes care of me as of old, and the children are charming and funny – but of course very different from pre-war children, the things they have heard and seen... The other day, when they overheard their mother telephoning to a florist's about a wreath for a dead child, one of the boys asked: "But Mummy, my Daddy said all the Germans have left Lillehammer by now. So how could Mathinson's baby be killed?"

The work of love the Bøes have done to make this place inhabitable and get it to look like it did once really is astonishing. But then they had had four washerwomen working here for three weeks to get rid of the dirt and retrieve and clean the things they found thrown out from the place... I am working on a short history of Norway, but severely handicapped because I have not my library. The books are safe in storage, but I have nowhere to put them, as my "lodgers" used the bookshelves for firewood.

In the letters that Undset sent to the States she wrote relatively little about her own situation, constantly reassuring her friends that "I am really very well off." She was mostly concerned with the country's situation – how they were going to increase the production of foodstuffs, obtain materials for construction, and restart trade across national borders. In these letters she did recount much of what she had learned about everything that had happened toward the end of the war. The children in Norway had largely made it through the five years with their health intact, but she thought that her old friends, those who were her own age, had aged terribly, and people were suffering from a great weariness and nervous exhaustion:

> But then, in this small town so many of the young men, and some young women, have been killed – during the war in Norway, on the ocean, as airmen in our forces overseas, and in the hands of the Gestapo or in German concentration camps. In my nearest neighborhood a son is missing in each of the seven nearest houses, and of the boys who used to come to this place to dance and play only my youngest son and the youngest son of my lawyer, who is also my very dear friend, are left of the old gang.

One of the people that Undset mourned the most was her godson Helge Frøisland. On a dark November day in 1945 she sat down and wrote a long letter to Marjorie Kinnan Rawlings in which she recounted his tragic story. By that time Helge's mother, Helene Frøisland, had also died:

> Yesterday Hans and I went to his mother's funeral. She literally died from a broken heart. Helge secretly left home some days after Christmas 1943 and for more than one year he lived up in the mountains, above the timberline, in a cave where they dared not have a fire, because of the smoke, spending their days and nights in a sleeping bag when they were sending secret radio messages to our army in England and receiving and hiding the armament that was dropped by airplanes for our home forces. It was a life like the lives of the outlaws of old, but Helge and his companions were used to mountaineering and skiing since they were tiny boys, and he was a splendid, strong and goodlooking and sunny boy. Some few times he managed to send his mother a message, even a little tea and candy dropped from the English planes. Then this winter they met with some Russians who insisted they were evaded prisoners who hoped to make their way to Sweden. His companions were against it, but Helge insisted, they must be given some food and clothing and helped to find their way over the border. When he arrived at the meeting place far into the wildest part of the mountains he ran into 14 Gestapo men – the Russians had been provocateurs (some were, they were executed at once

when the Russians arrived in Norway). The agreement was, that if some of the "boys in the mountains" were taken by the Gestapo they must keep their mouths shut for five days, afterwards they were to tell the Gestapo about those posts which would by then have been evacuated by the Norwegians. Helge and his comrade kept silent under the torture for eleven days. But the fatal thing was, an avalanche of snow had buried their post, and so the others believed that was why it had been silenced, and when Helge (with 60 kilo packing on his flayed back) took them to the nearest post. Fighting ensued where two Norwegians and four Gestapists were killed, a farmer's wife who had arrived with provisions was wounded – the rest of the Norwegians shot their way out. During the fighting Helge stood tied to a tree, and afterwards he was released and shot through the neck. However, nobody knew what had become of him. And when Norway was free and the boys from the mountains returned, Helge's mother went to every single train coming from the north for more than a week, looking for her boy. Then the snow in the mountains thawed a little, and they found him – lying with his ski[s] on his feet and the staves in his hand, his dead face looking towards the mountains he had loved all his life. His mother broke down completely, and some weeks ago her mind started wandering, then one week ago her heart gave way. We had been friends since we were young girls, she was an emotional and unbalanced, but exceedingly charming girl, very musical, brilliant and strange. There is one girl left, twenty four years [old], as lonely as anybody could be, but thank God, she is a gifted and levelheaded young woman, even if she is utterly heartbroken after the losses of her only brother and her mother.

Another person who was in deep mourning was Gunvor Hjerkinn, the young woman who had been engaged to Anders. Undset treated her as a member of the family and spoke of her as her daughter-in-law. Many of the presents that she had given to Anders she now passed on to Gunvor, including the silver napkin ring with his initials, books that were inscribed "To Anders from Mother," and the handwritten manuscripts for *Gymnadenia* and *The Burning Bush*. Undset admired the young woman who had taken part in illegal activities during the war and wrote to Ingeborg Møller:

Gunvor was here New Year's Eve but went back home on New Year's Day. She's working so hard at that office for war widows that I'm afraid it will be the death of her in the end. But she undoubtedly doesn't think about that – and she's glad to have a job where she feels useful. Her accounts of the war widows are unbelievable; they know so little of what they're entitled to of help from the State. Rolf Wickstrøm's widow received 100 kroner a month from a union fund for herself and her child, and she was delivering newspapers for *Aften-posten*. The office hadn't contacted her because they were sure that *she* at least had received all conceivable help and guidance – what with the monuments to her husband everywhere and his military funeral and the like. But no, nobody had taken any real interest in his widow. The office obtained for her the 12,000 kroner that she was *entitled* to receive. It undoubtedly takes a toll on Gunvor to go from house to house and investigate such matters, but she is so intelligent and tactful, I can't imagine anyone better suited to this work.

Sigrid Undset had her own tasks and official obligations to tend to, because in the wake of the war many special ceremonies were arranged, and she was asked to participate at the unveiling of several monuments. One of the memorial services she agreed to attend was held at Mesnali. To her old friend Ingeborg Møller she wrote, "Pastor Hauge will preside – you know, he lost his son in 1940, and for once I'm going to a Lutheran church service. Pastor Hauge came in person to invite me, and he was the one who presided at Anders' funeral, after all." It worried her that the graves of her son and daughter still had no headstones, but in November 1945 she told her stepdaughter Ebba that she was working on the matter:

> Now I've finally received from Dr. Harry Fett photographs of some of the lovely old wrought-iron crosses that were used so much out in the country during the eighteenth century. And now Bakken, who does artistic smithwork, is supposed to come up here one day so I can finally order crosses for Anders' and Mosse's graves. It will be good to put the gravesite in order. It's so exposed up there that it's no use planting much. In the summer I'll put in a couple of roses that I can bring home and keep in the basement during the winter, and otherwise I'll let periwinkles cover the ground...

It was satisfying to have the gravesites put in order at Mesnali. Nevertheless, Undset allowed herself to laugh a bit at the zeal her old aunt Halma in Trond-heim displayed with regard to her own burial arrangements. According to her niece, the busybody of a woman was so determined to have everything about her funeral proceed exactly as she wished, that she would have preferred to get it over with as soon as possible. A short time after Undset visited her during that first autumn after the war, Aunt Halma had her wish fulfilled.

Fortunately, there were also some stories with a "happy ending" that Undset could recount to her friends in the States. One of them was that Hans had made it through the years in London in one piece and was now eagerly involved in attending to his father's estate. Svarstad had left behind paintings, an apartment in Oslo, and some money, because during the first years of the war his work had sold quite well.

Another welcome piece of news was that Ole Henrik Moe had returned from Sachsenhausen. He had even saved his hands from injury so that he could immediately take up his career as a pianist. Martin Blindheim had managed to come home alive from imprisonment too, even though everyone except for his fiancée, Charlotte Thomas, had given up hope. Undset was happy for the young people, although there was a striking contrast between their hope-filled plans for the future and her own lack of energy. She felt worn out and often very alone, and even Signe Thomas, who had been widowed during the war, had little time for her sister. Now her grandson "Fredriksen" was the most important person in Signe's daily life.

What stung the most was perhaps the fact that the Authors' Union, of which Sigrid Undset had been such a loyal member for so many years, had "forgotten" her efforts when the first annual meeting was held after the war. Ten Nordic authors were named lifetime honorary members, but Sigrid Undset was not among them. The following year the board tried to make amends, but by then the damage was done. She never attended any of their meetings again.

Undset's desk was, as always, her steadfast workplace. The old green-painted desk that she had inherited from her father had been destroyed; only one drawer and a table leg remained of it. So she had a big table moved from the "priest's house" into the hearth room, and then she started in on the "ocean" of paperwork, dealing with matters both big and small, public and private, from Norway and abroad. Long before the war, after she'd been away for a few days, she once complained that she had to deal with "15 fathoms of letters and documents," when she came home. Now, after five years of a state of emergency, there were of course hundreds more that needed her attention.

Undset's business manager, Eilif Moe, had been appointed a circuit judge right after the war, and it was his job to handle the first stage of the cases of treason in the district. Diligent and conscientious as he always was, he nevertheless took time to help Undset with straightening out her financial situation. It was strange to think that as late as April 1945, Moe had received notice that

Next page: Ingvald Undset's old desk was destroyed, but Sigrid Undset moved another table into the hearth room and set to work.

a "liquidation of the estate's valuables" at Bjerkebæk was imminent. A couple of months later, the agenda had changed to questions concerning compensation, the return of assets, and a renewal of Undset's annual author stipend.

Figuring out her tax obligations after five years of war took some doing, because the tax office demanded a detailed accounting of all of Sigrid Undset's income for each separate year. Of course it was impossible to produce this information, but with Moe's help the bureaucrats accepted a compromise and found pragmatic solutions.

Some of the mail that found its way to Bjerkebæk was not at all welcome, and it was with raised eyebrows that Undset wrote brief messages to her business manager: "Saturday. Dear Eilif... I'm now receiving just as many letters from Germany as I did before this little disagreement between their country and ours caused a slight break. Asking me for permission to produce *East of the Sun and West of the Moon*, and inquiring about my health and whether I would write something consoling or encouraging for those who have always been so anti-Nazi... well, well. Your Sigrid."

One of the few German letters that did not end up in the wastepaper basket came from Gertrud Meyer, who had been a prisoner in a concentration camp for a long time. After her release, Meyer wrote to Undset to thank the author for all she had meant for the German anti-Fascists, both through her political work and as an artist:

> When I sat in solitary confinement, I received your *Master of Hestviken* from a kindhearted woman who was put in charge of the prisoners. Never before have I experienced how strongly a person is bound to his fate, and yet through his actions he is able to express eternal laws and truths. Another memory: The same woman brought me *Kristin Lavransdatter* – which I had read many years earlier. I trembled with joy and excitement when she gave me *Kristin Lavransdatter* – in all secrecy, because no one could know that I had the books; I had to hide them in my bed. After a long workday I read them in my cell, without light. But in the prison yard a searchlight had been set up, and the light shone through the bars on the windows. In the evening, when the guards had made their last rounds and the sound of the last rattling keys had subsided, I climbed up on the edge of my bed, pressed the book against the wall in the strip of light from the window, and read your *Kristin*. The shadow from the bars made it difficult, and I kept having to slide the book from one side to the other. In this strained position I read your work, sometimes half the night or even all night long, and was filled with an inner glow.

Undset kept Gertrud Meyer's letter, but when a German author asked her for a photo to replace the one he had lost during the Allied bombing of Koblenz, she swore loudly and tore his letter to shreds. She'd been skeptical of the German mentality ever since she was a little girl and heard about Denmark's defeat at the hands of the Germans at the battle of Dybbøl in 1864. It would take more than a few hurt individuals to arouse her sympathy. She felt a profound bitterness about so many disappointments – the Catholics' contact with the Fascists during the Spanish Civil War had shaken her, as had the failings of the Church with regard to the persecution of the Jews. But she noticed with satisfaction how the nuns in Hamar chose to punish their own:

> An old girl from Tretten, a Catholic, was a Nazi and the girlfriend of Sprekkenhusen, who was liquidated. She attended all the services at the church, but she was always accompanied by sisters who, contrary to their usual kindly demeanor, looked like prison guards. She was not allowed to talk to anyone in the congregation but was kept confined to her room when not at mass. I found it so edifying that the good and pious sisters refused to handle her with kid gloves – quite the opposite. In their view, people who were traitors and friends of the Gestapo cannot expect God to forgive them unless they accept their just punishment and acknowledge that it is nothing compared to what they deserve. The chief executioner from Hamar – his name starts with a T – had a number of battles with Sister Xavier during the war; she's not afraid of anything. Now he's locked up in the county jail, crying all day long and sending messages to Dr. Riise almost every day to complain to him. Some people are just unbelievable.

Hans was not as fierce as his mother, and he had his own thoughts about what should be done with traitors. He had become interested in jurisprudence, and in 1946 he wrote an article for the journal *Samtiden* with the title "Coming to terms with traitors – or with the constitution?" Here he argued strongly against a special law that was passed by the Parliament on February 22 of that year. The law made it possible to sentence a traitor to up to a year in prison – i.e., without a conviction. Hans felt that this went against the constitution, which states that no one can be imprisoned without trial. He also reminded readers that the Italian and German dictatorships during the years between the wars were made possible because of just such a misuse and undermining of their constitutions. This was of course a controversial point of view, and Sigrid Undset was cautious with her remarks. To Marjorie Kinnan Rawlings she merely wrote

It took time to put all the books in their place on the new shelves. On the table is a photo of Anders in uniform.

of Hans: "He is busy arranging a memorial exhibition of his father's paintings, and he has also started his career as an author, with an article on a question concerning the Norwegian constitution. It was very keen and well written too, but I wish he would think of getting his degree."

The distance between Hans and his mother was growing in so many ways. When they went to the ballot box, Undset voted for the progressive Venstre party while Hans voted for the conservative Høyre; she stayed mostly in Lillehammer, while Hans was in Oslo and seldom wrote home. After discussions with his half-sister, it was Ebba who moved into Svarstad's apartment on Gabels Gate. For his part, Hans solved his housing problem by taking over Ole Henrik Moe's apartment. Ole Henrik had just made his debut as a pianist in the concert hall at the University of Oslo and was now going to England to study art. This was a development that pleased Undset, in many ways:

> Ole Henrik was here to say goodbye. Hans is taking over his apartment, one big room with a bathroom and a small kitchen. I was over there one afternoon; it's terribly nice. And we're all overjoyed at Ole's triumphs. It must be wonderful to have the music inside yourself so that you can seek solace in prison and prison camps by thinking about exactly how you would play a work if

you someday manage to escape with your life and have access to a piano. Before he leaves he's supposed to give testimony in that informer case against Norsk Hydro, which was the reason he was locked up.

Undset tried to support Hans in his efforts to organize an exhibition of Svarstad's paintings. She realized how much it meant, not only to her son but also to Gunhild and Ebba, that they'd be able to honor their father's memory in this way. As a thank you she was invited to Svarstad's home at Ringerike and wrote to Hans: "I've never been there, you know. I would have liked to see the place someday, but I always had the distinct impression that your father didn't ever want me there." After much discussion back and forth, it became clear that the dream of a major retrospective was going to be realized, and Undset wrote to her son:

> Dear Hans, Thank you for your letter that came today, it made me very happy. And you must know that I'm glad the exhibition will happen as planned – an exhibition that will truly establish all that your father was as an artist. It also makes me sad, you know, when I think about how he had the unique ability to blot out his own place in the light – a suspiciousness, obstinance, and no doubt a sort of neurasthenic defiance toward real or imagined enemies; many of the latter were his friends or had been once and wanted nothing more than to be his friends again... I'm quite proud of you (read: extremely). I think you've been so diligent and loyal and I'm pleased with what you've accomplished. So long. Your devoted Mother.

To Rawlings, Undset wrote about what a strong impression it had made on her to see Svarstad's paintings all together:

> Our marriage was far from happy, but then, he too was never a happy man, he had a gift for turning love, friendship, even admiration into nothing. But how great an artist he was even I never really understood, until I saw this exhibition of some 130 of his very finest things... It was above all due to the tireless exertions of my son Hans that the exhibition came off, and a couple of young painters who admired Svarstad in spite of his strange ways and uneven production arranged it, refusing every picture (even some belonging to galleries, one or two belonging to me) in which they could discover a flaw. So it was an event, when it came off. I am really proud of Hans for his loyalty and energy – to him his father was just an acquaintance, as we separated when he was a baby, and he is perfectly aware that "life with father" would

have been rather miserable (his half-sisters, my stepdaughters, had a bad time in spite of what I was able to do for them), but I think he felt so keenly the tragedy of the man, who did everything in his power to frustrate himself, and yet was such a rare genius. So then, I spent an emotionally quite exciting ten days -- and feasting with "the children," Hans and the girls, and was very happy and relieved when it was all over.

Unfortunately, there was a postscript that was not quite as pleasant. When the celebration was over, Hans quarreled with his sisters about who owned the specific paintings and about who should pay the bill for the Svarstad exhibition. Undset felt resigned and wrote to Rawlings:

> Nothing came of it except bitterness and disappointments and expense – which ultimately I shall have to carry, but then, that's what I am used to. And two more years lost for his studies, after the five years in our army in England. Well, he seems to have settled down at last and is reading law now... Some-how my onetime husband seemed to blight everything he touched. He was not a bad man, nor vicious, nor mean, only cussed – the cussedest man I ever met or heard about. He did belong to one of these old farmers' families where the men get cusseder and cusseder in each generation, and he did not take the least after his mother, who was a sensible and bright, courageous old peasant women, whom I was very fond of. I think of her very often these days, among other things because she taught me spinning, though I never became very proficient at the spinning wheel.

Undset hoped that in the long run Hans would find some sort of goal to work toward, but she wasn't optimistic about the situation because her son was far more of a dreamer than a realist, and he loved creating castles in the air. But Hans was one of the few persons with whom Undset could let down her guard, and the bond between them remained strong. "Hans clings to me more now than ever," she wrote to Ingeborg Møller, perhaps with a trace of guilt because she felt an urge to retreat from all the problems of daily life, especially those that seemed to arise around Hans. She missed her older son, who had been so practical and calm. "Ever since Anders died, I've had this feeling that I'm not especially anchored to this earth. It's not a weariness with life or anything like that, I have a great deal to live for, yet there is still always this feeling that I'm just doing things while I'm marking time. I would love to see Hans happily married before then, of course."

Sigrid Undset, sketched by Hans.   Self-portrait of Hans.

However, there was no sign of a new daughter-in-law in sight, but then there was so much that Hans hid from his mother. To Ebba's despair, he had started inviting friends to her apartment on Gabels Gate, and among them were Tore Hamsun, the son of Knut Hamsun, and a journalist by the name of Christianne Daae Neeraas. Both had been members of National Unity and were therefore now frozen out of "decent society" in Norway. Christianne Daae Neeraas had worked as a journalist for several institutions controlled by the Nazis, and after the war she promoted herself as an impresario and art curator. She now took a great interest in Hans, and in 1948 she wrote a flattering article about Sigrid Undset's home for the Norwegian-American newspaper *Nordisk Tidende*. Nevertheless, Hans did not introduce her to his mother.

Hans was approaching 30. He made no bones about the fact that he enjoyed spending money, but he had no income of his own. "I feel sorry for the young people," Undset wrote to Ingeborg Møller:

We convinced ourselves that we grew up in a relatively stable world and believed that to a certain degree we could plan how we wanted to shape our future: It was a "fool's paradise," as events have shown, but children and youngsters growing up need to feel that they have strong roots under their feet. Yet those who are growing up now – can they feel that way? Or can a human child get used to being like a water plant that drifts along the surface of a stream and yet still blooms once in a while?

Undset made provisions for her son to be paid a regular monthly sum from Aschehoug, and without complaint she would give him money whenever he asked for larger amounts to cover unusual expenses. When Hans went to Stockholm, he would outfit himself with clothes from her ration quota and at her expense, because her own needs could wait. "I haven't bought anything since I came home from America except for a pair of galoshes – so far I've given my ration points to others."

Thea and Fredrik Bøe were the ones who handled the chore of obtaining essential goods for the household, in a market that was characterized by shortages of every kind, from building materials and fuel to eggs and meat and clothing. During a visit to Oslo, Undset tried to do some shopping, following the unfamiliar system of ration cards and stamps, but she soon gave up. The following report was presented to Thea: "I got two pairs of stockings, no. 9 ½ – that was all they had, you can't get stockings for more than one stamp on the clothing cards. In general, this game of cards... I realize that you spare me from a great deal by managing my cards, because here in Oslo, where I have to deal with them myself, I realize that I understand nothing."

At Christmastime during that first winter back home, Sigrid Undset received a surprising present from the United States. It was a small package from Magny Landstad-Jensen, who was a journalist at *Nordisk Tidende*. Undset sent a warm thank you and wrote back: "It was delightful to receive that elastic – it's one of the most costly things to try and find." Magny Landstad-Jensen was thrilled that the famous author in the Old Country had taken the time to write to her, and soon voluminous letters went back and forth across the Atlantic. The next thank you letter was for a gift of stockings. "They were truly welcome, I must tell you, and such a surprise, because there seems to be a shortage of stockings all over the world right now." Otherwise Undset could report that in Norway they weren't doing so badly when she compared the situation to what Helene Frøisland's daughter described from Paris:

Compared with the other countries that have been in the clutches of the Germans, we are doing fine. Folks have managed to get fuel – just barely, and now it looks as if spring is coming in earnest, just as the supplies of wood are beginning to give out. The cold is the worst, my goddaughter writes from Paris for the Associated Press – the French are freezing and starving. All winter long the young Norwegian girl has been living at a hotel without heat or hot water, but she eats at the journalists' canteen, not well but enough to get by. We've had a lot of lovely fish this winter (and lobster and shrimp for those who could pay, because we didn't export lobster this winter, and the catch was good), good margarine, one meat dish a week, and plenty of milk and bread. This summer we'll have cheese and butter too, once they get the milk production up and running, and eggs, once the three million eggs that are in incubators and under brooding hens are hatched (though of course more than half will be male chicks). Of course there is very little coffee or tea, and the fact that we don't have vegetables or fruit is partly due to the war – the lack of sprays, fertilizer and seeds – but mostly because of the scorching heat and dry summer, which did have some benefits in another way, since it was good for those people who were undernourished and without clothes and suffering from nerves after the war to really soak up the sun – and then they saved on clothing too.

Undset concluded by saying that she was going to give a reading at a public event – "there are events every evening and fund-raising" – and she adds that Magny Landstad-Jensen is welcome to use part of her letter in *Nordisk Tidende* if she likes. In a P.S. she adds a bit of advice: "If you send packages to any of your relatives in Norway, soap, good, perfumed soap, is one of the most refreshing things for us... We have plenty of soap but only two kinds, mostly made from fish oil, and what they call hand soap smells only slightly less nasty than the laundry soap."

In the winter of 1947, the citizens of Lillehammer had great problems with the electricity supply, because after the hot, dry summer, the water reservoirs were only half-full. Power was shut off from midnight until 5:30 in the morning and from 1:30 until 3:00 in the afternoon. The power could also go out at any other time without warning. "My candlesticks are the most valuable items in the house," reports Undset. "And the fact that I still have woodstoves in most of the rooms is a blessing that I can't praise highly enough – people who got rid of their old stoves and installed electric heat are freezing, in spite of all sorts of emergency measures."

Many of Undset's American friends sent packages to Bjerkebæk, containing everything from tea and coffee to rice and cigarettes, stockings and bars of soap. For her own part Undset sent packages to her friends in Finland twice a month. "But we can only send non-rationed items," she reports, "which means almost nothing but fish products. But sprat in herring oil is nothing to sneeze at when there's a shortage of fats."

Consumer goods were not the only things that found their way from America to Bjerkebæk. In one of her letters Undset sends a thank you for books sent to Thea's twins along with a booklet of children's songs. Fredrik Bøe was an able violinist, and his two sons liked to accompany him. "The little boys sing 'Rockabye Baby in the Treetops' and some of the other songs as loud as they can. Every Sunday their father has to play through all the American nursery rhymes on his fiddle." Once again she recalled the old words of wisdom: "It's better to have too little of the necessities than never to have had anything extravagant. Extravagances – that's what people work for and long for." She wrote these words in her novel *Jenny* a lifetime earlier, but they originally came from her mother, Charlotte Undset. Now her thoughts kept returning more and more often to those who had meant the most to her in life, and she recalled:

My mother was as hot-tempered as gunpowder, and patience was a virtue that she didn't know even by name (it was something I had to learn because it didn't come naturally to me, but someone had to do it if our house was to be a home and not a basket full of four quarreling cats). I was often fuming mad at her, but we all knew that when it came to really important matters, she was as dependable as a mountain – it was only concerning trivial things that she was unbearably fussy and unreasonable and ill-tempered, but then she was never boring. As poor as we were during those years after my father died, when I was eleven – even then Mama decided that the necessities weren't what mattered most; instead, once in a while you needed to grant yourself a little extravagance. A dinner that was probably rather similar to the dinners at Grini Prison – and then a new book or an excursion out to Bygdøy with coffee and cakes, or a ticket to the theater. And even if she was in the midst of a furious temper, if someone said something that made her laugh, she was done. My boys worshipped their grandmother, mostly because she was so marvelously temperamental – the old "she-tiger" they sometimes called her.

The ranks of those that Sigrid Undset had known in the old days grew even thinner. March 1947 brought the death of "Uncle Møller," who had been her steadfast contact at Aschehoug ever since her literary debut in 1907. Undset shared her grief with Magny Landstad-Jensen:

Old Møller died three weeks ago. He retired from the company right after the war – it had taken a terrible toll on him; he was a Jew, you know, although the Germans never discovered this. Every night he would make his apartment

During the war Thea had saved Sigrid Undset's favorite plant, her Crown-of-thorns.

available for "he knew not what." He always had his pockets full of illegal newspapers, and he was the soul of the enterprise that Aschehoug had set in motion – they gave every single employee, whether in the offices or the print shop or in the transportation division, a couple of herrings or something else to eat for lunch every day during the years when food shortages were at their worst. The last time I was in Oslo, in early February, I made an appointment to meet him at the office, and we sat and talked for an hour. Now I'm glad that we did.

She had to say goodbye to so many, and there was much in the past for her to remember. Once in while Sigrid Undset found herself – with a slight feeling of guilt – longing back to her simple life in the United States. But she looked forward to working in her garden, and that very first spring in Bjerkebæk she planted seeds and grew seedlings in pots and jars on the windowsill:

Among other things, I've planted quite a lot of seeds from America that I'm excited about: Milkweed, the yellow and red Columbine that grow wild along the Hudson and Mohawk Rivers, Blackeyed Susans (in pots ready to be planted when they get a little bigger), and several vines that I fell in love with up in Massachusetts, Indian cucumber is what they called them there, and the storekeeper sent me a packet of seeds that he had collected for me before I left last year. I don't know what it's like at the Rockaways, but otherwise I think there were such marvelous wildflowers up in Massachusetts, at least up near Oneida Lake, the places out in the country that I know best over there... But of course it's wonderful to be home and see the spring in Norway too. Blue and white anemones and cowslip and the bird cherry is just about to blossom.

A man came from the Gardening Club to prune the fruit trees and help Undset order new berry shrubs. She planted forsythia, the bush with the golden flowers that she had seen in the Botanical Garden in Brooklyn. She knew that it flourished in the Oslo area, and now she wanted to try growing it in Lillehammer. The vegetable garden was more important than ever in these postwar years, and so she planted peas, green beans, and big Italian fava beans, thyme, sage, parsley, chervil, lettuce, kale, and broccoli. Nothing much came of the maize she planted, but she got good crops of beets and chard.

The second spring after her return home, Undset saw that the garden was starting to look like a real garden again. From the nuns in Hamar she received cuttings that she used to make a border of auricula, because that had always been one of her favorite plants. They appeared so early in the spring and smelled so lovely. The nuns had gotten plants of all colors and shapes from their mother church in the Netherlands. To do the spadework in the garden, Undset hired a couple of young boys who had been sentenced to hard labor for treason. That helped, even though she found it sad to think that these youngsters had been on the wrong side during the war. "I almost feel as if I'm using slave labor," she confessed. "But the boys are treated well, of course. They look strong and healthy as they work with bare torsos; some of them are handsome, fair-haired Norwegian boys. The whole thing seems so sad – and so meaningless." Undset herself was plagued by back pain, but she still tried to work in the garden two hours each morning and two hours in the evening. The rest of the day she mostly spent at her desk.

In May 1947, Sigrid Undset turned 65. The day was celebrated in a subdued fashion, with the author Peter Egge and his wife joining her for dinner along with Eilif and Louise Moe. Hans was also home. The party that was supposed to be held at Aschehoug was canceled because the publisher was ill with pneumonia. Instead, Undset was invited to a simple morning event at the publishing house, but she missed Sir William Nygaard and Old Møller, and many of her other good friends and colleagues, such as Nini Roll Anker and Regine Normann. They too had passed away. After her birthday celebrations, Undset felt worn out and wrote to Ingeborg Møller that she had sunk so low that she was considering buying some "sensual" easy chairs for Bjerkebæk. She felt as if she'd grown so old that it would do her good to sit more comfortably.

During the summer they were busy at Bjerkebæk doing a major remodeling, but one day Mathea insisted that the Mistress needed to go to the hairdresser. Afterwards Undset was told to go upstairs and put on a nice dress. Anne-Marie Frøisland, who had just returned home from Paris, went with her godmother to help with the buttons in the back. Undset moaned and complained, as she usually did anytime someone pressured her; nevertheless, she put on her Sunday best. Later in the day the bell at the blue-painted gate rang, and in came the king's emissary to present a very special honor. In the past, Sigrid Undset had been named Knight of the Order of St. Olav. Now she received Norway's highest honor, the Grand Cross of the Order of St. Olav, "for distinguished literary work and for her service to her country." She was the first woman of non-royal blood to receive this honor.

Undset's literary work was not quite over, because before she left the United States she had signed a contract with Doubleday to write a biography of Catherine of Siena. Undset labored over this book, making slow progress as she struggled to understand the ideas of this saint from the Middle Ages:

> Unfortunately, I can't seem to follow St. Catherine's advice – to love everything in God and only in God, like the person who swims underwater and sees and feels only what is under the water; that is how the soul that has immersed itself in divine love should love everything in this sea, and only what is in it. She also talks about entering into God and allowing God to enter into yourself, the way that a fish is in water and the water is in the fish. Yet when she wrote that, she had apparently never seen the sea. She is undoubtedly one of the most remarkable women that has ever lived.

Late in the summer of 1947, Undset went to Oslo to finish the biography about St. Catherine. She was going to stay with the Dominican nuns in Oslo, because there she would be ensured peace and quiet to work. In the meantime, the workmen had taken over Bjerkebæk, and Magny Landstad-Jensen received a report about the work: "The house is now going to be painted and the roof repaired – it leaks like a sieve all over, and so on. Of course the houses and towns that were burned to the ground deserved first claim on the oil and paint and materials, but now my turn has finally come – and not a minute too soon, since everything is in terrible disrepair after the 'friends' and their 'girlfriends' played havoc with the place."

In late autumn Undset sent her manuscript of 237 pages to Doubleday and breathed a sigh of relief. She was glad that she had finished the work before winter set in with electricity rationing and unreliable lamps.

The book about Catherine of Siena represents the keystone of Undset's literary oeuvre if it is seen as a cohesive critique of culture. According to the scholar Astrid Sæter, her books seen as a whole represent "a gradual stripping away of the female role and gender, of the ego, a depersonification for divine purpose, to become a figure that serves the Great One only." But contemporary readers didn't understand the intent of the book about Catherine, and from the United States came only a deafening silence.

Undset found consolation in the fact that the exclusive "Golden-Age Club" was once again active. She and Ingeborg Møller were still the only members; the two authors would meet every so often to discuss religion and politics, plants and food, and they would confide in each other all their health problems and family worries as well as their views on literature, both old and new. In a "summons" to one of their sessions, Undset wrote that "The Golden-Age Club's next meeting should be dedicated to the poet Petter Dass. I read aloud from his 'Trumpet of Nordland' and 'The Catechism Songs' when I was in Oslo, and that was manna." Her old distrust of "development" and "progress" occasionally surfaced, but to Ingeborg Møller she could be quite frank: "According to what my teachers, both male and female, at Ragna Nielsen School predicted, along with other good folks, we should now be sitting in the land of milk and honey and smile sympathetically at our naive and brutal ancestors who engaged in such things as warfare and forming armies, and so on. Ah well..."

She had recurring problems with her health. After Easter in 1948, Undset was feeling so ill that she went to stay with the nuns in Hamar for several days. Sister Xavier's nursing, in particular, did her good, and little by little Undset got better. But she was a bit anxious when later that spring Ingeborg Møller managed to persuade her to come with her to Denmark. It turned out to be a trip rich in experiences and joys. On May 20, Sigrid Undset celebrated her birthday in the land of her birth, and the two old ladies enjoyed themselves at the Royal Theater and in Kalundborg. The one fly in the ointment was a letter from Hans, who was in need of 20,000 kroner – and it was urgent. His mother took care of the transaction, sighing heavily as she remarked: "He's always going to be dependent on his mother's money."

After Ingeborg Møller and Sigrid Undset separated to continue traveling on their own, Undset fell ill. Seriously ill. She had to get help in order to return home, because she was confused, had trouble walking, and found it difficult to talk – all the familiar signs of a stroke. At Bjerkebæk she was able to rest and receive nursing care, and by autumn she had recovered somewhat, although she felt more resigned and worn out than ever. Undset recalled what Ronald Fange had once told her: "We sow our seeds and hope that even if an avalanche overtakes the world tomorrow, there will come a time when the buried seedcorn takes in air and light again and begins to sprout."

Another avalanche caused Undset much distress. From the United States came word that the manuscript of her biography about Catherine of Siena had been rejected; the publisher didn't want to print it because he thought it would damage the author's reputation. Undset was deeply disappointed, but Hans refused to be deterred by this setback. He suggested to his mother that the two of them go to Hollywood together to produce a film based on *Kristin Lavransdatter*.

For a couple of years Undset had been negotiating with an American film company regarding the rights to the trilogy, and in March 1947, acting on advice from Attorney Moe, she had signed a contract with Cromwell Productions in California. The company later changed its name to Beilenson Productions. In a letter from Eilif Moe to Felix Guggenheim, who was also involved in the plans, it's apparent that large sums of money were under discussion: $200,000 in royalties were mentioned as a first payment. The year after signing the contract, Undset received the script for the film. It was written by a Mr. Talbot Jennings, who had limited the story to the first two volumes: *The Wreath* and *The Wife*. There were many things she would have liked to correct, but Undset didn't have the energy to get involved in the work. She left it up to Hans and her sister, Signe Thomas, to keep tabs on the film project.

In February 1949, they sent a nine-page memo to California in which they went through Mr. Jennings' script point by point and offered detailed suggestions for improvements. Their initiative was not well received "over there," and the whole film project threatened to fall apart. Hans thought the problems could be solved if they emigrated to the United States, but Undset bluntly refused. If she was going to move anywhere, it would be to Hamar so that she could be closer to St. Torfinn Chapel and the nuns who lived there.

Hans tried to get Eilif Moe to persuade Undset, since he himself was cautious about discussing the film plans with his mother. The reason for this was that he was hoping to place one of his friends, a Norwegian actor, in the role of Erlend, but he didn't want to mention this to Undset. For many years he had tried to hide from her what he called his "unfortunate tendency," or his "special trait." Yet she must have had her suspicions that he felt more attracted to men than to women. Hans realized that many people had an inkling about

Sigrid Undset is brought home for the last time.

this side of his character, but they had discreetly closed their eyes to it. As a result, he constantly felt threatened, and he was always seeking to arm himself with some sort of instrument of power that could give him the upper hand over anyone who might conceivably reveal his secret. Perhaps he feared his mother's reaction because of several intimations to be found in her novels. In *The Master of Hestviken*, Olav's first major misstep is caused by the accusation that he has gotten too cozy with one of the young men at the seminary. Einar sneers crudely and lashes out at Olav: "What a lovely story that is, I think, this friendship of yours with that fair-haired boy. We have heard a thing or two about the sort of friendship that all of you learn in school." Olav doesn't fully understand the accusation, but he can guess at the meaning and kills Einar by plunging his axe into the man's back.

Undset was always interested in the natural course of life and the importance of kinship, and she had hoped to experience the joys of watching her grandchildren grow up. Now it was up to her only remaining child to carry on the

The cortège from Lillehammer.

family, but Hans wasn't interested in marriage. He feared his mother's reaction, yet he may have underestimated her tolerance. Willa Cather and her female partner were among Undset's friends in the United States; she visited them many times at their home, and there is no indication that she was shocked by or critical of their relationship. Nevertheless, it was a breach of the law to live out "the love that dares not speak its name," as Oscar Wilde once expressed it. Homosexuality was, in the best case, synonymous with scandal and great vulnerability; in the worst case it might lead to a prison sentence.

Christianne Daae Neeraas gladly assumed the role of "beard" for her friend. She needed someone who could help her get back on her feet after the war, and she was unconventional enough to push the boundaries when it came to sexuality, also her own. Both of Hans' half-sisters knew about his preference, Ole Henrik and Eilif Moe recognized the signals, and Signe Thomas was eventually told. It was a tense situation and there was a great deal at risk. Hans realized that he was trying to hide behind a poorly kept secret and finally felt that the situation had become intolerable. After an agonizing conversation with his mother in the late spring of 1949 – a conversation during which harsh words were said on both sides – he left for Paris.

And then, all of a sudden, Sigrid Undset died.

Standing next to the bier: Arne Skouen, Claes Gill, Nils Johan Rud, Einar Skjæraasen, Tarjei Vesaas, Thorolf Elster, Odd Eidem, and Georg Brochmann. Martin Blindheim and Ole Henrik Moe, holding ceremonial staffs, stand in front of the coffin.

A young nurse was the one who found her. Kirsten Aas started her shift at Lillehammer Hospital on the morning of June 10. She was told that Mrs. Undset had been diagnosed with a kidney infection and had been given a bed in a shared room, although she had the room to herself. She had been admitted the day before, and a nun from Hamar had sat at her bedside all night, but no one in the family had been summoned. Now Sister Xavier had gone to Bjerkebæk to rest. They assumed that the patient must be hungry, so Kirsten Aas took a food tray into the room. There on the floor next to the bed lay Sigrid Undset, and there was no sign that she had tried to call for help.

Hans was informed, and he immediately flew from Paris to Copenhagen. He was in a terrible state, but his cousin Clara Hasselbach consoled him as best she could. She found him a dark suit and helped him on his way to Oslo. The

Bishop Jacob Mangers offers a blessing for the deceased.

Ragnhild Wiberg, Hans Undset Svarstad, Signe Thomas, and Clara Hasselbalch followed the coffin.

newspapers were filled with obituaries, and the authorities announced that the funeral would take place on June 19, at the government's expense, at St. Torfinn Church in Hamar.

Four days before the funeral, two cars drove up to the main entrance of Lillehammer Hospital. One of them was the hearse, the other was Frederik Bøe's cab. A short time later the doors opened and four men carried a white coffin out into the drizzling rain, followed by Signe Thomas, Louise Moe, Sister Xavier, and several nurses in blue-and-white uniforms. The coffin was quickly placed inside the hearse, while Fredrik Bøe made sure that the entourage was settled in his cab. Then the two vehicles drove the short distance up to Bjerkebæk. A few flags were flying at half-mast. When the cars arrived, the coffin was carried to the entrance of the hearth room. Signe Thomas nodded to Fredrik Bøe, and the gate was again closed, keeping out the reporter from *Dagbladet*. Sigrid Undset's body would rest in peace at home for the next three days.

Hans booked a room at a hotel in Hamar on the night before the funeral, and Ole Henrik Moe kept him company, trying to console him. He was deeply unhappy and filled with self-reproach. He couldn't fathom how his mother could have died before they had finished their discussion and become friends again. The fact that they had parted with such harsh words was more than he could bear.

The following day the coffin stood in the chancel of the new St. Torfinn Church, draped in a Norwegian flag. A special card was required to come inside, and many had to make do with standing outdoors. At the foot of the catafalque lay a magnificent wreath from His Majesty the King with a white ribbon and an inscription in gold. Next to it was a wreath from the Crown Prince and Princess with a ribbon in the national colors: red, white, and blue. The church was filled with summer flowers and the pillars were adorned with green foliage. *Hamar Stiftstidende* wrote: "The funeral was conducted as a high mass by Bishop Dr. Jacob Mangers with all the solemnity, gravity, and ceremony that have been part of Catholic tradition for almost two thousand years. With the placing of the wreaths, the memory of the deceased was honored by the powers of the State as well as the Catholic institutions, the literary institutions, and prominent individuals."

The mass was performed in Latin by the bishop attired in splendid vestments, assisted by prelates and ministrants. The hymns of Judgment Day were sung: "*Dies irae*" and "*Agnus Dei.*" Then the bishop spoke: "The death of Sigrid Undset did not come as a surprise, either to herself or to those of us who knew her. We all knew that illness had set its mark on her and that her strength had begun to fade. She was prepared for this and accepted it with the equanimity and quiet joy that is given to those who have surrendered themselves and all they possess into the hands of God."

At the placing of the wreaths, eight members of the Authors' Union stood next to the bier, with Martin Blindheim and Ole Henrik Moe in front, holding ceremonial staffs. According to the newspaper, Peter Egge was deeply moved as he carried forward a wreath from Sigrid Undset's personal friends. "Anyone who has managed to enter her closed world knows that a nobler soul has never lived among us. We thank her with love and admiration," said her old friend. The entire mass took two and a half hours, with a long series of speeches and tributes.

After the ceremony in the church, the bier was carried out to the waiting car, with Sigrid Undset's sisters Ragnhild Wiberg and Signe Thomas, her son Hans, and his cousin Clara leading the ranks of mourners. Along the entire route of the cortège, flags were lowered to half-mast, and in a few places flowers had been set up in the shape of a cross. At the cemetery in Mesnali the coffin was taken to the family gravesite. There the bishop swung his censer over the bier, and then at last he sprinkled it with holy water.

Epilogue

"... and the hedge grew so high"

Two years after Sigrid Undset's death, Mathea and Fredrik Bøe once again moved out of Bjerkebæk. This time their twin boys were ten years old and could hardly remember living anywhere else than on Nordseterveien. Bøe built his own house nearby, while Hans and Christianne moved into the old and sun-scorched timbered buildings of Bjerkebæk. They married the same year that they moved in, and along with this unconventional couple came a large and motley group of family members, friends, and acquaintances. It soon became clear that the new owners were not particularly interested in maintaining the buildings or taking care of the plants. Nor was it easy for them to find compe-tent and reliable household help. After a short time their business relationship with Eilif Moe became so strained that Undset's old friend withdrew and left the job to his colleague, Haakon Thallaug.

For several years Undset's son and daughter-in-law tried to keep alive the plans for a film based on *Kristin Lavransdatter*. They even contacted Ingrid Bergman with the idea that she would play the leading role. But nothing ever came of the project, and the dream of millions in income vanished like a fata morgana. On the other hand, they did realize the idea of creating a gallery for Svarstad's paintings. For this purpose, the small guesthouse was slightly enlarged, and in the main room the walls were covered from floor to ceiling with Svarstad's paintings. But to the disappointment of the owners, "The Svarstad House" never attracted much atten-tion. The building was still mostly used as a guesthouse and as a banquet room whenever large numbers of people gathered to celebrate one thing or another.

The couple at Bjerkebæk received a growing number of inquiries from people interested in literature who wished to see Sigrid Undset's home. Eventually Hans and Christianne became primarily the stewards of the Nobel Prize winner's legacy, while their inheritance from Svarstad receded into the background. Hans Undset Svarstad never completed his studies, nor did he ever hold a job in the usual sense. Yet the royalties from his mother's work provided him with a nice annual income, since her books continued to sell well in many different countries. Nevertheless, the couple had constant money problems. They traveled a good deal and preferred to finance their stays abroad with royalties paid directly to them in the currency of the country in question. From Eastern Europe it was difficult, if not impossible, to transfer large sums to Norway, but by traveling to the countries themselves and spending the money there, the couple was able to finance many luxurious trips. Hans and Christianne once bought a fancy car upon their arrival and then gave it to the driver as payment when they departed. In this way they were able to use the royalties from Sigrid Undset's literary work.

The garden and houses at Bjerkebæk were either left in the care of friends or simply abandoned for extended periods of time. On other occasions all rooms were fully occupied. Ebba Svarstad lived in the attic of the guesthouse for a long time, and for several years a single mother and her daughter lived in the basement beneath the living room. A bodega was set up in the space under the hearth room and put to much use when the guests were in their younger years. Damage to the property as well as general wear and tear became a growing problem, the perennials and roses disappeared, and weeds and trees were allowed to flourish unpruned. It was clear to everyone who passed by on the road that the buildings were in great need of repair. Those who had been inside the gate and seen the old rooms reported leaks in the ceilings, dubious electrical wiring, and a party life that was taking a heavy toll on the interior. Whenever the money ran out, a few of the home's most valuable objects would be sold, and over the years many paintings and rare antiques disappeared.

The activities of Christianne Undset-Svarstad during the war in organizations controlled by National Unity never became generally known in Lillehammer. The police had dismissed the charges of treason against her in December 1946 "for lack of evidence"; they undoubtedly had bigger fish to fry. It's unclear how much her husband knew about her past, but the couple went through many crises. They never had any children, because Hans was firmly opposed to the idea. Nor was it generally known that he preferred male lovers. All his friends discreetly looked the other way, which was possible because he largely restricted that side of his life to his travels abroad. In this way both spouses managed to hide a dark secret from the rest of the world, and that may have created some sort of balance in their relationship, as well as a bond that kept them together.

Hans expressed his bitterness toward his mother in a play that he wrote but never finished. It was a one-act play that Christianne published after her husband's death. In *Stemorsblomst. Intermesso i en akt* (Stepmother's Flower. Intermezzo in One Act), he tells the story of a crippled old spinster who grew up in the shadow of her extraordinarily talented and morally superior stepmother. The main character, who is confined to a wheelchair, constantly brings up the differences between her father's and stepmother's families. The former consists of lively business people who have seen better days, while the latter family is composed of conscientious academics and pillars of society. And as the "plot" – which is largely a monologue – unfolds, the mother's funeral takes place in the next room. The play is marked more by immature rebelliousness than any literary art, and it's easy to understand why the author himself did not wish to have it published.

Hans never became a writer, although he clearly had talents in that area. But he was always afraid of being compared with his mother, and he lacked her discipline when it came to work. Half jokingly he said that his only ambition in life was not to bore his fellow human beings, and that he never did. Most often he played to the hilt the role of the quick-witted and amusing eccentric, and in his immediate surroundings the stories about him were both numerous and funny. His closest friends were also able to report on other sides of his character, including his remarkable intelligence; his vast knowledge of history, politics, and art; and especially his kindness and heartfelt generosity. In more than one crisis he proved himself to be a staunch friend.

After some years, Hans wanted to move away from Lillehammer, but first he had to dispose of Bjerkebæk. On one occasion he tried to persuade the Catholic Church to buy the property, but the church politely declined. Another time, it was the Nobel Prize winner Alexander Solzhenitsyn who received an offer to move into Sigrid Undset's house. But after a brief visit in the winter of 1974 Solzhenitsyn moved on, trailing a whole entourage of journalists in his wake.

Hans Undset Svarstad died on Christmas Day, 1978, while staying in Spain. According to his own wishes, he was laid to rest in his father's grave in Vår Frelser Cemetery in Oslo. Almost twenty years later, Christianne Undset-Svarstad's ashes were buried in Gamle Aker Cemetery, in the grave of her twin brothers, Henrik and Carl Gabriel Neeraas. In reality, the couple had parted ways long before they ended up in separate gravesites, because by the time Hans died, he had been living apart from his wife for several years. Yet as the gentleman that he was in so many ways, he had continued to support her financially. His widow inherited most of his estate, including the right to live at Bjerkebæk, and she made it clear to the rest of the family that she didn't wish to move. Instead she chose to buy out the shares in the property inherited by her husband's half-siblings.

Over the years Christianne made many attempts to take care of Bjerkebæk. She took the initiative to have the property declared a heritage site protected by law, and she wrote articles about how important it was to preserve the house and garden for posterity. She had no interest in Maihaugen's suggestion that some of the furnishings should be moved to the museum. In general, she was very concerned that Sigrid Undset's estate might be misused or exploited for commercial purposes. With reluctance she allowed the municipality to tend to the garden and fix the fences in time for Lillehammer's anniversary celebration in 1977, and in connection with the 1982 centenary of Sigrid Undset's birth, Christianne also allowed the county to repair the roofs of the old buildings. But as the years passed, her relationship with the local authorities became quite strained, both because of unresolved tax issues and because of the construction of a new road that prompted the expropriation of the bottom section of the garden.

Whenever scholars and teachers from the Nansen College in Lillehammer came to Bjerkebæk, Christianne was happy to show them around the property, provided she was home and in the proper frame of mind. A few were given access to the books and documents in the house, while others had to leave empty-handed. Borghild Krane lived at Bjerkebæk for long periods of time while she was working on her biography of Undset, but Sherrill Harbison, who knew that there were many letters from the American author Willa Cather somewhere in the house, traveled twice to Lillehammer from Massachusetts in vain. The letters were later found among old newspapers and rubbish in the basement.

In many ways Christianne thrived in her role as Sigrid Undset's daughter-in-law and proprietor of Bjerkebæk. It gave her an income as well as something to live for; it was a role that she had chosen herself and to which she clung. When Hans wanted to get rid of the property, she was always the one who resisted. But occasionally she would sigh heavily and say that it felt as if she'd lived her life solely through her famous mother-in-law and not through her own resources. That was a sensitive issue – and a strange situation for someone who had never actually met Sigrid Undset.

In the fall of 1996, Christianne Undset-Svarstad died after a lengthy illness. At the time, many expected that she had made good on her plans to leave Bjerke-bæk in her will to a foundation. Royalties from Undset's work would provide the operating funds and ensure that the property was made accessible, but only to a limited degree and for those with special interests, such as Catholics, writers, and friends of Undset. Christianne had talked about this to many people over the years, also to lawyers, yet no will was ever found, in spite of a thorough search. The result was that Christianne's two nieces in Sweden, the daughters of her sister, inherited Bjerkebæk. The mayor of Lillehammer contacted the Swedish heirs, and in 1997 the heritage site buildings along with the household contents and the garden were sold for 6.8 million kroner to a consortium consisting of the Norwegian government, regional and local authorities, Andres Jahre's Humanitarian Foundation, and the Aschehoug Publishing Company.

The Norwegian Cultural Department became the formal owner of Sigrid Undset's home, and their expressed goal was that Bjerkebæk should be made accessible to the general public. The supervision of the property was put in the hands of Maihaugen and the Sandvig Collections, which immediately began the physical restoration and documentation of the site's history. An architectural contest was announced to build a visitor's center at the back of the property, and in 2002 Carl-Viggo Hølmebakk and his colleague Gyda Drage Kleiva were chosen the winners. They called their entry "God's Beautiful Daughters." As Undset biographer Tordis Ørjasæter emphasized when she presented the prize to the winners, there was every reason to celebrate the fact that a new building would now be constructed in the service of Sigrid Undset's life and work. On May 20, 2007, marking 125 years after Undset's birth, the public building was dedicated by Her Majesty Queen Sonja. With that, Bjerkebæk opened to the public as a museum.

At the opening, Maihaugen's director acknowledged that the justification for the new museum was not based on the physical estate left by Undset but rather on her art. For this reason the ambition is to link Undset's life and literature, and to make manifest the author's writing and the values and views expressed through her work.

Sigrid Undset had her own favorite writers, and one of them was the great nineteenth-century Danish author Steen Steensen Blicher. When she edited a collection of his short stories, she wrote in the foreword that people who know an author's work inside and out, and yet still can find new joys in it, will always find each other in "a sort of joyous freemasonry." Let us hope that in the future many such meetings will take place inside the gate of Bjerkebæk – and not just for those who at the Millennium chose *Kristin Lavransdatter* as the best Norwegian novel of the twentieth century, but also for new generations of readers who discover the work of Sigrid Undset.

Notes

Unless otherwise noted, Sigrid Undset's books are published by H. Aschehoug & Co. (W. Nygaard), Oslo. The Norwegian titles are given here in their original spelling, whereas the modern spelling is used in the main text. All quotations are taken from first editions, unless other source information is cited. The letters quoted are archived, as originals or copies, at the National Library in Oslo, with the exception of those where another source is indicated.

Lillehammer Station — Disembark on the right

"Clemenceau is of the opinion that Germany...": *Gudbrandsdølen*, 22 May 1919.
"I think I need to lie down...": Letter to Nils Collett Vogt, 2 March 1910.
"no love turns out as...": *Jenny*, part III, chapt. XII.
"anatomical defects of this race": A. C. Svarstad: "The Revenge of the Jews" in *Samtiden*, Feb. 1918.
"Every once in a while...": Nini Roll Anker: *Min venn Sigrid Undset*, p. 37.
"There he is in Kampen...": Letter to Nini Roll Anker, August 1919.
"the sun brought forth...": "Emma and Gunvald" in *De kloge jomfruer* (1918).
"from the thickets lining the road...": *The Wreath*, part III, chapt. IV.

Sigrid Undset makes herself a home

"Now everything looks brighter...": Letter to Nini Roll Anker, 10 June 1919.
"The sky was a heap of tangled...": *The Wreath*, part III, chapt. IV.
"Sigrid Undset herself recounts...": "Sigrid Undset's home and family" in *Politiken*, 11 December 1928.
"until they knew every nook and cranny...": "Henrik Mathiesen" in *Norsk folkekultur*, pp. 49-54.
"As if smeared with melted lard...": "De hine" in *Nordmannsforbundet*, Christmas 1942.
"The little people who clamber up a slope...": *Morgenbladet*, 4 September 1910.
"The whole time, you see...": Letter to Dea Hedberg, 23 April 1902.
"The Movement for Home Ownership...": *Et kvindesynpunkt*, p. 132.
"could no longer deal with...": Letter to Nini Roll Anker, 17 September 1921.
"The boards of the walls...": *Den trofaste hustru*, pp. 41-42.
"People do not have to kneel...": in *Lundemøbler*, undated catalogue.
"old and new attitudes...": quoted in Sunniva Hagenlund: *Portrett av et vennskap*, p. 4.
"salvationists and anarchists...": Roll Anker, p. 14.
"For customs and traditions may change...": *Kong Artur og ridderne av det runde bord*, p. 252.
"and it was much easier to see them...": *Tolv år*, p. 16.
"See to it that you have the walls painted...": *Urd*, 1907, quoted in *Nye hjem*, ed. Morten Bing and Espen Johnsen, p. 18.
"Mother, why aren't you wearing...": Letter to Nini Roll Anker, 13 August 1919.
"But stroke of luck no. 2...": Letter to Nini Roll Anker, 10 June 1919.
"If I get some help...": Letter to Nini Roll Anker, 4 July 1919.

"That meticulous little woman...": Christian Elling: "De norske" in E. Nielsen, ed.: *Dansk skrivekunst*.

"And yet she's incomparable...": Letter to Nini Roll Anker, 4 July 1919.

With an office in "Norway's most beautiful home"

"I had it painted the exact...": Letter to Dea Hedberg, 6 November 1901.

"It was often so difficult...": *Aftenposten*, 21 January 922.

"I thought life was so enormous...": Letter to Dea Hedberg, 8 March 1902.

"I have filled all the windows...": Letter to Nini Roll Anker, 8 August 1920.

"rather nerve-wracking companion...": Letter to Nini Roll Anker, 21 December 1921.

"I wrote eight different versions...": Karin Leander: "Sigrid Undset, Nobelpreisträgerin und Mutter," in *Düsseldorfer Stadt Anzeiger*, 29 May 1932.

"Hans is starting to rebel...": Letter to Dea Hedberg, 6 September 1922.

"The Nobel Prize? She'll certainly...": Erik Rudeng: *William Nygaard*, p. 292.

"Send me the bill,": Sigrid Braatøy to Nan Bentzen Skille.

"given by Mrs. Sigrid Undset...": Document dated 27 February 1926 in Thallaug and Moe's archives, Opplandsarkivet.

"She'd been coming here...": *Oslo Illustrerte*, 2 March 1935.

"so there's not much peace to work...": Letter to Gösta af Geijerstam, 11 August 1923.

"Wish to purchase, for removal...": Advertisement in *Gudbrandsdølen*, 12 July and 19 July 1923.

"I can afford it.": Letter from Rasmus Stauri, Jr. to Nan Bentzen Skille, Bjerkebæk archives.

"For one thing...": Letter to Gösta af Geijerstam, quoted in Hagenlund, p. 57.

"The new house has turned out...": Letter to Nini Roll Anker, quoted in Roll Anker, p. 62.

"My library turned out to include...": Letter to Nini Roll Anker, quoted in the same work, p. 64.

"I had a guest arriving...": Letter to Ingeborg Møller, 17 October 1925.

"This week I move in...": Letter to Nini Roll Anker, quoted in Roll Anker, p. 63.

The "guesthouse" that became the "priest's house"

"Ora pro nobis! Virgo Maria": In Tordis Ørjasæter: *Menneskenes hjerter*, p. 51.

Mathea Bådstø: The information is mainly from Elin-Dagny Bådstø's school paper from 1972.

"Is there anyone outside the circles...": Edvard Bull's letter in *Social-Demokraten*, 12 December 1920.

"even the temperaments of the people...": Edvard Bull quoted in H.Rieber Mohn: *Sten på sten*, p. 37.

"We always arrived early...": Hetty Henrichsen to Nan Bentzen Skille, Bjerkebæk archives.

"Where are the deeds that should bear witness...": *The Wife*, part I, chapt. V.

"in order to receive his reward...": *Den brennende busk*, p. 132.

The garden — "the third loveliest thing" in the world

"How lovely it is to have a garden...": *Fru Marta Oulie*, p. 65.

"memories of fields where they played ball...": *Splinten av trollspeilet*, p. 97.

"I think you are so fortunate...": Letter to Nini Roll Anker, 8 September 1920.

"a proper gardener...": *Vaaren*.

"This formative principle...": Liv Bliksrud: *Natur og normer hos Sigrid Undset*, p. 79.

"No heavenly dreams could the soul create...": *Vaaren*, p. 27.

"I think my heart is like...": *Splinten av trollspeilet* (1966), p. 165.

"Last week I had a great deal to do…": Letter to Ragnhild Wiberg, 4 March1923.

"This summer I had the ground…": Letter to Gösta af Geijerstam, 4 February 1923.

"desolate gardens with a gazebo…": *Fru Marta Oulie*, p. 59.

"stock in one, asters and carnations…": *Elleve år* (1982,)p. 62.

"But most fun of all was the flower bed…": same work, pp. 63-64.

"People around here are imitating us…": Conradi, et al: *Gjennom hageporten*, p. 23.

"Without a doubt, I've caught…": Letter to Signe Thomas, 18 February 1933.

"Well, we certainly have chickens now…": Letter to Mathea Mortenstuen, 30 January 1928.

"My garden is looking lovely…": Letter to Signe Thomas, 1 June 1932.

"Those who have a weak sense of smell…": Erik Axel Karlfeldt: *Lukt och doft. En sommarpredikan*, Karlfeldtsamfundet 1995, p. 31.

"The garden is my summertime joy…": E. A. Karlfeldt "*I Dalarne*", Karlfeldtsamfundet 1995, p. 26.

"We've had sunshine now…": Letter to Astri af Geijerstam, 16 March 1926.

"We've had terrible weather…": Letter to Gösta af Geijerstam, 5 September 1928.

"We have summer here…": Letter to Astri af Geijerstam, 26 June 1930.

"of a type of squill…": Letter to Astri af Geijerstam, 17 January 1929.

"filled with hyacinths and daffodils…": Letter to Mathea Mortenstuen, 24 April 1935.

"Here the winter is…": Letter to Astri af Geijerstam, 17 January 1929.

"I'm going to send home some flower seeds…": Letter to Mathea Mortenstuen, 26 April 1937.

"A strange thing…": Letter to Signe Thomas, not dated.

"No, no, my child…": Signe Ollendorff to Nan Bentzen Skille.

"Sigrid Undset communed with plants…": Ole Henrik Moe, quoted in Charlotte Blindheim: *Moster Sigrid*, p. 32.

"I am sure that in the years to come…": Letter from Willa Cather to Olav Paus Grundt, quoted in *Urd*, No.23, 1946. Provided in the original English by Sherrill Harbison, Amherst, MA.

The children at Bjerkebæk

"We don't like this Lillehammered place…": Charlotte Blindheim and Sigrid Braatøy to Nan Bentzen Skille, Bjerkebæk archives.

"*Hossi kan grase paa jori gro…*": *Et kvindesynspunkt*, font page.

"to this one, the mother who…": "Efterskrift" in *Et kvindesynspunkt*, p. 157.

"the poor Norwegian children…": "Barna I Araceli"[sic] in *Morgenbladet*, No. 66, 1910.

"The cultural work has to be started…": "Det fjerde bud" in *Et kvindesynspunkt*, p. 61.

"knick-knacks and flotsam…": Letter to Katti Anker Møller, 1 December 1915, quoted in Kristin Johansen: *Hvis kvinner ville være kvinner*, p. 184.

"in the midst of all the family's…": "Begrepsforvirring," in *Et kvindesynspunkt*, pp. 105-106.

"This physical fact means…": "Nogen kvindesaksbetraktninger," in the same work, p. 23.

"The higher a person's culture…": "Det fjerde bud," in the same work, p. 36.

"the desperate plight of those women…": "Efterskrift," in the same work, p. 159.

"the weakness of the movement…": in the same place, p. 160.

"gets plenty of exercise…": Letter to Nini Roll Anker, 4 July 1919.

"Extremely charming…": Letter to Nini Roll Anker, 13 August 1919.

"it's no exaggeration…": Letter to Nini Roll Anker, 7 November 1919.

"That's not why I brought you up here…": Gunvor Stendahl to Nan Bentzen Skille.

"Opening available…": Household archives at Bjerkebæk.

"She has tomorrow afternoon off…": Letter to Nini Roll Anker, 17 September 1921.

"She will never be like other children…": Letter to Nini Roll Anker, 10 January 1921.

"I can hear the maids giggling…": in the same letter.

"I'm so tired…": Letter to Nini Roll Anker, 13 February 1921.

"When I came to Lillehammer…": Letter to Gösta af Geijerstam, quoted in Hagenlund, p. 170.

"But I wanted nothing else." "Vårskyer," in *Julehelg*, 1920.

"Most of them came from well-to-do families…": Hetty Henrichsen to Nan Bentzen Skille, Bjerkebæk archives.

"In some sense children stay children…": Letter to Dea Hedberg, 6 September 1922.

"Hans is terribly sweet now…": Letter to Nini Roll Anker, 21 December 1921.

"Believe me, Hans is lively and sweet…": Letter to Ragnhild Wiberg, 4 March 1923.

"Hans is pestering me…": Letter to Ingeborg Møller, 20 December 1925.

"Here I come with my father…": Sigrid Braatøy to Nan Bentzen Skille.

"but he spends most of his time with Brit…": Letter to Mathea Mortenstuen, 26 June 1926.

"She's actually completely unchanged…": Nini Roll Anker's diary, 2 November 1935.

"Here in Italy I've had very little time…": Letter to Nils Anker, 15 April 1925.

"Father Lutz, what exactly happened…": Hetty Henrichsen to Nan Bentzen Skille, Bjerkebæk archives.

"Why does he have that hat…": Sigrid Braatøy to Nan Bentzen Skille.

"I'm trying to make it an offering…": Letter to Gösta af Geijerstam, 5 September 1928.

"He no doubt intends to propose that…": Letter to Astri af Geijerstam, 16 March 1926.

"Hans is in Hamar…": Letter to Signe Thomas, 19 August 1926.

"Tomorrow I'm going out to buy a gramophone…": Letter to Ragnhild Wiberg, 4 March 1923.

"Dear Signe…": Letter to Signe Thomas, 5 September 1922.

"if the practice of throwing oneself off a cliff…": *Ida Elisabeth* (1999), p. 99.

"My sister who lives in Stockholm…": Letter to Gösta af Geijerstam, 11 August 1923.

"For as long as I live…": Letter to Gösta af Geijerstam, 28 August 1928, quoted in Hagenlund, p. 107.

"She chatters endlessly…": in the same place.

"Sometimes I think I know exactly…": in the same work, p. 153.

"to all the horticultural…": Letter to Ingeborg Møller, 15 January 1926.

"With regard to Trond's clothes…": Letter to Mary Andersen Stendahl, 12 July 1939.

Mathea Mortenstuen

"May the blessings of the Holy Family…": Hetty Henrichsen to Nan Bentzen Skille.

"The eternal discord between my maids…": Letter to Signe Thomas, 19 August 1926.

"I'm doing well in school…": Letter from Hans to Sigrid Undset, 11 February 1927.

"Dear Mathea, Of course I'll lend you the sum…": Letter to Mathea Mortenstuen, 5 July 1927.

"You must know that it would be a great joy for me…": Letter to Mathea Mortenstuen, 30 January 1928.

"My dear Goddaughter…": Letter to Mathea Mortenstuen, 19 March 1928.

"A child's welfare requires…": "Efterskrift," in *Et kvindesynspunkt*, p. 156.

"They mustn't be allowed to taste the dried fish…": *The Wife*, chapt. IV.

"grouse on a spit…": *The Wife*, part II, chapt. II.

"The key principle behind Anine's concept…": *Tolv år*, p. 48.

"the ungodly marvelous wine here…": Letter to Karen Gude Müller, 1 March 1910.

"frozen and starving, wrapped in a blanket…": Letter to Signe Undset, 1910.

"I *am* starting to grow tired of roast mutton…": Letter to Ragnhild Undset (later Wiberg), quoted in *Samtiden*, No.30, 1959, p. 285.

"When I came back from my visits…": Regine Normann: "To middager hos Sigrid Undset" in *Urd*, No. 47, 24 November 1928.

"Didn't the Mistress say that…": Sigrid Nordby to Nan Bentzen Skille, Bjerkebæk archives.

"too bad about the camellia…": Letter to Mathea Mortenstuen, 12 July 1935.

"Thea met me at the station…": Sigrid Bøe Nordby to Nan Bentzen Skille, Bjerkebæk archives.

"You all look like you're waiting…": in the same place.

"You meant so much to my mother…": Letter from Hans Undset Svarstad to Mathea Bøe, 1 July 1949.

"in the grand style". Letter to Ingeborg Møller, 9 June 1947.

Miniature theaters and other sorts of drama

The Troll Queen: *Østenfor sol og vestenfor måne*, pp. 64-65.

"It's only natural that a work such as…": *Lillehammer Tilskuer*, No. 139, 1928.

"Public performances are difficult…": same source, 19 September 1928.

"Soon — hopefully very soon…": same source, No. 139, 1928.

"was performed for an overwhelmingly adult…": R.H.S. in *Tidens Tegn*, quoted in *Gudbrandsdølen*, No. 298, 1929.

"It's not meant to be a dramatic play…": Kristian Elster in *Nationen*, quoted in *Gudbrandsdølen*, No. 298, 1929.

"We see here to a persistent degree…": Anders Stiloff in *Aftenposten*, quoted in *Lillehammer Tilskuer*, No. 149, 1929.

"They never let me keep anything…": Sigrid Braatøy to Nan Bentzen Skille.

"It's sad not to have Hans here…": Letter to Astri af Geijerstam, 27 April 1927.

"So I'm trying to make it a penance…": Letter to Gösta af Geijerstam, 5 September 1928.

"He has a hard time getting along…": Letter to Signe Thomas, undated.

"I think it actually gets worse…": Letter to Astri af Geijerstam, 17 January 1929.

"one of the worst attacks of bigotry…": *Gudbrandsdølen*, No. 276, 1927.

"Catholicism was foreign and dangerous…": *Den katolske kirke i Norge*, p. 306.

"Send all the Norwegian Bolsheviks…": interview in *Aftenposten*, 6 May 1925, quoted in Borghild Krane: *Sigrid Undset. Et liv*, p. 223.

"about the idolatry that is called Church of Rome…": *Gudbrandsdølen*, 6 May 1927.

The Nobel Prize comes to Lillehammer

"the best work of an idealistic bent…": Sture Allén: "Överträffa Shakespeare?" in *Artes*, No. 3, 1997, p. 65.

"With great admiration for Sigrid Undset's indefatigable…": Svenska Akademien: *Nobelpriset I litteratur*, part II, 1921- 1950, pp. 107-130. All information concerning the discussions within the Swedish Academy comes from this source.

"It was agreed that they would put in two salted…": "Katholsk propaganda," in *Vor Verden*, 1927, p. 127.

"which risks being more royalist than…": Nathan Söderblom: "Et brev," same source, p. 222.

"a single sympathetically tinged memory…": Sigrid Undset: "Svar til Ärkebiskop Söderblom," same source, pp. 294-304.

"Well, I've been awarded the Nobel Prize…": Sigrid Braatøy to Nan Bentzen Skille.

"Just say that I'm happily surprised…": *Oplandenes Avis*, 14 November 1928.

"a heartfelt thank you…": *Hamar Stiftstidende*, 17 November 1928.

"The rooms at Bjerkebæk almost look like…": same source.

"Mrs. Undset's housekeeper answered…": *Tidens Tegn*, 15 November 1928.

"letters from people pleading for money…": *Hamar Stiftstidende*, 17 November 1928.

"Sigrid Undset to use…": *Aftenposten*, 26 November 1928.

"Mrs. Undset's marvelous plan…": Ronald Fangen in *Aftenposten*, 26 November 1928.

"My dear Sigrid, Many thanks for…": Letter from Charlotte Undset, 29 November 1928.

"when we were in Stockholm…": Ole Henrik Moe to Nan Bentzen Skille.

"Then Mrs. Undset stood up…": *Morgenposten*, 10 December 1928.

"a dark gold dress, she descended the stairs…": *Dagens Nyheter*, 11 December 1928.

"When the train approached Lillehammer…": *Lillehammer Tilskuer*, 19 December 1928.

"When she arrived at the station gate…": *Gudbrandsdølen*, 18 December 1928.

"In the proud dale a castle looms…": Frimann Clasen in *Lillehammer Tilskuer*, 7 December 1928.

"New Foundation from Sigrid Undset…": *Arbeiderbladet*, 26 March 1929.

"Even in Sweden the state religion is…": *Morgenbladet*, 27 March 1929.

"for the assumption that she had…": *Aftenposten*, 27 March 1929.

"The only stipulation with regard to…": *Morgenposten*, 27 March 1929.

The difficult thirties

"Dear Aunt Kirsa…": Letter to Kirsa Gyth, 13 December 1929.

"Get out of my way!": Sigrid Braatøy to Nan Bentzen Skille.

"I live in perpetual fear…": Letter to Astri af Geijerstam, March 1928, quoted in Hagenlund, p. 114.

"Thanks for the birthday greetings…": Letter from Hans Undset Svarstad to Mathea Mortenstuen and Anders Svarstad, 8 September 1930.

"Well, Mrs. Undset…": Sigrid Braatøy to Nan Bentzen Skille.

"A Trip Abroad…": School essay by Hans Undset Svarstad, 1931. Private owner.

"Well, here we sit…": Letter to Mathea Mortenstuen, 27 July 1931.

"Anders didn't feel like waiting…": Letter to Mathea Mortenstuen, 30 June 1932.

"brown and black and blue…": Letter to Mathea Mortenstuen, 10 July 1932.

"Dear Mathea, I've received some unhappy news …": Letter to Mathea Mortenstuen, 18 July 1932.

"Is that really true?" Sigrid Bøe Nordby to Nan Bentzen Skille.

"The Devil in all his glory…": Ole Henrik Moe to Nan Bentzen Skille.

"I've been reading the essays written by…": Letter to Ingeborg Møller, 14 March 1934.

"I would rather know that my son lay…": "Det fjerde bud," in *Et Kvindesynspunkt*, p. 62.

"Finally he was accepted as an apprentice…": Letter to Ingeborg Møller, 14 March 1935.

"Well, let's hope that people are interested…": Sigrid Bøe Nordby to Nan Bentzen Skille.

"she always goes to such extremes…": Letter to Signe Thomas, 1 June 1932.

"She won't finish her book this year…": Nini Roll Anker's diary, 2 November 1935.

"So I've started a treatment again…": Letter to Mathea Mortenstuen, 30 June 1935.

"Her income has shrunk considerably…": Nini Roll Anker's diary, 2 November 1935.

"There was no radio at Bjerkebæk…": Signe Ollendorff, private recollections.

"I'm going to Birmingham on Saturday…": Letter to Mathea Mortenstuen, 14 April 1937.

"[It] must have *once* been simply magnificent…": Letter to Mathea Mortenstuen, 26 April 1937.

"Anders went to Germany today…": Letter to Mathea Mortenstuen, 15 May 1937.

"Hans has detention again…": Hans Svarstad's school report, 1937, Bjerkebæk archives.

"instead of at this sorry place…": Letter to Mathea Mortenstuen, 26 July 1938.

"They can't even get the children…": Letter to Ingeborg Møller, 19 September 1938.

"worn out from trying to gain admittance…": Letter to Ingeborg Møller, 15 November 1938.

"I remember Max Tau…": Signe Ollendorff, private recollections.

"It's pitiful to see her now…": Letter to Mary Stendahl.

"Even that she begrudged me": Anne-Cath. Vestly to Nan Bentzen Skille.

"Dear Mary, Mosse died peacefully…": Letter to Mary Stendahl, 13 January 1939.

"Hans is at Maribu right now…": Letter to Mary Stendahl, 12 July 1939.

"This presented many possibilities…": Letter from Signe Thomas to Bjarne Winsnes, 28 November 1971.

"Dear, dear children — be friends always…": *Madame Dorthea*, chapt. 12.

"Fight for all that you hold dear"

"So now I don't know…": Letter to Ingeborg Møller, 14 March 1939.

"release us from the chains…": Letter to Ingeborg Møller, 15 December 1939.

"We have disarmed ourselves…": Letter to Ingeborg Møller, 25 March 1940.

"happy, compliant, gentle, and sweet…": Krane, p.105.

"We met many Englishmen who…": Ole Henrik Moe to Nan Bentzen Skille.

"Her clarity of vision and perspective…": Astrid Sæther: "Sigrid Undsets eksildiktning," in *Literature and the Second World War*, Workshop 2, p. 142.

"Wedding at Bjerkebæk": Petra Bækkevold: *Et århundre. Gode og onde dage – slik jeg husker dem*. Recollections privately distributed within Bækkevold's family.

"Refusal, evasion, or failure to comply…:" Letter from Fåberg Police, 22 September 1941. Documents referring to Bjerkebæk during the Second World War come from Eilif Moe's archives at Opplandsarkivet, when no other source is given.

"Inasmuch as I herewith remit…": Letter from Eilif Moe to Fåberg Police, 18 October 1941.

"gradually slip away some of the things…": Letter to Hans Undset Svarstad, 7 October 1940.

"Signe and I have talked a good deal…": Letter from Ingeborg Møller via Ragnhild Wiberg, 5 October 1940.

"Perhaps the Bøes won't be allowed…": Letter to Hans Undset Svarstad, 7 September 1940.

"people who are interested in the same things…": "Skjønne Amerika," in Winsnes, ed.: *Artikler og taler fra krigstiden*, p. 200.

"Thea is unbelievably kind and sweet…": Letter from Signe Thomas via Ragnhild Wiberg, 28 October 1940.

"Kündigung Ihrer Wohnung…": Letter from Max Krüger to Fredrik Bøe, 26 January 1942.

"Director Sandvig and his entire family are…": Letter from I. Müller, Ministerialrat.

"The Sandvig Collections have at all times…:" Letter from Eilif Moe to S. Heggstad, 14 September 1942.

"3 of the board's 7 members belong…": Letter from Guldbrand Lunde to Der Reichskommissar, 6 September 1942.

"work on an air-raid shelter…": Bill from Oluf Olsen, 25 November 1943.

"He even drove off with a truckload of perennials…": Letter to Ingeborg Møller, 12 September 1945.

"an extraordinarily valuable collection…": Letter from W.Munthe to Fritz Meyen, Reichskommissariat, 11 November 1941.

"Have you heard anything…": Letter from Eilif Moe to John Ansteinsson, 6 October 1943.

"Twice librarian Ansteinsson traveled…": *Fjell-Ljom*, 16 May 1943.

"I think it was just in the nick of time…": Letter from Eilif Moe to John Ansteinsson, 20 September 1945.

"THE BOOKS THAT LAST FOREVER": in *The New York Times Book Review*, *The Christmas Book List Number*, December 1943.

"You know, Mother, if we get our country back…:" *Happy Times in Norway*, p. viii.

"You must be prepared for the fact…": Letter to Hans Undset Svarstad, 22 September 1943.

"I simply don't have the pounds…": same place.

"I have a mind to try and plant some dogwood…": "My American Garden," in *Harper's Bazaar*, May 1944.

"As to returning to my old home…": Letter to Marjorie Kinnan Rawlings, 25 May 1945.

"DEAREST WOULD LOVE TO MEET YOU…": Telegram to Hans Undset Svarstad, 19 May 1945

The curtain falls

"The stories I have heard…": Letter to Marjorie Kinnan Rawlings, 21 July 1944.

"where the Germans destroyed everything…": same place.

"it's unbelievable what Thea and Bøe…": Letter to Ingeborg Møller, 12 September 1945.

"The Bøes have moved into the old house…": Letter to Ingeborg Møller, 12 September 1945.

"It was my luck that this house lacked…": Letter to Marjorie Kinnan Rawlings, 24 November 1945.

"But then, in this small town…": same place.

"Yesterday Hans and I went to his mother's funeral…": same place.

"Gunvor was here New Year's Eve…": Letter to Ingeborg Møller, 3 January 1948.

"Pastor Hauge will preside…": Letter to Ingeborg Møller, 12 September 1945.

"Now I've finally received…": Letter to Ebba Svarstad, 13 November 1945.

"15 fathoms of letters": Letter to Gösta af Geijerstam, 3 July 1928.

"liquidation of the estate's valuables…": Letter from Kultur- og Folkeopplysnings-Departementet to Eilif Moe, 23 April 1945.

"Saturday.Dear Eilif…": Letter to Eilif Moe, undated.

"When I sat in solitary confinement…": Letter from Gertrud Meyer to Sigrid Undset, 24 December 1947.

"An old girl from Tretten, a Catholic…": Letter to Ingeborg Møller, 24 April 1946.

"He is busy arranging a memorial exhibition…": Letter to Marjorie Kinnan Rawlings, 3 July 1946.

"Ole Henrik was here to say goodbye…": Letter to Ingeborg Møller, 29 September 1946.

"I've never been there, you know…": Letter to Hans Undset Svarstad, 20 September 1945.

"Dear Hans, Thank you for your letter…": Brev til Hans Undset Svarstad, 20 January 1947.

"Our marriage was far from happy…": Letter to Marjorie Kinnan Rawlings, 17 February 1947.

"Nothing came of it except bitterness…": Letter to Marjorie Kinnan Rawlings, 3 December 1947.

"Hans clings to me more now than ever…": Letter to Ingeborg Møller, 23 April 1947.

"Ever since Anders died, I've had this feeling…": same place.

"I feel sorry for the young people…": Letter to Ingeborg Møller, 5 March 1948.

"I haven't bought anything since I came home…": Letter to Magny Landstad-Jensen, undated.

"I got two pairs of stockings…": Letter to Mathea Bøe, 1 October 1947.

"It was delightful to receive that elastic…": Letter to Magny Landstad-Jensen, 10 January 1946.

"They were truly welcome…": Letter to Magny Landstad-Jensen, 26 March 1946.

"Compared with the other countries…": same place.

"My candlesticks are the most valuable…": Letter to Marjorie Kinnan Rawlings, 3 December 1947.

"But we can only send non-rationed items…": Letter to Magny Landstad-Jensen, 17 February 1947.

"The little boys sing 'Rockabye Baby'…": Letter to Magny Landstad-Jensen, 23 March 1947.

"It's better to have too little of the necessities…": *Jenny*, part I, chapt. III.

"My mother was as hot-tempered as gunpowder…": Letter to Magny Landstad-Jensen, uncertain date.

"Old Møller died three weeks ago…": Letter to Magny Landstad-Jensen, 23 March 1947.

"Among other things, I've planted…": Letter to Magny Landstad-Jensen, uncertain date.

"I almost feel as if I'm using slave labor…": Letter to Marjorie Kinnan Rawlings, 12 May 1947.

"for distinguished literary work…": Quoted in Ørjasæter, p. 354.

"Unfortunately, I can't seem to follow…": Letter to Ingeborg Møller, 12 November 1947.

"The house is now going to be painted…": Letter to Magny Landstad-Jensen, 30 July 1947.

"a gradual stripping away of the female role…": Sæther, p. 144.

"The Golden-Age Club's next meeting…": Letter to Ingeborg Møller, 12 November 1947.

"According to what my teachers…": Letter to Ingeborg Møller, 3 April 1948.

"… and the hedge grew so high"

"a sort of joyous freemasonry": Introduction to *Steen Steensen Blicher*, p. 42.

Chronology

1881 – 29 July	Charlotte Gyth (from Kalundborg, Denmark) is married to the archeologist Ingvald Undset (from Trondhjem, later Trondheim, Norway). The wedding takes place in Kalundborg. The newlyweds go to Italy. In the winter Ingvald Undset is taken ill.
1882 – 20 May	Sigrid Undset is born at the home of her maternal grandfather in Kalundborg.
1884 - 12 April	Sister Ragnhild is born. In July the family moves to Kristiania (later Oslo) in Norway.
1887 – 7 March	Sister Signe is born.
1893 – 3 December	Father, Ingvald Undset, dies at the age of 40.
1897	Passes the intermediate school exam.
1898	Passes the exam after a one-year secretarial course. Starts writing to her pen pal Dea Hedberg in Sweden.
1899	Employed as secretary for an engineering company in Kristiania.
1900	Starts writing *Svend Trøst*, a historical novel set in Denmark.
1902	Puts aside *Svend Trøst* and starts writing *Aage Nielssøn til Ulvholm*, also a historical novel set in Denmark.
1904	Has a short essay published in *Aftenposten*.
1905	*Aage Nielssøn til Ulvholm* is rejected by the Gyldendal Publishing Company in Copenhagen.
1907	*Fru Marta Oulie* (published in English by the University of Minnesota Press as *Marta Oulie*) is published by Aschehoug in Kristiania. All subsequent books by Undset are also published in Norway by Aschehoug.
1908	*Den lykkelige alder* (The Happy Age), short stories.

1909	Gives notice as secretary and goes to Italy on a stipend. Lives at Via Frattina 138 in Rome, where she meets the painter Anders Castus Svarstad on Christmas Day. *Fortællingen om Viga-Ljot og Vigdis* (published in English as *Gunnar's Daughter*), a novel set in the early Middle Ages in Norway.
1910	Meets Svarstad in Paris. Publishes *Ungdom* (Youth), a collection of poems.
1911	The novel *Jenny*, marks Undset's breakthrough as a writer.
1912 – 30 June	Married to A. C. Svarstad at the Norwegian consulate in Antwerp.
1912	Spends four months in London and goes to Via Frattina 138 in Rome. *Fattige Skjæbner* (Poor Fates), short stories.
1913 – 24 January	Anders Castus junior is born in Rome. Sigrid travels back to Norway with the ill infant. Settles in Kristiania.
1914	Visits her husband in Paris. Becomes a member of the Council of the Writer's Association. *Vaaren* (Spring).
1915 – 29 October	Maren Charlotte (Mosse) is born. *Fortællinger om kong Artur og ridderne av det runde bord* (Tales of King Arthur and the Knights of the Round Table).
1917	Mosse is examined at the state hospital. *Splinten av Troldspeilet* (The Splinter from the Troll's Mirror).
1918	*De kloge jomfruer* (The Wise Virgins).
1919 – 27 August	Hans Benedikt Hugo is born in Lillehammer, where Undset has rented a house at Nordseterveien 1. *Et kvindesynspunkt* (A Woman's Point of View) (essays).
1920	*Kristin Lavransdatter. Kransen (The Wreath).*
1921	Buys the house in Lillehammer, calls it Bjerkebæk. *Kristin Lavransdatter. Husfrue (The Wife).* She dedicates the book to the memory of her father.
1922	*Kristin Lavransdatter. Korset (The Cross).* Is awarded an annual stipend by the Norwegian government.
1923	Translates *Tre sagaer om islændinger* (Three Sagas about Icelanders).
1924	Buys the Dalseg house and has it reconstructed at Bjerkebæk. Is separated from Svarstad and converts to the Roman Catholic Church.

1925	Goes to Italy with her son Anders and her mother. *Olav Audunssøn i Hestviken* (published in English as *The Master of Hestviken*, vol. 1–2).
1926	Translates Robert Hugh Benson: *Christ in the Church (Kristus i Kirken).*
1927	Hans is sent to the St.Sunniva Catholic school in Oslo and boards at St.Joseph's Institute. Writes *Østenfor sol og vestenfor måne* (East of the Sun and West of the Moon), a play for a miniature theater. *Olav Audunssøn og hans børn* (published in English as *The Master of Hestviken*, vol. 3–4).
1928	Becomes a lay Dominican and takes the name Sister Olave. Visits her stepdaughters in England, where Ebba converts to the Roman Catholic Church. Translates Robert Hugh Benson"s *The Friendship of Christ (Kristi Venskap).* Writes *De tre kongsdøtrene i berget det blå* (The Three Princesses in the Mountain Blue), a play for a miniature theater. Awarded the Nobel Prize in Literature for 1928, specifically for her historical novels.
1929	*Etapper* (Stages), essays, *Gymnadenia* (Gymnadenia).
1930	*Hellig Olav. Norges konge.* (Saint Olav. King of Norway), written for the 900th anniversary at Stiklestad. *Den brændende busk* (The Burning Bush), a sequel to Gymnadenia.
1931	Translates G. K. Chesterton's *The Everlasting Man (Det evige menneske)*. Travels to Gotland and to Iceland. Hans comes home to go to school.
1932	Celebrates her 50th birthday alone in Sweden. *Christmas and Twelfth Night* (religious essays), *Ida Elisabeth*, a novel.
1933	*Etapper. Ny række.* (Stages. New Series).
1934	*Saga of Saints.* Travels to northern Norway. *Elleve aar* (Translated into English as *The Longest Years*), an autobiographical novel.
1935	Hans is sent to a reformatory school near Oslo. Anders goes to Birmingham to become a trainee at the Austin car factory. Supports Ossietzky's candidacy for the Nobel Peace Prize. Elected head of the Norwegian Authors' Union.
1936	Hans returns to become a student at Lillehammer Secondary School. *Den trofaste hustru* (The Faithful Wife).

1937	Travels to England, Scotland and the Orkney Islands. Turns down an offer of $50,000 from Metro-Goldwyn-Mayer for the film rights to *Kristin Lavransdatter*. Anders engaged to Gunvor Hjerkinn. *Norske helgener* (Norwegian Saints).
1938	*Selvportretter og landskapsbilleder* (Self-Portraits and Landscape Pictures).
1939 – 12 Jan.	Mosse dies
– 23 Aug.	Charlotte Undset dies, 84 years old.
– 1 Sept.	Second World War begins. *Madame Dorthea,* a novel.
1940	Three children from Finland are evacuated to live at Bjerkebæk.
– 9 April	The German occupation of Norway begins. Undset flees to Sweden.
– 27 April	Anders is shot in battle and buried at Mesnali near Lillehammer. Undset and Hans travel across the Soviet Union and Japan to San Fransisco. Undset settles in New York.
1941	Begins a series of lecture tours. Visits Monterey in Massachusetts, this summer and the following ones.
1942	*Return to the Future*, a political essay. *Happy Times in Norway*, memoirs written for young readers.
1943 – 22 Aug.	A. C. Svarstad dies at a hospital in Oslo. *Sigurd and his Brave Companions. A Tale of Medieval Norway.*
1945	*Twelve Stories by Steen Steensen Blicher* (edited and with an introduction by Undset), *True and Untrue and other Norse Tales* (edited and with an introduction to folk tales by Asbjørnsen and Moe). Leaves Brooklyn on the freighter *Montevideo*, returning to Norway on 30 July. *Return to the Future* is translated into Norwegian as *Tilbake til Fremtiden*, but publication is stopped by the Soviet Embassy.
1946	*Steen Steensen Blicher* is published in Danish.
1947	*Lykkelige dager* (Norwegian translation of *Happy Times in Norway*). Undset is awarded the Grand Cross of the Order of St. Olav.
1948	*Caterina av Siena* is rejected by Doubleday in the United States. Goes to Denmark with her friend Ingeborg Møller.

1949 – 9 June	Is taken ill and is admitted to Lillehammer Hospital.
– 10 June	Dies unexpectedly from kidney infection.
– 15 June	Is buried at the cemetary in Mesnali, between the graves of Mosse and Anders.
Nov.	*Tilbake til fremtiden* is published.
1951	*Caterina av Siena* is published in Norwegian.
1955	*Sigurd og hans tapre venner* is published in Norwegian.
1998	*Tolv år*, an unfinished tekst (found at Bjerkebæk), is published, edited and with an introduction by research librarian Tone Modalsli.
2008	*Sigrid Undset. Essays og artikler*, four volumes edited and with introductions by Professor Liv Bliksrud.

Photo credits

Maihaugen: 8, 11, 15a, 18, 19, 26, 27, 28–29, 30, 41, 44, 54, 58, 61, 62, 64, 66, 68, 70, 71, 73, 74, 84, 86, 89, 100, 102, 112, 119, 121, 123, 125, 130, 139, 149, 160, 163, 178, 194, 199, 211, 212, 219, 225

Allan and Karsten Bøe: 13, 17, 22, 31, 32, 46, 55, 76, 77, 88, 91, 95, 106, 108, 110, 111, 126, 134, 136, 137, 141, 142, 145, 153, 156, 168a, 189, 190, 205, 206, 215, 234, 235, 238, 241, 246–247, 250, 257, 263, 264, 265, 266

Aschehoug Publishing Company: 51, 78, 98–99, 120, 172, 183, 208, 227, 231
Manuscript collection, Norwegian National Library: 182, 185, 188, 201, 203, 236
Sigrid Undset Society: 162, 168b, 197, 253b
Oluf Fagstad: 16
Nan Bentzen Skille:17b, 75
Botanical Museum: 81
Dagbladet: 262
Anna Eggen: 83
Tom Resvoll Holmsen: 80
Oppland Archives:253a
Nils Frøisland: 181

In spite of numerous attempts, in some cases it has not been possible to track down the copyright holders for some of the photos used in this book. Any questions should be directed to the publisher.